INCARCERATED JUVENILES IN GHANA

Respecting Lived Experiences Through Confinement Ethnography

Lilian Ayete-Nyampong

With a Foreword by
Andrew M. Jefferson

BRISTOL
UNIVERSITY
PRESS

First published in Great Britain in 2026 by

Bristol University Press
University of Bristol
1–9 Old Park Hill
Bristol
BS2 8BB
UK
t: +44 (0)117 374 6645
e: bup-info@bristol.ac.uk

Details of international sales and distribution partners are available at bristoluniversitypress.co.uk

DOI: 10.51952/9781529264159

This book will be made open access within three years of publication thanks to Path to Open, a program developed in partnership between JSTOR, the American Council of Learned Societies (ACLS), University of Michigan Press, and The University of North Carolina Press to bring about equitable access and impact for the entire scholarly community, including authors, researchers, libraries, and university presses around the world. Learn more at https://about.jstor.org/path-to-open/

British Library Cataloguing in Publication Data
A catalogue record for this book is available from the British Library

ISBN 978-1-5292-5475-4 hardcover
ISBN 978-1-5292-5476-1 ePub
ISBN 978-1-5292-6415-9 ePDF

Cover design: Bristol University Press
Front cover image: iStock/Favor_of_God
Bristol University Press uses environmentally responsible print partners.
Printed and bound in Great Britain by CPI Group (UK) Ltd, Croydon, CR0 4YY

FSC
www.fsc.org
MIX
Paper | Supporting responsible forestry
FSC® C013604

Bristol University Press' authorised representative in the European Union is:
Easy Access System Europe, Mustamäe tee 50, 10621 Tallinn, Estonia,
Email: gpsr.requests@easproject.com

I dedicate this book to my late father, Rev. William Otu, whose values of hard work and integrity shaped my life. I also dedicate it to my mother, Mrs Rose Otu, as she approaches the celebration of 97 years of fruitful life in 2026. Mum, your resilience, optimism, and steadfast faith have been a pillar of strength for all of us. The joy and fulfilment of family moments with you remain priceless.

Contents

Acknowledgements

Correctional centres are usually bound with walls, gates, labels, locks, etc., and they can be difficult to penetrate. I am therefore much indebted to the detaining authorities of the correctional centres in Ghana as well as their oversight bodies, the Ghana Prisons Service, under the auspices of the Ministry of Interior, and the Social Work Department of the Ministry of Gender, Children and Social Protection, for granting me access to the centres.

Physical access does not automatically guarantee social access; sometimes, the latter can be more difficult as one can obtain permission or a nod from an ethical committee to interview inmates or staff but interviewees especially in a detention environment may decide to remain silent. Gaining social access to various informants in correctional centres or prisons is therefore as important as negotiating access to a physical setting. In this respect, I am thankful to the children, young people, their staff and related actors in the correctional centres.

I am grateful to CHRAJ, under Dr Joseph Whittal's leadership, for facilitating access to correctional centres, and to Her Excellency Ms Anna Bossman, who supported my research at its inception. I also acknowledge the Netherlands Fellowship Programme (NUFFIC) for sponsoring my initial studies from 2008 to 2013, culminating in my PhD. My later visits in 2019 and 2023 were self-funded, with the Commission assisting through letters of introduction.

Professors Leontine Visser and Roy Gigengack, your supervisory support during my doctoral research remains unforgettable. Though more than a decade has passed since I earned my PhD, your guidance and encouragement continue to inspire me.

Dr Andrew M. Jefferson, I am grateful for your invitation to the inaugural meeting of prison ethnographers in Copenhagen in December 2009, which led to the creation of the Global Prisons Research Network. Your support in conferences and publications, including the special edition *Everyday Prison Governance in Africa* in Her Majesty's Prisons Service Journal, has been invaluable.

Dr Rod Earle, your inspiration has greatly contributed to the realization of this book. Since our first meeting at the Milton Keynes symposium in

2012 – *Resisting the Eclipse: What Prison Ethnography Has to Offer in an Age of Mass Incarceration* – you have remained a steadfast source of encouragement. Your invitation to contribute to *The Palgrave Handbook of Prison Ethnography* proved pivotal.

Finally, I owe immense gratitude to my husband, Reverend Professor Samuel Ayete-Nyampong, and my children, Dr Daisy Ofori, Dr Angelina Klinogo, and Mr John Ayete-Nyampong, together with your lovely spouses and children. Your unwavering support, reassurance, and inspiration have sustained me throughout this journey. May this book continue to inspire you in your own pursuits.

Foreword

Andrew M. Jefferson
DIGNITY – Danish Institute Against Torture

The last couple of decades have shown a resurgence of ethnographic work on prisons and other sites of confinement, also in sub-Saharan Africa (Jefferson and Martin, 2014, Drake et al., 2015, Martin, 2015, Martin and Jefferson, 2019, Weegels et al., 2020, Morelle et al., 2021, Stuit et al., 2024). In 2009 when the fieldwork that lies at the heart of this book was initiated this was not the case. At that time prisons in Africa were still considered by some to be off limits due to their inherent difficulty, dangerousness, or incomparability – unworthy of inclusion, for example, in a book comparing prisons internationally (South and Weiss, 1998).

Thankfully this is no longer the case as this book bears witness.

Ethnography is typically thought of as a method characterized by immersion in the social worlds of research participants, deeply reliant on observation and participation. It is commonly associated with the discipline of anthropology but today utilized by researchers across the social science spectrum. But it is more than just a method; it is also an orientation or way of thinking. To employ an ethnographic sensibility is to approach the social worlds of research participants attuned to the significance or meanings they attach to their own everyday lives and practices. And to the taken-for-granted assumptions and structural drivers of their practice and the practices that frame their lives (Schatz, 2013).

Prisons may be thought of as amplifying institutions, that is institutions that simultaneously compress and intensify experience (Jefferson and Schmidt, 2019), often exacerbating pre-existing deprivations (Jefferson et al., 2021). They are also totalizing, with (almost) all aspects of life subject to confining, punitive, external controls (Schliehe, 2016). Further, prisons are fundamentally relational institutions, on the one hand, circumscribing relational possibilities by reducing the opportunities for people in prison to interact with those they choose (their families and friends, for example) and, on the other hand, obliging prisoners to mingle with people they have not themselves chosen to associate with. As Sykes (1958) observed, in one of the earliest prison studies, prisons compromise autonomy, radically limit opportunities, and thrust people into unavoidable social webs.

Along similar lines and going against the grain of common understandings (of prisons as isolated and isolating institutions), Rhodes (2010) has emphasized the social nature of imprisonment. Prisons may have anti-social effects on individuals, their families, and even society – but they are deeply social environments. Indeed, following Rhodes, they can be thought of as producers of sociality (Jefferson and Gaborit, 2015). But what kinds of sociality, under what specific conditions, and with what effects?

The everyday, relational qualities of prisons and other sites of confinement and their generative effects are what make ethnography an optimal approach. Ethnographic immersion is designed to look behind the scenes, a desirable quality in spaces that are often heavily defended and where subtlety and persistence is required to manage the many boundaries that must be continually negotiated to enable and maintain access. As evidenced by this study, ethnography enables access to institutional underlives.

While human rights actors (understandably) view prisons from a norm-driven, deficit-oriented point of view attentive to the ways in which everyday prison practices (often focused on 'conditions and treatment') fail to live up to norms and standards, ethnography directs attention to the full pallet of everyday institutional experience. Prison ethnographers attend to the entirety of prison experience, not only to conditions and treatment but also to experiential 'climates', that is the conditioning conditions that underlie everyday experiences of imprisonment.

Tomas Max Martin and colleagues identify three central dimensions of prison climates worth attending to if 360-degree accounts of prison practice are to be generated. These are survival, governance, and transition. Directing attention to survival involves looking at how the occupants of prisons (prisoners and staff) manage and cope with their everyday situations. Focusing on governance comprises examining the way authority is distributed and experienced, that is essentially answering the question: who is (really) in charge. Finally, being oriented towards transitions is to be attentive to the way prison practice 'persists and mutates', that is changes but also stays the same.

These conceptualizations and realizations emerged from conversations between prison ethnographers working in the Global South in the 2000s. Lilian Ayete-Nyampong, the author of this book, was a contributor to those conversations and a key participant in the inaugural meeting of the *Global Prisons Research Network* established in 2009. The network was set up recognizing that prisons in the Global South (or 'beyond the west') was an emerging, insurgent field of research where researchers were often relatively isolated and collegial support and intellectual sparring was desirable.

At the inaugural meeting in Copenhagen, Lilian brought her experiences of Ghanaian sites of confinement into conversation with the experiences of other researchers looking at prisons in Brazil, India, Nigeria, South Africa, Uganda, and Zambia. She was always conscious of her positionality, situated within a human rights agency but keen to push the boundaries of rights discourse and to privilege the experience of the prisons' occupants, to demythologize, we might say, the penal experience, and the experience of the prisons' inhabitants. As evidenced by this book, Lilian came to grapple with themes that other founding members of the network were grappling with – entangled encounters; everyday experiences; the relational and porous nature of prisons; prisoner–staff relations; prison governance; and the way prisons are not timeless institutions located outside of society but are, in fact, inherently situated in history and society. What she uniquely brought to the table was her former experience of monitoring sites of confinement in Ghana and a specific interest in young people and their experiences of penal power.

She also embodied care and compassion, or, to use a shorthand term, heart. At the time, Lilian was still learning the ethnographic research trade, but brought with her years of experience in the field of human rights and a long-standing commitment to confronting systemic injustices. Her research focus – the topic of this book – grew out of a desire to better understand and make sense of dynamics she had seen in practice. It reflected a desire to link efforts to improve the world with efforts to understand the world, to inform and qualify interventionist praxis with knowledge anchored in experience. She sought to challenge commonly held assumptions and counter bias and prejudice especially about incarcerated young people, by refusing, for example, to accept accounts of the 'African child' that render them inherently 'bad', choosing instead to listen to their own accounts of what led them to prison.

Ethnography in sites of confinement is a high risk-high gain endeavour to be entered into cautiously if at all. It is no easy task but with the right combination of humility, persistence, and steadfastness – and with adequate support networks for the ethnographer – it can serve an invaluable purpose, nuancing understandings, and challenging commonly held beliefs about institutional legitimacy and the way incarcerated people are rendered incarcerable. Ethnographies of sites of confinement in under-researched peripheralized contexts such as Ghana also serve to challenge the hegemony of western representations of imprisonment reminding us of the diversity of forms of confinement that exist globally, albeit often sharing a colonial heritage.

By its very existence this book helps to 'southernize' prison studies – empirically and conceptually – thus furthering the necessary agenda of academic decolonization. By furnishing us with new insights into the lived worlds of detention centres for young people in Ghana it enables the possibility of new cross-country comparisons. By 'fashioning facts'

(MacLean, 2022) through careful observation and heedful listening this book offers scholars, policy makers, and activists new ways of thinking about youth detention in sub-Saharan Africa and by extension new ways of understanding how penal pain might be mitigated and how young people living in compromised circumstances might be enabled to flourish in freedom rather than end up confined. It is thus a welcome addition to the literature on sites of confinement in sub-Saharan Africa and beyond.

1

A Decade of Research: Framing the Enquiry

Introduction

The chapters of this book are built on insights from four years of sociological research, carried out between 2008 and 2013, through ethnographic work in Ghana's correctional centres for young offenders and juveniles.[1] This research culminated in earning my PhD in the Netherlands. A decade after my initial fieldwork, I undertook a follow-up visit in 2019, followed by another in 2023 (Ayete-Nyampong, 2013a, 2019, 2023). The primary purpose of these subsequent visits was to evaluate the changes that had taken place since my first engagement.

Drawing on two decades of human rights work with the Commission on Human Rights and Administrative Justice (CHRAJ), this chapter frames the book's rationale by highlighting the limited impact of reforms despite strong legal foundations. It reflects on my shift toward ethnography – initially isolating given the scarcity of confinement studies in Africa but later enriched through scholarly networks. Before this reflection, I outline key interpretive concepts and trace Ghana's juvenile justice evolution from community practices through colonial ordinances to post-independence custodial measures. I reflect on an initially isolating trajectory shaped by my shift towards ethnography and the scarcity of confinement ethnography in Africa, though later enriched through the development of meaningful scholarly networks.

At the heart of this book lie narratives of children in conflict with the law, a serendipitous and yet crucial focus that brings to the fore the experiences of youngsters prior to committal. These accounts are marked by troubling memories of rejection, neglect, and abandonment, most often inflicted by parents and extended family. Youngsters' agency, however, exists alongside ongoing exposure to neglect and harm. Many actively navigate their circumstances: leaving school, relocating, shaping new relationships, working informally, or turning to spiritual and supernatural practices as strategies of survival. Through their stories, children reveal who they are, where they come from, and the divergent ways they process their differentiated experiences before and during committal. Narratives of youngsters also complicate simplistic explanations linking neglect to poverty alone. While economic hardship is relevant, many children see their abandonment by family and state as intentional, infused with emotional meaning and moral judgement. Their interpretations shape how they attempt to reclaim control and rebuild relationships, while in committal in correctional centres. Thus, from the very moment of committal to correctional centres, youngsters demonstrate a clear awareness of their circumstances. They often describe themselves as victims of familial irresponsibility, particularly by fathers and other relatives who failed to meet their basic needs. Their resentment extends beyond the private sphere of kinship: it targets state actors, especially the police, who they feel have misidentified the source of wrongdoing by arresting them rather than holding their families accountable.

The title of this book signals a challenge to foregoing narrative: it calls for recognition and respect for children's perspectives and lived experiences, including their candid, often fierce verbalizations of anger and betrayal. Male children, for instance, declare from behind the wall of confinement: 'We shall jail our fathers'; 'We shall jail the police' (Ayete-Nyampong, 2013a). Girls, too, express their discontent, though often through defiance and disengagement from rehabilitative activities intended to reform them.

Through an ethnographic lens, I discuss how life stories of young detainees reveal how pre-custodial experiences shape their confinement, while analyses of correctional centres as 'total institutions' expose both disciplinary aims and the persistence of children's agency. The text uncovers the mortification procedures of a total institution, the hidden social underlife, the tactical sidetracking and appropriation of institutional programmes, and the paradoxical role of escapes in reinforcing control. In sum, everyday relational life in correctional centres is complex, marked by boundaries that are permeable and fluid – constantly shifting between confinement and society. These boundaries are not fixed; rather, they are continually negotiated and renegotiated through the routines, interactions, and relational practices that shape daily existence in correctional centres.

A decade on, revisiting these institutions reveals only modest progress, while entrenched neglect and violations persist, fuelling ongoing critiques of the rehabilitation and correctional capacity of correctional centres.

This book arrives at a pivotal moment in Africa's demographic history when approximately 70 per cent of sub-Saharan Africa's population is under the age of 30[2] (Nugent, 2005, Bah, 2025, Begho and Daubry, 2025). Ghana reflects this youthful trend[3] not only in its general population but alarmingly in its prison population as well[4]. The question that easily comes to mind is, whether Ghana's juvenile justice system and related legal framework are genuinely committed to rehabilitating children in conflict with the law, or inadvertently producing cycles of recidivism that swell the ranks of the adult prison system?

Before examining how Ghana's system of social control evolved from informal practices to codified laws, and questioning whether these laws have translated effectively into practice, I first outline in the next section a set of concepts that frame the discussions in this book. My ethnographic interpretive framework draws on insights such as mortification procedures within total institutions, the hidden social underlife, tactical sidestepping and appropriation of institutional programmes, and the paradoxical interplay of power, resistance, and defiance during escapes. Together, these perspectives, stemming from diverse theoretical paradigms, enrich the analysis in this book.

Multiplicity of concepts

The concepts I deploy emerge from my ethnographic interpretative framework that draws together diverse theoretical paradigms illuminated by the differentiated lived realities within Ghana's correctional centres. While these conceptual strands may at times appear contradictory, they offer a lens through which to grasp the paradoxes and relational complexities that define everyday institutional life, rendering it anything but linear, predictable, impermeable or neatly structured. No single theoretical perspective could fully account for the contradictions, ambiguities, entanglements and complex dynamics that marked my ethnographic data. It is precisely this multiplicity of realities that led me to embrace an actor-oriented approach, allowing for greater attentiveness to complexity and contextual nuance embedded in young people's lived experiences (Long, 2001).

Total institutions

Correctional centres illustrate Goffman's concept of total institutions, defined as places where individuals live and work under enclosed, formally administered routines, separated from wider society (Goffman, 1968). Although institutions vary in their degree of 'totalness', correctional centres remain total insofar as barriers to outside contact exist, marked by walls, locked doors, and large groups of inmates engaged in uniform, routinized activities (see Chapter 5). For young people, institutionalization begins with initiation ceremonies and mortification procedures, intended to shape them through rules, routines, and interventions, and to deliver them as 'corrected' and reformed at the end of confinement. Warders, psychologists, social workers, justice professionals, and human rights actors all play roles in facilitating these interventions.

Underlife

Mortification in total institutions strips inmates of roles, names, and identities. To cope, Goffman describes 'secondary adjustments' – unauthorized practices that provide inmates satisfaction without directly resisting staff authority (1968). Unlike primary adjustments, which involve fulfilling expected roles, secondary adjustments may seek to alter institutional structures, and yet fit within existing routines. Contained adjustments form the 'underlife', which I liken to a concealed social world in correctional centres (see Chapter 6). This underlife is complex rather than a uniform inmate subculture. I do not therefore equate the underlife (Goffman, 1968) in correctional centres with an inmate subculture that is entirely homogenous (Hensley et al., 2003, Agozino and Dastile, 2022, Dvoryanskov and Sika, 2022, Higgins et al., 2022, Petrus et al., 2022).The social underlife in correctional centres, which to some degree is also shared by staff, is a complex one, shaped by punishment, rituals, and patronage practices characterized by the sharing of material and non-material resources. While Goffman highlights underlife as a response to institutional authority, he seems to stop short of recognizing inmate agency. My analysis therefore draws on Foucault's notion of everyday resistance to capture the dynamics of power in Ghana's correctional centres.

Power and resistance: Foucault's notion of power

Drawing on Foucault's notion of power, I show that power is not possessed but enacted, usually intertwined with resistance (Foucault, 1978). My research illustrates this through escape incidents involving Afua, Theresa, and James, where everyday life in confinement is marked by both power and resistance or defiance (see Chapter 7). For Foucault (1978), power permeates disciplinary sites, which in the context of my research might represent correctional centres, police cells, courts and so on, and resistance emerges wherever power operates. Though he draws on Bentham's panopticon to explain disciplinary power (Foucault, 1977), Foucault moves beyond the simple oppressor–oppressed dichotomy, emphasizing power's multiplicity. It is worthy of note that, in Ghana's correctional centres, the panoptic control is less architectural than social, expressed through constant reminders of rules and routines and the sense of being watched. Here, power is exercised through people rather than structures, revealing its dynamic interplay in everyday relational life.

Scott's notions of domination and resistance

Scott's concepts of hidden transcript and public transcript come from his influential work *Domination and the Arts of Resistance* (Scott, 1990). They describe how power relations are expressed differently in public versus private contexts, especially under conditions of domination. Drawing on Scott's notions of domination and resistance, I explain how staff, in the formal and open performance of their roles, exercise authority, yet privately – in the hidden transcript – they admit difficulties in managing youngsters (see Chapter 5). Scott's framework is mostly bound to the dominator–oppressor dichotomy, which tends to overlook the complexity of how power relations also involve compromise and cooperation. My analysis in this book, draws predominantly on an actor perspective (Long, 2001), which gives meaning to the complexity of everyday interplay of power, defiance, negotiation, and compromise that transcends dichotomies and binaries.

An actor-oriented perspective and the underlife

The interpretative framework of my ethnographic data mostly aligns with an actor perspective, even though I have utilized multiplicity of concepts as earlier discussed. Professor Norman Long is the pioneer of the actor-oriented approach (Long, 2001), one of the perspectives of the internationally recognized tradition of the Wageningen School of Sociology, where I conducted my initial research from 2008 to 2013.[5] Norman Long's actor-oriented perspective shifts focus from individual mental and psychological states to what they actually do in the messy, negotiated reality of confinement practice. The actor-oriented perspective is different from actor-oriented rational choice models. The latter emphasizes individualism rather than the differentiated socially situated experiences of actors (Long, 1992, 2001, Hebinck et al., 2001). The actor-oriented perspective positions itself differently from a systems approach by portraying knowledge as fragmentary and diffused, rather than interconnected subsystems that constitute a unified whole. Long locates the experiences and practices of social actors, within a contextualized socio-cultural and political setting. A social actor, in this respect, is not merely a synonym for an individual, nor is it a fixed social category such as social class or gender, but a social construct (Long, 2001).

From an actor-oriented perspective, discussions in this book do not treat young and juvenile offenders as a homogenous group, hampered by structural constraints before and during committal. I recognize children in conflict with the law as social actors, having differential responses to similar structural causalities of crime and delinquency (see Chapters 3–8). As social actors, they are not merely passive recipients of planned criminal justice reforms or linearly following laws or human rights conventions. On the contrary, the efforts of social actors of juvenile and young offenders are invaluable to any change concerning them. The agency of youngsters in this regard attributes them to process social experience and devise ways of coping with life, even under the most extreme forms of confinement. Agency can also be equated to the power to pass on a command or enlist the involvement of others in a scheme, by the ability to influence others, for instance socially. Thus, whereas juvenile offenders are structurally constrained, and their lives wrapped in rejection, abuse, abandonment, they demonstrate the capacity as social actors to negotiate the structural and everyday challenges they encounter.

As earlier indicated, I illustrate how from an actor-oriented perspective, complex dynamics prevalent in entangled relationships and hierarchies are not restricted to dualities, binary oppositions or fixed boundaries between officer and inmate. This notion of entanglement was employed in discussions following the presentation of conference papers at a Global Prisons Research Conference in 2010 on the theme: 'Dissecting the "non-western" prison'[6]. Entanglement was meant here to deconstruct the dyad of prisoner–staff relations. While the connotation behind this usage is beneficial, the image of an 'entangled web' may suggest a kind of trap from which one cannot free oneself. A similar usage is by Callon (2007), who in the context of how ties are constituted with market transactions, explains the notion of entanglement as a web of relations in which one never quits, and one cannot escape. A broader usage of an 'entangled social logic' is employed by Olivier de Sardan (2005), and yet, his use of 'logic' tends to also suggest some sort of rationality, thus missing out on the uncertainties and ambivalences of everyday relational social life in detention committal. A more flexible and preferable usage is evoked by Arce and Long (2007) in their reference to complex entanglements of social relationships from an interface perspective, one that entails social relations that are fluid or constantly on the move, characterized by negotiations within and across loose boundaries.

Generally, an actor-oriented perspective practically brings to the fore the diverse complex entanglements, contestations, contradictions, and ambiguities that are prevalent among actors of various hierarchical and social positions. Methodically, this requires listening and respecting the complexity and sometimes messiness of everyday confinement practice, a process that is dynamic and far from being linear or predictable. This stands in contrast to traditional theories, which tend to prioritize systems and structures, top-down linear processes, and one-size fits all approaches.

Appropriation and sidetracking

The book also briefly discusses forms by which youngsters and related actors divert from institutional goals by means of appropriation and sidetracking (Olivier de Sardan, 2005). Sidetracking is seen as different from resistance

(Foucault, 1978, Scott, 1985, 1990), as sidetracked and appropriated efforts do not directly oppose or confront institutional goals head on; sometimes there is even an accommodation of institutional goals. I draw on the conceptualization of development projects (Olivier de Sardan, 2005) to demonstrate how institutional goals of reform and correction are appropriated by youngsters as they devise practical methods, drawing on their own local resources (see Chapter 8). The central motive being that youngsters manage to appropriate institutional goals for their own interests and, in the process, institutions sometimes tend to be beneficiaries. The case of William, an inmate teacher discussed in Chapter 8, who sidetracked from and appropriated formal approaches of educational instruction, emphasizes that youngsters are not passive recipients of educational and religious instruction, knowledge, or reform. On the contrary, they sidetrack from and appropriate interventions that align with their realities. William's case demonstrates that effective education requires attentiveness to learners' micro-behaviours, lived contexts, and shared experiences. Viewed through the lens of convict criminology (Ross and Richards, 2003, Jones et al., 2009, Earle, 2016, 2018, 2019, 2020, Richards et al., 2018, Davies and Earle, 2020), William's case of appropriation underscores the value of engaging inmate teachers and peer instructors both during custody and after release. These individuals combine lived experience, contextual pedagogy, and practical innovation, enabling them to connect with juveniles more effectively.

Largely, youngsters' understandings of education, reform, and related constructs stand in contrast to the interpretations held by institutional actors and agents of change. Rather than conforming to formally prescribed goals, children in conflict with the law frequently navigate towards appropriated, locally constructed alternatives that reflect their lived experiences and aspirations.

In the section that follows, I briefly trace how Ghana's system of social control and juvenile justice[7] has evolved from informal community mechanisms through colonial ordinances to the current legal framework that formalized juvenile justice.

From informal systems of social control to codified laws

Both the pre-colonial and colonial periods in Ghana featured distinct informal and formal systems of social control (Riby-Williams, 1954, Odetola, 1980, Mensa-Bonsu, 1990, 1995, Ame, 2018, Adewale and Schepers, 2023, Nyarko, 2023). In the pre-colonial era, mechanisms of social regulation varied across ethnic groups, even as they shared common values, communal responsibilities, and belief systems. Across these diverse groups, local deities, ancestors, chiefs, clan and family heads, and the extended family played central roles in ensuring adherence to cultural norms, belief systems, and traditional codes of conduct (Riby-Williams, 1954, Odetola, 1980, Mensa-Bonsu, 1990, 1995, Ame, 2018, Adewale and Schepers, 2023, Nyarko, 2023).

Families sought to pass down occupational skills to their children directly or through fosterage, and child work was valued as children were intentionally trained to take over from their parents and other adults within the family. The phenomena of homelessness, *streetism*, child labour, and institutional systems such as children's homes and orphanages were virtually non-existent in the pre-colonial era (de Graft-Johnson, 1965, Ame, 2018). In this era, crime usually assumed a broader definition and was not only considered against the individual but against the family, ancestors, the gods, and entire community. Serious offences attracted harsh and sometimes inhumane sanctions such as atonement, pacification, and related rituals. Other times, ridicule, banishments, social ostracism or 'social death' (Abotchie, 1997) and so on, were utilized as forms of punishment. For instance, if a family member who contracted a debt was unable to pay under the traditional system of communal responsibility, the onus was on other members of the family to do so (Sarbah, 1904, Ame, 2018). This was exemplified within the *trokosi* system, which is still prevalent, where mostly female children commonly referred to as *trokosis* were made to serve in shrines to cover or atone for the sins or offences of other members of the family (Ababio and Mawusinu, 2000, Boaten, 2001, Ame, 2013, 2018, Arthur-Ewusie, 2024, Ayete-Nyampong, 2025b).

The measures of social and crime control by various ethnic groups including the communal family and extended family system, however, experienced a gradual weakening during the period of the slave trade between the 15th and 19th century. Further, the rise of colonialism and related changes in the 19th and early 20th century in the Gold Coast further impacted the traditional mechanisms of social control (Reid, 1978, Arowolo, 2010). For instance, the administrative structure and system employed during colonial rule could not entirely support the large numbers who migrated to the cities and towns to be educated (Tooth, 1949, Ame, 2018) Most migrants therefore remained unemployed, giving rise to children who needed care and protection, which resulted in social problems such as homelessness, petty thefts and so on (Sarbah, 1904, Tooth, 1949, Riby-Williams, 1954, Ame, 2018).

Petty theft was said to be the most frequently committed offence according to a survey of juvenile delinquency in the Gold Coast based on information obtained from police records (Tooth, 1949).[8] This situation of petty thefts by juvenile delinquents, which has persisted until now, was not peculiar to the Gold Coast. Fouchard reports that petty thefts and other social problems encountered by the youth in Nigeria similarly emerged within the same period of the early 20th century (Fourchard, 2006). Generally, some contributing factors to such social problems during the colonial period as earlier indicated were urbanization and the weakening of the family system due to administrative structures that promoted migration of large numbers to the cities and towns (Tooth, 1949, Riby-Williams, 1954, Ame, 2018). These challenges led to the enactment of ordinances and laws that formally defined child delinquency and legitimized custodial measures as the state's response to behaviours such as petty theft.

Formal recognition of child delinquency

A set of ordinances were passed in Ghana by the colonial administrators in the early 20th century, specifically, from 1928 through to 1946,[9] to address social problems by young people (Riby-Williams, 1954, Ame, 2018, Hynd, 2018). Within this period, custodial measures were employed and industrial homes,[10] including the Borstal institution in Accra, were established. Courts were mandated to commit children who had committed offences to training schools and juvenile courts of summary jurisdiction were constituted (pursuant to the courts ordinance of 1945) resulting in the creation of a juvenile justice system that gave formal recognition to juvenile delinquency and to custodial practices (Riby-Williams, 1954). Fouchard (2006), in commenting about custodial measures employed in Nigeria, indicated that such measures contributed to a judicial machinery that criminalized a large portion of urban youth and formally employed the label 'juvenile delinquency' in Nigeria. After independence, the Criminal Procedure Code of 1960 (GOG, 1960) was passed in Ghana and this saw the repeal of earlier statutes and the incorporation of what was contained in previous ordinances. The Criminal Procedure Code of 1960 saw amendments in 1994 and 1998 as the period after 1970 saw the crucial need to shift from committal to the strengthening of non-custodial options such as probation and community service. This was partly on account of budgetary constraints in maintaining juvenile institutions and partly due to the realization that incarceration did not pose enough deterrence to juvenile crime (DSW, 2005b). An innovative amendment worth noting is Section 4 of the Criminal Code Amendment Act (Act 554) of 1998 (GOG, 1998b), which raised the age of criminal responsibility from 7 to 12 years. This aligned with international human rights standards and the guidance of the UN Committee on the Rights of the Child, which recommended 12 years as the absolute minimum age at which a child may be held criminally responsible.[11] Most of the foregoing ordinances, laws, and institutional frameworks were based on practice in the United Kingdom (Riby-Williams, 1954, Fourchard, 2006), and so implementation in local contexts was difficult. In order to promote effective rights-based reforms and strengthen non-custodial options, Ghana in 2003 passed the Juvenile Justice Act 653 (GOG, 2003), a comprehensive Act that introduced innovative provisions on probation work and alternatives to custodial sentencing as well as rights-based approaches, which gave prominence to the best interest of the child.[12] Despite that the Juvenile Justice

Act and related international, regional, and domestic frameworks emphasize diversion, and related non-custodial approaches to juvenile crime, custodial measures have remained entrenched for children in conflict with the law.

The discussions that follow briefly outline the legal framework that supports Ghana's juvenile justice system.

The legal framework that supports Ghana's juvenile justice system

Ghana has a robust legal framework for ensuring justice and protection for children. The Juvenile Justice Act, Act 653 of 2003 (GOG, 2003); the Children's Act 560 of 1998[13] (GOG, 1998a), and other related international human rights instruments constitute the basis for promoting the human rights of children in conflict with the law in Ghana. Ghana was the first country in the world to ratify the United Nations Convention on the Rights of the Child (CRC) (UNCRC, 1989) and has ratified various human rights treaties, such as the International Covenant on Civil and Political Rights (ICCPR) (UNICCPR, 1966), and the International Covenant on Economic, Social and Cultural Rights (ICESR) (UNICESCR, 1966), and those relating to child protection including the only region-specific child rights instrument, namely the African Charter on the Rights and Welfare of the Child (ACRWC) (AUACRWC, 1990). This unique treaty emphasizes the reform, reintegration, and social rehabilitation of children in conflict with the law who are in committal. Other non-treaty international and regional standards of relevance are the United Nations Standard Minimum Rules for the Administration of Juvenile – Beijing Rules 5 (UN, 1985); the UN Guidelines for the Prevention of Juvenile Delinquency – Riyadh Guidelines (UN, 1990a); the UN Rules for the Protection of Juveniles Deprived of their Liberty – Havana Rules (UN, 1990b); UN Minimum Rules for Non-Custodial Measure – Tokyo Rules (UN, 1990c); the Guidelines for Action on Children in the Criminal Justice System.[14] General Comment No. 24 of the Committee on the Rights of the Child[15] underscores a critical concern in custodial practice, urging that the deprivation of liberty be used strictly as a measure of last resort for children in conflict with the law.

Indeed, international and regional legal instruments, alongside national frameworks and policies such as the 1992 Constitution of the Fourth Republic of Ghana (GOG, 1992), Ghana's Children's Act (Act 560, 1998) (GOG, 1998a), the Criminal and Other Offences Act, 1960 (GOG, 1960), the Courts Act, 1993 (Act 459, 1993) (GOG, 1993), Ghana's Juvenile Justice Act (Act 653, 2003) (GOG, 2003), and policies such as the Child and Family Welfare Policy (GOG, 2015a) and the Justice for Children Policy (GOG, 2015b), provide a relatively robust legal foundation for protecting the rights of children in conflict with the law in Ghana. The 1992 Constitution of Ghana obliges the state to be guided by international human rights instruments in fulfilling its responsibilities. Furthermore, Article 28 of the 1992 Constitution of Ghana specifically addresses children's rights, mandating Parliament to enact laws that guarantee special care, assistance, and protection for children.

In discussions that follow, I briefly outline, under Ghana's Juvenile Justice Act of 2003, who constitutes a child in conflict with the law.

The child in conflict with the law

Under the UN Convention on the Rights of the Child (UNCRC) and Ghana's Children's Act, a child is defined as any person under the age of 18. Children in conflict with the law are those alleged, accused, or found to have committed an offence, or any other breach of the law. The passage of Ghana's Juvenile Justice Act resulted in specific definitions pertaining to age and who constituted a 'child in conflict with the law'. According to sections 46 and 60 of the Act, a juvenile offender is a child under the age of 18 in conflict with the law who has been convicted of an offence. In accordance with the Act, a young offender is 18 or more years of age but below 21 years and has been convicted of an offence.

The Act does not set a lower-level limit for a juvenile offender; this gap is, however, filled by Section 4 of the Criminal Code (Amendment Act 554 of 1998) (GOG, 1998c), which sets the legal age of criminal accountability at 12 years. The Juvenile Justice Act, Section 47 (3) sets the upper limit for children in conflict with the law at 21. The legal definition of juvenile and young offenders in detention in accordance with the relevant laws in Ghana thus covers persons between the ages of 12 and 21.

Female juvenile offenders aged 12 to 18 are confined in Ghana's sole female Junior Correctional Centre, located in Osu, Accra. The Senior Correctional Centre (SCC) is also Ghana's only institution for male young offenders. In line with the Juvenile Justice Act, it also houses juveniles aged 12 to 18 who have committed serious crimes, resulting in a mixed population of juveniles and young offenders between 12 and 21 years.[16]

I use the terms children, youngsters, youth, young people, juveniles, young offenders, inmates, detainees, boys, girls, and related terms interchangeably throughout the chapters of this book, to refer to children in conflict with the law. Of these terms, youngsters appear most frequently in both my fieldwork and writing, reflecting a preference for its more informal and contextually resonant tone. While I acknowledge that the majority of these youngsters are under 18 years and are categorized legally as children, the predominant usage of youngsters reflects both the diverse institutional and social framings of juveniles and young offenders in the Ghanaian context.

In the next section, I share reflections as a practitioner who has had oversight in the past two decades of monitoring visits conducted by the

CHRAJ to adult prisons and correctional centres for juveniles and young offenders in Ghana.

Reflections as a practitioner

As a practitioner with CHRAJ, I have spent over two decades overseeing research projects and conducting monitoring visits to prisons and correctional centres. This long engagement prompted me to reflect on the effectiveness of our work. Between 2007 and 2008, I observed that human rights professionals working with children often approached them primarily as a legal category, relying heavily on statistical data and survey-based research. While such data provided valuable insights, it frequently lacked the qualitative depth needed to capture children's own perspectives and lived experiences. For example, harmful cultural practices such as *trokosi*, child labour, trafficking, neglect, and abuse had received significant advocacy and research attention, yet the voices of the children themselves were not always central to these efforts. At the same time, little focus was placed on incarcerated children and young people in detention (DSW, 2005a, Hoffmann and Baerg, 2011). Even within CHRAJ, initial monitoring visits focused on prisons and police cells, with correctional centres for juveniles and young offenders added only later[17]. Yet, by being lawfully confined, incarcerated children and young people faced particularly difficult circumstances that demanded closer engagement. This neglect may have stemmed from the stigma of criminal guilt attached to juvenile offenders and the challenges of accessing detention institutions.

As a result, issues concerning children in conflict with the law were often relegated to the margins of Ghana's child protection priorities (Mensa-Bonsu, 1990, Abotchie, 1991, Amenyendzie, 1998, DSW, 2005a, Asare, 2009, Hoffmann and Baerg, 2011), and they received minimal attention from monitoring bodies, practitioners, government agencies, civil society, researchers, and philanthropists alike.

I decided in 2008 to explore the meanings that incarcerated children and young people attached to human rights. Years of collaboration between my employer, the CHRAJ, and the oversight bodies governing correctional institutions proved vital to this research. My senior position at CHRAJ, followed by my transition to social science research in the Netherlands, facilitated substantive access to institutional spaces, administrative data, the incarcerated youngsters, and the actors charged with their supervision.

No sooner did I commence preliminary fieldwork in 2009 than I realized that official human rights discourse, rooted in international treaties and conventions, rarely aligned with the everyday language, meanings, and lived realities of children in conflict with the law. This warranted an epistemological shift towards privileging children's own voices and experiences, distinct from my practitioner orientation, which had focused on employing deductive approaches to assess whether the human rights of incarcerated youngsters were being upheld. This shift required that I strive to immerse myself partially in the everyday confinement worlds of child detainees, to listen, to respect, and to recognize them as right-bearing individuals rather than merely subjects of policy or enquiry. The methodological adjustment called for a suspension of normative assumptions about human rights, justice, and even my own formal role as a practitioner. Throughout the research process, I was often confronted by the intricacies and complexities associated with my dual role of an academic researcher and a human rights practitioner who needed to move beyond conventional monitoring mechanisms, to appreciating the views and lived experiences of children in committal.

Through listening closely to children's narratives, participating in their daily routines within correctional centres, and engaging with the various actors around them, a series of gaps in the implementation of the Juvenile Justice Act (Act 653, 2003) became serendipitously visible. These gaps included prolonged pre-sentence detention, weak parental contact and support, low interest and engagement in educational activities, gender-based disparities in educational provision particularly for girls, and inadequate reintegration support after discharge. As a human rights practitioner, I could not ignore the indication that, despite the passage and review of various laws, children in conflict with the law continued to face multiple human rights violations and challenges.

My ethnographic evidence points to an implicit assumption embedded in laws and associated reforms – that children originate from stable, supportive nuclear and extended family structures support. This, however, does not reflect the lived realities of youngsters who engaged the attention of my research. While this study is limited in scope and does not permit broad generalizations, it nonetheless underscores a critical lesson, namely, that implementing laws such as Ghana's Children's Act and the Juvenile Justice Act, without integrating children's perspectives about their lived realities, such as their continual neglect by family, can result in significant shortcomings and further gaps.

Youngsters' lived accounts expose a pronounced disjuncture or disconnect. For these young people, both the family and the state appear delinquent, institutions that have failed them morally and functionally. Yet within institutional and professional domains, children in conflict with the law are rather cast in the role of the delinquent, the criminal, the subject in need of reform. While these children may indeed have committed offences, their accounts unsettle conventional ideas of crime and correction. They reveal a disconnect between institutional understandings of reform and children's own interpretations, highlighting divergent constructions of culpability, responsibility, and justice. This disconnect has profound implications, when children experience 'correction' as misdirected or misaligned, it risks undermining efforts intended to rehabilitate them. Thus, children's pre-committal experiences tend to influence the meanings and interpretations they attach to their stay in committal as well as to concepts such as justice and correction.

Besides children's accounts, I demonstrate throughout the chapters of this book how youngsters in correctional centres actively assert their needs and challenge the authority of both family and state. Their seeming acts of defiance, ranging from non-compliance with institutional rules to disengagement from educational, religious, and counselling initiatives, serve as subtle yet potent critiques of the systems designed to rehabilitate them. These strategies reveal how youth not only subtly resist correction but, in effect, offer their own forms of critique and reformation directed at the institutions themselves. Alongside this, I detail the practical realities of correctional centres and the strategies staff employ to navigate daily challenges while maintaining an outward image of effectiveness. These approaches, often involving negotiation, coaxing, and compromise, can somehow diverge from official and institutional goals. Yet these practical methods tend to be the means by which staff manage youngsters who do not conform to institutional goals. Through these everyday practical realities or norms, correctional centres tend to sustain a semblance of functionality, thereby presenting themselves as spaces of correction and reform.

Largely, lived realities of everyday correctional life as discussed in my book resist simple binaries between staff and inmates, different from Goffman's indication that in total institutions, '… social mobility between the two strata is grossly restricted' (Goffman, 1968: 19) and an inmate-staff split is conspicuous. My ethnographic evidence establishes that the relational life and dynamics in correctional centres go beyond staff–inmate, formal–informal, official–private, oppressor–oppressed binaries and divides. On the contrary, relationships are entangled, and manifest compromise and cooperation of a hierarchy of inmates and staff in a mutual exchange of material and non-material resources. Predominantly therefore, discussions in this book illustrate from an actor perspective the complex dynamism of the everyday relational (Long, 2001), dotted by power, defiance, negotiations, and compromise.

Taken together, the chapters of this book highlight the disjuncture between institutional narratives that label youth as delinquent and the perceptions of children who often see themselves as victims of adult neglect. The book challenges oversimplified accounts of childhood that reduce street life, labour, or migration to criminality, thus missing out on the social and relational meanings that children associate with these contexts. The analysis underscores the continuity between pre-confinement, custodial, and post-custodial worlds, showing that young offenders are not merely legal subjects but social actors with interconnected life trajectories. Everyday correctional life is marked by porous physical boundaries (Martin and Jefferson, 2019, Cunha,

2020, Weegels et al., 2020, Ellis, 2021), as well as fluid social boundaries (between peers, staff, and wider society), where alliances, hierarchies, and external networks constantly reshape experiences of confinement. These dynamics reveal multiple realities, and seeming contradictions, that defy simplistic categorization, while exposing the performative logic of institutions that must appear in control even when disciplinary power falters.

Rather than reductively and simplistically portraying Ghanaian and broader African correctional centres and prisons as inherently inhumane institutions, characterized by overcrowding, poor ventilation, and minimal food rations in need of external correction or reform, this book grounded in small-scale, non-generalizing research, centres the voices and experiences of detainees themselves. I offer insights into Ghana's seeming closed institutions characterized by *mortification* procedures (Goffman, 1968), where youngsters attempt to carve out autonomous spaces, rewrite rules, and sometimes contribute to the governance of correctional structures. By what I term an *ethno-inductive* approach – an inside-out, inductive, and ethnographically grounded perspective – I deliberately move away from the normative, human rights, and legalistic language that has shaped my practitioner orientation in previous years. Compendiums of human rights treaties and laws are plentiful and firmly established within international human rights frameworks. What remains critically scarce, however, are the perspectives, lived realities, and the context of the very people these laws are designed to protect. Both dimensions – the legal frameworks of protection and the lived experiences – must be considered together; without this balance, implementation risks being devoid of context.

The novelty of the discussions in this book lies in the complementarity they offer to conventional and legalistic approaches to prisons in Africa as well as to the wider ethnographic scholarship on children and youth in Africa and the Global South. Generally, academic literature on African youth as social actors has been mostly preoccupied with 'free youth' in contexts of war, conflict, violence, and politics. My book is innovative as it contributes scholarly work in Africa on confined youth as social actors. I go beyond the axiomatic recognition of youngsters as 'bad' social actors to demonstrate the practical ways by which youngsters attempt to negotiate everyday boundaries in correctional centres. At the same time, however, these agentic youngsters are still within the grip of confinement. Their relative powerlessness is equally relevant and indicates their need for support and protection.

Through the period of ethnographic fieldwork, characterized by observation and participation, I came to distinguish ethnography as a methodological approach distinct from the broader category of qualitative methods familiar to me as a practitioner (Hammersley, 1994, 2018b). By extending my fieldwork over a prolonged period, my study marked a pioneering contribution to confinement ethnography in Ghana. As noted earlier, ethnography was not my initial methodological choice. Through an unexpected epistemological shift, I found myself re-examining not only my methodological stance, but also my orientation towards knowledge itself. I emphasize here the value of ethnographic narratives as a layered and vital resource, drawing on rich qualitative data (Heikkilä, 2020) that provides contextualized knowledge of differentiated perspectives about confinement practice. My ontological and epistemological shift landed me on a lonely pathway as scholarly work on confinement ethnography in Africa was skeletal.

In the next section, I reflect on my own positionality, my early isolation in this field, and the gradual development of meaningful networks that deepened and strengthened my engagement with ethnographic approaches.

From isolation to networks: making African prisons ethnographically visible

Primarily, ethnography seeks to appreciate the perspectives and lived experiences of people under study, by listening to them and observing their activities in everyday life (Hammersley and Atkinson, 1995). It has assumed various shifts in meaning over the years and does not lend itself to a singular definition. This approach to the study of human cultures and society was employed predominantly within the discipline of anthropology, but has evolved over the years, through the mid-20th century, to being transdisciplinary in the 21st century – its shifts and transdisciplinary focus does not undermine its worth.

Some research employing ethnographical approaches has been done in the United States, Canada, United Kingdom, and other parts of Europe, Asia, Latin America, and Africa (Stein, 1955, Wacquant, 2002, Liebling, 2004, Piacentini, 2004, Jewkes and Johnstone, 2006, Bandyopadhyay, 2007, Jefferson, 2007, Crewe, 2009, Lindegaard, 2009, Martin, 2009, Rhodes, 2009, Sauls, 2009, Darke, 2012, Earle, 2012, Garces, 2012, Hammersley, 2015, Jefferson, 2015, Drake et al., 2015a, Abbott and Scott, 2019, Cunha, 2020, Rowland et al., 2025).

Generally, a review of existing literature at the outset of my fieldwork in 2009 revealed a striking paucity of scholarly work on prison ethnography in Ghana as well as in Africa. Literature reviewed at the time focused on normative aspects of reforms within Ghana's juvenile justice system (Mensa-Bonsu, 1990, Abotchie, 1991, Mensa-Bonsu, 1995, Arthur, 1997, Mensah-Akorah, 2005). This scarcity of ethnographic fieldwork in prisons and confinement sites rendered the initial phase of my journey isolating, until I encountered the work of Dr Andrew Jefferson (Jefferson, 2007). His nuanced insider reflections on Nigerian prisons resonated with my preliminary impressions from the field in Ghana. That same year, Andrew invited me to an inaugural gathering of prison ethnographers in Copenhagen, aimed at fostering dialogue on local carceral contexts across the Global South. At this conference, we exchanged ethnographic experiences from Uganda, Nigeria, Ghana, Sierra Leone, Zambia, South Africa, as well as India and Brazil. I was the only African participant, and the event offered a rare and invaluable opportunity to engage with a small group of scholars. Whereas most participants were not from the continent, they nevertheless brought insightful ethnographic lenses to confinement spaces in Africa (Jefferson et al., 2009). At the conference, one key consensus emerged, it was no longer sufficient to merely document poor conditions in prisons, as human rights frameworks had long done. We needed to make prison experiences and everyday confinement practices, which were often inaccessible, ethnographically visible.

A pivotal outcome of the gathering was the formation of the Global Prisons Research Network (GPRN) in 2009, envisioned as a platform for amplifying ethnographic perspectives on confinement in the Global South. The network aspired to challenge reductive portrayals of Global South prisons as merely sites of failed compliance with international norms. Instead, it aimed to foster scholarly exchange, encourage reflexive interaction among researchers, and expand the field of prison studies beyond the epistemic frame of the Global South, towards a more grounded and contextually attuned knowledge base.

The GPRN began to expand its influence as I participated in another conference in Amsterdam in 2010, as well as a big symposium held in Milton Keynes, United Kingdom, from 18 to 19 September 2012, under the theme *Resisting the Eclipse: What Prison Ethnography Has to Offer in an Age of Mass Incarceration*. The symposium was well attended, with over 100 delegates representing approximately 12 countries. Ethnographic work in Africa and other non-Western spaces such as Brazil and Ecuador featured.

It was a great opportunity to establish contact with Dr Rod Earle, a seasoned researcher in the area of youth justice with long years of experience of lectureship at the Open University. A sequel to the Milton Keynes conference in 2012 was another conference in Bordeaux, France in September 2013, which saw an array of scholars with approximately 35 presentations and discussions by 50 participants in areas of confinement such as refugee camps, psychiatric institutions, migrant centres, shelters and so on, that were not limited to prisons. This conference was themed '*Confinement Viewed through the Prism of the Social Sciences: Contrasting Facilities, Confronting Approaches*'. The Bordeaux conference further deepened transdisciplinary engagements. A few of us presented on African contexts (Curtis, 2013, Gillepsie, 2013, Ayete-Nyampong, 2013b), contributing to a growing body of scholarship across the continent.

A useful accomplishment following these conferences was a collection of field-based ethnographic insights from seven African countries published by

Her Majesty's Prisons Service Journal in 2014, and edited by Dr Andrew Jefferson and Dr Tomas Martin, and under the special edition 'Everyday Prison Governance in Africa'. Based on extensive fieldwork in Rwanda, Zambia, Ghana, Sierra Leone, Uganda, and Ivory Coast, various scholars offered insightful insider perspectives on African prisons, complementing conventional and dominant accounts of dehumanizing conditions and human rights abuses.

Soon after this publication came another opportunity at the invitation of Dr Rod Earle for another book project stemming from the conference in Milton Keynes in 2014, the publication of the Palgrave Handbook of Prison Ethnography in 2015 (Drake et al., 2015b). The book featured diverse and rich contributions mostly from methodological and epistemological perspectives from 24 researchers based in the United Kingdom, United States, Canada, India, Scotland, The Netherlands, Belgium, France, Norway, Denmark, India, South Africa, and Ghana.

Thus, from a lonely start, the landscape of confinement ethnography in Africa and globally has undoubtedly expanded and the discussions in this book are largely situated within this growing body of scholarship on confinement ethnography. Confinement ethnography spans diverse custodial settings, including even non-legal forms of confinement, such as camps for accused witches, religious prayer camps, fetish shrines, and so on, which have engaged my professional interest and shaped recent writings (Ayete-Nyampong et al., 2025a, 2025b).

While confinement ethnography is gaining ground rapidly in Africa, it is important to acknowledge that much of the debate, scholarly exchange, and discourse continue to occur outside the continent. I look forward to seeing more scholarly engagements about Africa, on African soil.

Contributing some ethnographic perspectives to Ghana's child justice reform

Being a member of the National Advisory Committee on Child Protection provided me the opportunity to contribute some of my ethnographic perspectives to child justice reform processes between 2014 and 2015. In that period, I shared narratives from young people whose experiences revealed the neglect of children by both parents and the state. By the time of my second field visit (2009–19), significant developments had already taken place at the national level. I was part of a three member national research team in 2014 that examined the effectiveness of child panels in Ghana (Ame et al., 2020a, 2020b) by drawing mostly on actors' voices and perspectives, and was also part of national stakeholder consultations that contributed related juvenile justice reforms, including the drafting, and launch, of the Justice for Children Policy (GOG, 2015b) and the Child and Family Welfare Policy

(GOG, 2015a). The story of 'Kwesi' (see Chapter 3), for instance, was included in my employer's presentation at the official launch of the Justice for Children Policy.

My ongoing preoccupation with institutional research as a human rights practitioner also led me to adapt methodological approaches in projects I supervised, aiming to generate more practical outcomes. Some of these outcomes included insights into informal economies within overcrowded prisons, particularly around sleeping arrangements, which emerged during my employer's monitoring visits (CHRAJ, 2021a). While advocacy against overcrowding had long been part of reform agendas in prisons, no prior research in Ghana had sought to explain how incarcerated individuals managed daily life under such conditions through informal economic practices. These findings, though rarely included in official reports due to their apparent non-compliance with human rights standards, nonetheless revealed how prisons and correctional centres kept up appearances and sustained their functioning amid structural constraints.

From an ethnographic standpoint, CHRAJ's research on child labour in fishing communities (CHRAJ, 2021b) also yielded practical recommendations informed by local actors. One innovative arrangement involved a school with its Parents and Teachers Association to allow early closures on market days, enabling children to participate in fishing-related work while still attending school. This compromise, which acknowledged the financial realities of families, resulted in the school becoming the best performing in its district despite shortened hours. The CHRAJ report suggested that such arrangements could be piloted more widely, provided they did not harm children's health or wellbeing.

While in the past years, I have continued to reflect on findings from my ethnographic research spanning 2009 to 2023 and the way forward for children in conflict with the law, I also have created visibility about systemic abuses of children in conflict with the law and shared these views at a conference organized by the Child Research and Resource Centre (CRRECENT, 2024) in 2024. In a recent publication (Ayete-Nyampong, 2025a), I shared similar concerns about the pervasive denial of the human rights of incarcerated juveniles and young offenders. The next section focuses on these findings.

Years of neglect and systemic gaps

This section highlights critical and enduring shortcomings within Ghana's juvenile justice system, deficiencies that call for urgent decisive intervention by policy makers, practitioners, and advocates. Drawing on insights from my initial fieldwork in 2009 (Ayete-Nyampong, 2011, 2013a), subsequent consultations with key stakeholders[18] in child protection and juvenile justice, and a recent publication (Ayete-Nyampong, 2025a), inspired by a conference convened by CRRECENT (2024), I share, in the discussions that follow, some systemic challenges that have confronted children in conflict with the law for over a decade.

Children accused of minor offences are seldom granted bail, often because parents or guardians are unavailable to guarantee their return to court (Ayete-Nyampong, 2025a). Likewise, diversion provisions under Section 23 of the Juvenile Justice Act are rarely applied, as families expected to support such processes are frequently untraceable (see Chapter 7). Access to timely legal assistance is also limited: support typically begins only after arrest and at the first court appearance, rather than beforehand. This delay prevents children from benefiting from diversionary options early in the process and undermines their legal rights. Juveniles who are neither bailed nor diverted often endure prolonged stays in police custody or remand homes under harsh conditions (Ame et al., 2020a)[19]. In some instances, male juveniles are detained alongside adult suspects, further heightening their vulnerability.

Other scholars have also documented comparable challenges encountered by children in conflict with the law, particularly the routine denial of bail, the limited availability of legal aid, and the infrequent application of diversionary measures (Mensa-Bonsu, 1990, 1995, Mensah-Akorah, 2005, Ame et al., 2011, Hoffmann and Baerg, 2011, Boakye, 2012, Abrah, 2014, Ame, 2019). These findings reinforce a broader consensus within the literature that systemic shortcomings continue to undermine the rights and welfare of children who came in conflict with the law.

The chapters of this book discuss additional challenges confronting children in conflict with the law. These include the emotional distress experienced during the first six months of committal, persistent gender inequalities that limit educational opportunities for female juvenile offenders, and the general lack of interest among many youngsters in formal educational provisions. It also shares the perspectives and lived experiences of committed juveniles during periods of police detention prior to committal, shedding light on the systemic issues that shape their encounters with the justice system.

A major contributing factor to these challenges is the sustained absence of parental support, beginning in children's early lives and continuing through the point of arrest. When parents or family members are absent during trial proceedings, there is little assurance that a juvenile granted bail will be accompanied to court regularly. Similarly, without parental involvement, the supervision required for diversionary measures is often lacking. Yet, as the chapters of this book reveal (see Chapter 9), most laws and policies fail to acknowledge the lived reality of many children, such as those engaged in my research, who grow up without a stable family structure and are compelled to fend for themselves from as early as three years of age (see Chapters 3 and 4).

Although the scope of my research is limited and not intended for broad generalization, it underscores an urgent need for practitioners and policy makers to move beyond labels and statistics, and instead engage with the lived realities of young people. Preventative strategies must be prioritized, alongside transgenerational approaches that empower parents, grandparents, and guardians to nurture children from their earliest years, creating environments that foster healthy, meaningful, and fulfilling childhoods.

In my capacity as both practitioner and researcher, I have sought to bring ethnographic insights into the lived experiences of young people, extending their influence across reform processes, institutional practices, and scholarly discourse.

Conclusion

Ghana's history of social control demonstrates how juvenile justice has been shaped by both informal traditions and formal legal frameworks. Yet, my long engagement with correctional centres revealed that legal and statistical approaches alone cannot capture the lived realities of children in conflict with the law. Ethnographic narratives, by contrast, illuminate the micro-behaviours, perspectives, and experiences that are often overlooked.

The shift towards ethnographic approaches underscores the importance of moving beyond essentialized categories to embrace contextualized understandings of confinement. Though initially isolating, this pathway has opened opportunities to build networks and foster deeper engagement with qualitative methods. Ultimately, ethnography enriches juvenile justice reform by grounding policy and practice in the lived experiences of children, ensuring that interventions are not only legally sound but also socially meaningful and responsive to the realities of confinement.

In sum, my book calls for deeper scholarly and policy engagement with the complex, lived realities of youth in correctional settings, and a move beyond unitary, punitive framings towards approaches that acknowledge agency, vulnerability, and the need for innovation. It urges professionals and policy makers to take children's views and everyday realities seriously, rather than relying predominantly on institutional assumptions. Practitioners are challenged to pause, confront their biases, and acknowledge past shortcomings in youth justice interventions. Such reflexivity can open the way to more responsive approaches.

2

Confinement Ethnography: Methodological and Ethical Reflections

Introduction

In this chapter, I offer methodological and ethical reflections that problematize the research reality encountered during my initial fieldwork. It marked my first engagement with an ethnographic approach, and several of the experiences and insights gained are valuable for both practitioners and researchers working within prison or confinement contexts. Towards the end of the chapter, I briefly outline the methods employed during two subsequent field visits, which align closely with the standardized approach adopted by my institution.

Methodically, this chapter underscores the importance of ethnographic stories as a vital, multi-layered tool that draws on rich qualitative data (Heikkilä, 2020), offering differentiated perspectives of juvenile and young offenders, that should not be ignored by criminal justice and related practitioners and professionals.

Initial adaptations

During my initial interactions with youngsters, I observed that they articulated their needs and human rights in ways that diverged from my normative, practitioner-based understanding of rights. For example, during preliminary field interactions, informal conversations revealed their use of both official and unofficial ages. Such disclosures, alongside other forms of local knowledge gleaned from the field, challenged my prior assumptions and revealed that the 'research reality' was far less fixed or unitary than I had anticipated.

The emerging ambiguities, ambivalences, and contradictions could not be easily accommodated within my initial deductive framework, which relied on structured questions, structured checklists, and short intervals of observation and focus group discussions. Instead of imposing my formal methodological approach as well as my conceptualization of human rights on youngsters, I recognized the need to learn from them, deliberately listen to their stories, and participate in their everyday activities so as to make meaning of the diverse realities that confronted me. As a practitioner who had oversight of the mechanisms of annual visits to prisons and police cells countrywide and quite acquainted with assessing material conditions such as feeding, health, and sanitation, spacing in cells, and so on, and their compliance with human rights standards, this new road meant a completely new modification for me.

Generally, my new pathway entailed new learnings as I also needed to strengthen my knowledge base about the conduct of participant observations and other methods typical of ethnographic approach. I sought to do what ethnographers usually do by employing participant observation, unstructured and in-depth interviews, and studying youngsters and their everyday experiences. I watched what happened daily, listened to what was said, asked questions and, based on that, prepared in-depth fieldnotes (O'reilley, 2005).

Listening, observing, participating, and so on seemed simple and constituted commonalities that are shared by other ethnographers and could easily be taught or learned, on the face of it. In practice, however, complex dynamics plagued the everyday relational that was characterized by inconsistencies and serendipity and required reflection and reflexivity. I could not entirely rely on books for the appreciation of such emergent local knowledge that evolved from a field that was being continuously impacted locally and externally. In drawing interpretations, I could not aim at generalizations or statistical representations (O'reilley, 2005) such as in respect of pre-custodial experiences, the period of observation, underlife, escapes, and appropriation of educational objectives. On the contrary, I recognized the need to identify themes and codes that emerged from my data; addressed patterns and variations, and sometimes observed the same or different situations continuously. I utilized a variety of methods for the full import of diversity of empirical data from which my theoretical and interpretative frameworks emerged (Emerson et al., 1995, Hammersley and Atkinson, 1995, 2007, McGranahan, 2018, Hammersley, 2018a, 2018b). Central to my new pathway was an ontological stance and an epistemological perspective that did not assume that reality was singular or fixed, but recognized that that juvenile and young offenders actively constructed diverse meanings from their everyday experiences of detention. Stemming from this viewpoint I avoided the idea of developing a fixed set of questions from the outset. Instead, the study lent itself predominantly to an inductive approach, based on grounded theory (Glasser and Strauss,

1967) aiming to generate theory from observations, interviews, and related methods rather than testing pre-existing hypotheses.

Building trust and acceptance was vital to gaining both physical and social access. Factors such as the dynamics of the culture of the field as it was impacted locally and externally, researcher skill and expertise, level of immersion, the length of time spent in the field, and so on contributed to building trust and acceptance. Based on the differentiated ways that knowledge was constructed, I could not arrogate to myself complete local knowledge or a prefect insider. I conceptualized my dual role as a practitioner and a researcher, though the latter constituted my foremost and predominant role. By paying tribute to my monitor status as staff of the Commission on Human Rights and Administrative Justice (CHRAJ), which facilitated access to institutions, I also acknowledged that this double role was fraught with challenges that I grappled with throughout the entire research process. Predominant among the challenges were the effort to carve out a role for myself and the need for a continual negotiation of access and realizing that access, whether physical or social, as well as trust and acceptance, was not a one-off attainment but a process. I was not resident at the correctional centres but visited virtually daily for two years.

Generally, this research study, from an actor-oriented perspective, focuses on perspectives of juvenile offenders as social actors (Long, 2001), who construct diverse meanings of daily detention practice, while they interact with themselves and staff of correctional centres within the context of their immediate and wider environment.

I share the view that ethnography does not lend itself to a singular definition but has assumed various shifts in meaning over the years (Chopra, 2020, Côté-Boileau et al., 2020, Davis and Craven, 2020). The findings presented in this chapter suggest that, whereas practitioners ought to build their knowledge base about the science of doing ethnography, they do not have to be classic anthropologists in order to study everyday dynamics pertaining to carceral spaces and other related phenomena.

Methodological and ethical considerations

Before initiating this research, the information I typically sought from officers and young people, as a practitioner or monitor, mirrored that of human rights and criminal justice professionals. It centred on categories such as the nature of offences, evidence of abuse, disciplinary measures, physical conditions of confinement, and officer–inmate relationship. However, during my preliminary fieldwork, I came to recognize that these enquiries were shaped by a dominant view of the child or young person as a detained offender. This singular framing risks obscuring the broader lived realities of these individuals, including their growing-up narratives, everyday understandings of confinement, and the social identities that precede these legal categorizations. In essence, the predominant emphasis among legal and human rights actors on standards, laws, and institutional compliance can result in a reductive treatment of crime as a discrete incident, casting juveniles solely in the role of offenders. Such a lens fails to acknowledge the multiplicity of their social worlds. In contrast, my early findings illuminated young people as social actors with varied life trajectories and experiential understandings. Following this realization, my researcher stance diverged markedly from the structured and agenda-driven approach of my practitioner role and employer. Rather than adhering to pre-set questionnaires used during institutional visits, I reimagined correctional centres from the inside-out, seeking to access dimensions of confinement life largely invisible to external monitors, including professionals like myself.

My enquiry thus evolved into an inductive process, led by emergent empirical insights. I engaged ethnographic methods such as narratives, in-depth interviews, participant observation, and immersive involvement in daily routines. It was through sustained, iterative engagement with similar and contrasting situations that the richness and diversity of the data came into view, allowing my interpretive frameworks to naturally take shape. Decisions around what data to collect and from whom largely stemmed from on-the-ground observations and informal, dialogic exchanges, what I came to refer to as 'conversational interviews'.

While this inductive approach yielded moments of serendipity and unexpected revelation, it also entailed a dual vulnerability for me as the researcher and the youngsters (Ayete-Nyampong, 2015). Confronting my practitioner predispositions required ongoing reflexivity and thoughtful engagement throughout the research, through listening, participating, observing, and journaling.

Ultimately, my ethnographic evidence revealed practical practices within detention institutions, such as how correctional centres, in response to young people's resistance to institutional norms, deploy practical strategies to create the outward impression of a well-managed facility. Largely, I observed that everyday detention life features social interactions that are mundanely relational and does not always exhibit a neat, marked boundary between officer and inmate.

Delineation: avoidance of fixed boundaries at the outset

In deciding the delineation or scope for my research, some concepts and variables were identified as useful starting points in line with the thinking that data hardly stands alone. In other words, analysis pervaded all spheres of the research process. While reflecting on research questions, listening to narratives, observing and recording notes and coding, analysis was unavoidably inductive and deductive, and I tended to move from one to the other (Emerson et al., 1995, Tracy, 2012, Buscatto, 2018, Ziman et al., 2018, Sibeoni et al., 2020). However, on the whole, the process was predominantly inductive and I remained open to emergent issues.

In guiding the search for meanings that juveniles employ as they make sense of their world of detention, I entered the field with a design that had loose boundaries so as to make room for flexibility while at the same time preventing a confused or vague start devoid of purpose. The research questions that were developed initially served as a starting point in order to resist the temptation of just going in any direction and falling prey to a study that was either too broad or too restrictive. Delineations were not rigidly fixed from the start, though limited to the only female correctional centre and the only male correctional centre in Ghana. The study did not cover juveniles in adult prisons. While issues of rehabilitation and reintegration presented themselves, this study was not at the outset predicated on these issues. As a practitioner, I was familiar with actors' views at the broader level pertaining to rehabilitation and integration and related interventions, though the ethnographic evidence of my research pertaining to rehabilitation and reintegration challenged some previous notions I had held as a practitioner. Generally, I dwelt mostly on the perspectives of internal actors within the confines of juvenile correctional institutions.

Selection of correctional centres

Among the institutions I encountered during the preliminary phase of my study, only three were operational, with two ultimately selected as the core sites for my fieldwork. These choices were deliberate: both institutions stood out not only for their functionality but also for their distinctiveness and the diversity they represented. The Senior Correctional Centre (SCC) is Ghana's sole facility for young male offenders, while the Junior Correctional Centre (JCC) remains the only institution for juvenile female offenders.

Marked contrasts existed between the two, particularly in staffing levels and the number of incarcerated youth. At the SCC, both the daily number of detained boys and the size of the staff consistently exceeded those at the JCC. According to official records, the SCC had, since 2001, maintained an average daily lock-up of fewer than 150 young males. During my fieldwork from 2009 to 2011, daily figures ranged from 100 to 140. Over time, during subsequent follow-up visits in 2019 and 2023, the institution witnessed a gradual increase in committals. The SCC at the time of my initial visit had six dormitories (dorms), this number increased by two dorms during follow-up visits. Each dorm measured 13 by 70 feet and held a minimum of 15–20 male youngsters. The average daily lock-up at the JCC, on the other hand, had not exceeded ten in the last couple of years. The average number of girls held in detention during the period of fieldwork was eight. The JCC had two dorms, each held a minimum of four female youngsters. The main shift at the SCC ran from 7 am to 4 pm and hosted an average of 80 staff. At the JCC, six officers who were supported by part-time instructors on an as-and-when basis, who oversaw activities of female youngsters. Staff at the JCC were predominantly female. Similarly, the majority of dorm warders at the SCC were female[1].

Technically these institutions were also manned by different oversight authorities. This required some skill in negotiating access to actors who differed in terms of gender and in professional expertise, besides the official bureaucracies that characterized the institutions. Methodologically, this diversity suggested some differences in terms of methods employed and questions posed.

Research context and its ramifications

Collecting empirical data in natural settings of juvenile offenders entails becoming part of their natural settings and feeling part of their daily lives and routine. Therefore, I could not neatly separate the context within which narratives, interviews, and focus group discussions in the correctional centres were held from the empirical data gathered. This contrasts with the positivist viewpoint that the social world should be studied in the naturalness of the state devoid of the researcher's influence and methods, and that sources of data must lend themselves to analysis independent of the context of study. Conversely, Hammersley and Atkinson maintain that the same set of experimental questions lend themselves to diversity of responses on different occasions as people interpret stimuli differently and these interpretations differ as 'events unfold and shape their actions' (Hammersley and Atkinson, 2007: 8).

My aim was to make meaning of emergent data that lent itself to different interpretations. However, I could not equate my insider role to an inmate role as inmates constructed differentiated meanings of their everyday life. Even among inmates or youngsters, they shared and exhibited differentiated meanings on the same issues as has been established in this book, particularly regarding the occurrences of escapes.

Reflexivity was central to the research process as my intentions and emotions were not only inaccessible to the various actors in detention but even to me as researcher. I needed to reflect constantly so as to assess the extent to which my biases and beliefs could impact the research process. I needed to remind myself that I was not the story, my role was to tell the story and yet I was constantly part of the process (Bourdieu, 1990, 2000) representing the story in my style of writing and sharing in emotions of tears, anger, sadness, and so on, that characterized youngsters' narratives. The research process was therefore plagued by the interpersonal, relational, and institutional contexts that could influence the data collection, interpretation, and write-up processes. Additionally, I needed to maintain a delicate balance between my pre-existing practitioner self and researcher self (Angrossino, 2007: xvii, xii, McGranahan, 2018, Ziman et al., 2018).

From the outset of my preliminary research, I was acutely aware of occupying a dual position, known within correctional centres due to my prior engagement as a human rights educator and monitor, and now entering as a researcher. This varied positioning prompted persistent self-questioning throughout the fieldwork: *How was I perceived by those I sought to understand? In what guise did I present myself?* The issue of researcher positionality remained with me throughout; I never assumed full insider status.

At various points, I stepped away from the field to reflect on the direction of the study. During one such break, a journalist published a report, including graphic images, documenting incidents of staff physically assaulting detained youth. The exposé prompted an official investigation, which implicated certain staff members. When I returned to the field, one officer immediately asked whether my research was connected to the journalist's enquiry. This moment crystallized the ongoing tension around how I was perceived, not simply as a neutral observer but as a potential threat or ally, depending on one's vantage point. The consistency of my visits and the extended period of visit were helpful in this respect. Navigating these intersecting roles demanded a careful balance, a delicate but intentional interplay that shaped both my methods and my relationships in the field.

Gatekeeping

Prisons and correctional centres are usually clearly bound with gates, labels, locks, and walls, and can be difficult to penetrate. Physical access does not automatically guarantee social access; sometimes, the latter can be more difficult as one can obtain permission to interview inmates or staff but interviewees especially in a detention environment may decide to remain silent. While silence in itself can constitute data, long periods of silence can be frustrating to a researcher. Gaining access to informants in correctional centres or prisons is therefore as important as negotiating access to a physical setting (Hammersley and Atkinson, 2007, Buscatto, 2018, Ziman et al., 2018, Hammersley, 2018a). Initial long periods of participant observation were useful in establishing acquaintance and trust, thereby facilitating social access to inmates. Officers at the outset of my fieldwork were more familiar with my practitioner status despite attempts to clarify my research purpose. This familiarity determined what information they would provide. My switching into a researcher status and being able to sustain this status – which practically was not entirely possible – demanded reliance not only on insiders who could facilitate physical access, but also on insiders who were acquainted with everyday life in committal. Identifying certain people who police such formal physical and social boundaries was vital in the conduct of participant observation and interviews. I encountered several such gatekeepers, depending on the setting. The setting in this regard is not limited to physical place or a geographically bounded place, but gave consideration to social, political, and other contexts besides the interest of the gatekeeper (Hammersley and Atkinson, 2007, Buscatto, 2018, McGranahan, 2018).

My initial point of contact was one officer who usually conducted visitors around the centre and who was keen on introducing me to other officers, as this afforded him more social interaction than his repetitive office work. However, he became less interested when he realized that I was less keen on tours but rather sat more often with youngsters and other staff in the yard. I encountered another officer who seemed pleasant and showed me around the centre's educational facilities yet was circumspect as to the information he released to me. His responses and information were more idealized than what actually pertained (Rubin and Rubin, 1995). I noticed that most information he provided contradicted with what I observed; while he would say for instance that the centre had an abundance of textbooks and teachers, I realized that the opposite prevailed when I visited classrooms. I realized that generally what people say, what people do, and what they say they do are entirely different things (Ewing et al., 2011). He continued to facilitate my access to youngsters and to staff, but I no longer relied on him for information when I noticed his insistence to project a particular image of the institution. I however maintained the friendship with him as he continued to facilitate physical access to both youngsters and officers.

A senior officer was equally helpful in terms of providing access to youngsters and officers. Unlike the previous officer, the information he provided tallied mostly with my observations. However, upon his assumption of a management status (the second-in-command), this officer assumed a more formal stance in terms of his relationship with me as his interests tended to be steered towards that of management and those in authority. Another officer who was friendly and commanded some level of authority among subordinate and senior staff facilitated access to youngsters and staff during interviews and focus group discussions. He promptly ensured that whenever I requested to interview certain youngsters, hold focus group discussions, or speak to an officer, these persons were readily made available. During one of the initial focus group discussions, he arranged that we could sit in his office, while he was present. I tried to conduct the discussion being careful of his presence and this to some extent determined what questions I posed and how these questions were answered. To my surprise, however, youngsters spoke without much inhibition.

Nearly every day I visited the centres, I spent time in the yard interacting with both officers and young people, even when interviews were not planned. These informal engagements proved valuable, gradually building familiarity and rapport with both groups. Over time, some officers leveraged this relationship to advance their own interests, occasionally requesting that I relay their concerns to higher authorities.

While private interviews and individual narratives were conducted discreetly, focus group sessions were typically observed by dormitory officers. These presences were officially justified as necessary for security; however, I often noted that such occasions allowed staff to rest, sitting apart from the discussions, sometimes nodding off or engaging in separate conversations. At the time of my initial field visit, Ghana had not yet ratified the Optional Protocol to the Convention Against Torture (OPCAT) (UNOPCAT, 2002). Nonetheless, I was able to conduct private interviews with young detainees without resistance. Officers rarely enquired into the substance of these discussions. I attribute this openness primarily to the foundation of trust and acceptance that had been cultivated well before formal interviews began.

Interviews, participant observation, focus group discussions, and narratives

I employed a variety of research methods characteristic of ethnographic research such as unstructured, open, and conversational interviews, focus group discussions, narratives, participant observation, and examined official records. In all I conducted 95 interviews at the SCC and 90 interviews at the JCC; I also conducted 51 participant observations at the JCC and 65 participant observations at the SCC.[2] I held 15 focus group discussions at each of the institutions. Narratives were provided mostly by male youngsters. Conversational interviews were virtually held daily for the two-year period.

By virtue of my field research, I recognized that interviews in closed institutions could pose a tremendous challenge, as noted by Halsey (2006: 152), that anyone familiar with conducting interviews in custodial settings will know the vast and varied range of factors apt to influence the tenor of the interview on any particular day, such as suitability of interview settings and the prospect that the interview will be interrupted by the noise and commotion associated with admitting inmates. I also observed that escape occurrences, visits by various professionals, as well as the mood or disposition of youngsters also impacted the interview process.

Generally, finding space for interviews was difficult amid the regimentality of daily confinement life. I did not always decide the time of the interview, though my suggestions were usually not turned down by officers. Given that I had undertaken participant observation for prolonged periods prior to the conduct of my individual interviews, I was quite familiar with daily routines and activities, so I managed to squeeze in interview slots. Familiarity with staff, officers, and youngsters also offered an immense advantage in accessing youngsters. However, daily detention practice could seldom be programmed based on some sustained acquaintance or some acquired skill as regular surprises are thrown up, sometimes requiring a further negotiation of access to the youngsters. While following a set of methodological principles could be a useful guide as to what to do within a particular context, yet confinement practice could not always be anticipated; each day presented a practical experience that required the exercise of judgement in a particular context (Hammersley and Atkinson, 2007, Cramer et al., 2011, Buscatto, 2018, Hammersley, 2018a).

Whom to interview and what questions to ask

In virtually all cases, I dwelt on non-random convenient sampling and chose who to interview but I had to rely on gatekeepers who could facilitate my access to youngsters and officers. Interactions with senior officers and certain key people required that I prepare questions ahead of time to ensure that issues discussed were covered by a set of questions. My objectives and research questions were a good guide though I also drew on certain issues that stemmed from participant observation, narratives, and conversational interviews and which required further clarification. For instance, selection of whom to interview and what questions to ask were based on participant observation that I had previously undertaken. My first one-to-one interview with youngsters followed my participation in a church service, which was more or less an initiation ceremony. I was motivated to speak to youngsters who were keen to tell their story and yet unable to do so in the public weekly church audience gatherings.

As youngsters related their diverse experiences, I also identified certain commonalities, which I further pursued in subsequent interviews. The conduct of narratives also unearthed some occurrences in certain dormitories such as dorms one and two, which I followed up through further interviews, focus group discussions and participant observation. For instance, I spent a relatively longer period sitting by the officers-in-charge (OIC), in front of the first and second dorms due to youngsters' alleged experiences in such dormitories. The selection of questions and cases about escapes and dwelling for instance on Afua's case also determined the duration of interviews, the social and physical setting, spontaneity of the interactions, and who provided what information.

Since fieldwork in a correctional centre demands careful treading and patience, selection and sampling of cases was not predetermined, homogenous, nor a one-off activity but it evolved with the progress of the research process. My aim was not to seek a representative sample but to elicit as much diverse information on a particular theme and from as many different sources as possible. While, on some occasions, I targeted people who could have the desired knowledge, I relied mostly on unsolicited responses particularly in researching about escapes. Such spontaneity of responses did not only make a vital contribution to the theme I researched, but also provided the social distribution of knowledge and power among the various actors in correctional institutions (Hammersley and Atkinson, 2007, Cramer et al., 2011, Buscatto, 2018, Hammersley, 2018a).

I participated in church services, educational lessons, workshop sessions, staff durbars, garden work, and daily parades of both staff and inmates. Observations did not always dwell on predetermined discrete behaviour to be observed. I assumed the status of a participant as well as an observer, whose role was not entirely known to those involved in the research. I could not give a detailed introduction as to what I intended to do from the outset as I entered the field only with loose notions. This approach sometimes kept detaining authorities in some sort of suspense. For instance, in the course of my fieldwork, one OIC asked what I was up to and demanded that I clarified certain processes again.

Each day in the field, I engaged in 'conversational interviews' with both staff and incarcerated youth. These informal exchanges emerged naturally, often during shared activities or routine interactions, and with a few gentle probes, such conversations frequently surfaced insights that might otherwise remain hidden. My time was predominantly spent with warders (all of whom were subordinate officers) and young inmates, though I occasionally held interviews with senior staff.

One of the primary challenges of conversational interviewing lay in navigating the direction of dialogue. Officers and young people largely controlled what was shared and how. Given their familiarity with formal interrogations, most youths resisted any conversational drift towards offence-related topics. Matters of personal history, such as family life or the nature of their offences, were rarely disclosed, largely due to the lack of privacy, as discussions often occurred in the presence of peers or staff. The confinement context itself was saturated with suspicion. As explored further in this book, young people routinely distrusted one another, as well as the officers, and vice versa. This pervasive uncertainty shaped how information was withheld, managed, and disclosed.

Gaining social access to boys proved somewhat easier than with girls. The social environment within the JCC was notably less open, making in-depth interviews with female juveniles particularly difficult. Interestingly, focus group discussions offered a contrasting dynamic: girls participated with greater openness. In a setting rife with surveillance and suspicion, the simple act of gathering outdoors in a less regulated format created a space for freer expression. Focus group discussions may also have helped displace individual accountability, enabling young people to speak without the fear that any single person would bear the consequences of a comment.

Overall, both male and female participants were especially guarded when it came to personal background details, such as their parents' occupations or marital status, largely out of concern over ridicule from peers. Despite these sensitivities, focus group discussions proved doubly valuable: they not only served as a source of collective insight but also helped me determine which individuals to follow up with and what lines of enquiry to pursue in one-on-one interviews.

Critically, I came to regard familiarity and trust as prerequisites for meaningful dialogue. Unlike transient practitioners or visiting officers, whose presence often elicited reserved or selective responses, my sustained engagement seemed to cultivate greater openness. Even so, young people remained discerning in what they shared. Their capacity to steer conversations, sometimes in strategic directions, is explored further in my later reflections in Chapter 8.

Unsolicited and spontaneous responses

Youngsters' accounts and those of officers, although guided by semi-structured and unstructured questions, were to a large extent unsolicited and spontaneous. Youngsters related their experiences with limited prompts and questions, enabling them to describe and recall events uninterrupted. I sought clarifications from youngsters through follow-up interjections. These clarifications facilitated details and elaborations, thereby reducing the effect of my own invented meanings, that which Becker (2001) and Hammersley and Atkinson (2007: 101) refer to respectively as researcher influence. I attribute spontaneity of responses to long periods of participant observation in promoting acquaintance with the various settings. While unsolicited responses have a greater likelihood of curtailing the researcher's influence on responses and narratives, one could easily lose focus. I regard youngsters and staff and other respondents as actors participating in a social world and capable of constructing their own views as they participate in their social world and I do not seek to falsify or make truth claims merely because their accounts are subjective. Relatedly, I consider such subjective accounts a useful contribution to scholarly work on deviancy in ensuring that the juvenile is not disconnected from his total life experiences and social formations (Plummer, 1983). These stories emphasize the human person behind the legal label and dwell on the wider life experiences of juvenile offenders beyond the walls of correctional institutions. While I sought to reduce researcher influence, my aim was not to collect data that was devoid of bias, as I am well aware of the fact that my presence and that of others have an influence on my data. My preoccupation was to gather data employing a variety of methods but without disregarding the influence that various settings had on the data I produced.

Discrepancies and gaps in information

Throughout the fieldwork process, notable discrepancies emerged between official documentation and other forms of data. For example, recorded ages in institutional files often conflicted with the self-disclosed ages offered by young people during interviews. Many were upfront in stating that their official ages differed from their actual ones. Similarly, official names listed in administrative records sometimes masked other names they were known by or chose to identify with, revealing an identity that official documents failed to capture. Everyday events such as escapes, while significant to lived experience, were often absent from the formal record. In this way, official data tended to reflect institutional identities that diverged markedly from those revealed through conversational interviews and participant observation.

I also paid close attention to how information was shaped in interactions with other practitioners. Young people frequently withheld responses, not just out of distrust, but often due to how questions were structured or framed. Following sessions with a clinical psychologist, for instance, I witnessed youths privately reveal how they had managed to disclose little, resisting the encounter through silence or ambiguity (see Chapter 7). During CHRAJ monitoring visits, I observed officers administering highly structured questionnaires to detained youths. In sitting through these sessions, I became increasingly aware of the qualitative silences embedded in this format, nuanced personal narratives were effectively squeezed out by rigid question structures.

These insights were further complicated by differences in data collected from various staff categories. Informal conversations with officers I engaged daily painted a different picture from the more occasional, formal interviews I conducted with other staff. Over time, my fieldwork sharpened its focus on youngsters preparing for release. Here, too, contradictions emerged. Although some teachers at a vocational and technical workshop spoke of parental involvement and successful reintegration, my direct observations suggested otherwise. Only a handful of male youths were met at the gate by relatives upon discharge and, even in those cases, there was no assurance they would resettle with family. They sometimes lacked clear directions to their destination and did not have sufficient funds to pay for transportation.

On some occasions, I personally accompanied them to lorry stations, sometimes needing to assist with directions and fares. These moments not only exposed infrastructural and logistical gaps but also raised unsettling questions about institutional narratives surrounding rehabilitation and reintegration. One of the teachers said:

> When youngsters are discharged from correctional centres, many a time parents are invited to the centre to see the progress of their children, what they had done during the period. Upon discharge, parents are

> invited to accompany their wards home and in the absence of that officers accompany young offenders to entrust them to their parents. And so far most students settle well. (Ayete-Nyampong, 2013a)

Triangulation in terms of employing a variety of methods was invaluable for my research process in terms of disclosing these discrepancies, inconsistencies, and gaps in information. Further, I underscored the usefulness and relevance of ethnographic approaches in sensitive contexts or settings such as confinement sites where information is regularly monitored.

Some ethical considerations

Navigating practitioner–researcher ambiguities

During my institutional visits, my status as a CHRAJ practitioner was clearly known, I made a point of distinguishing between my past role as a human rights monitor and my current position as a researcher (Ayete-Nyampong, 2015). Nonetheless, I presumed that most officers perceived me as both practitioner and researcher, while I understood myself primarily in the latter capacity.

Over time, however, I was increasingly seen as a researcher. This may have reflected the unusual duration of my engagement; practitioners rarely immerse themselves in a single setting for such extended periods. Alternatively, I may have been perceived as a different kind of practitioner, one whose methods and intentions did not fit conventional expectations.

At the outset, I was formally introduced to staff and youngsters by the OIC as someone who had worked with CHRAJ, but who was now engaged in long-term practitioner research aimed at improving professional practice. From there, both officers and young people constructed diverse understandings of my role, locating me within a social landscape shaped by their own experiences, institutional dynamics, and interpersonal readings (Hammersley and Atkinson, 2007, Buscatto, 2018, McGranahan, 2018, Hammersley, 2018a).

Young people variously construed my presence as a staff member or a social worker, and at times as 'the CHRAJ lady'. Over time, and partly due to the extended duration of my engagement in the institution (or 'the field'), I came to occupy a 'mummy' role, one that resonated with youngsters, many of whom had lost familial connections. This maternal association became a conduit for meaningful social access, as they shared narratives and participated in conversational interviews with relative ease. Yet it also entailed expectations: I was counted on to meet occasional material needs and offer celebratory gestures, such as birthday treats.

Among officers, particularly those stationed in the yard, my sustained presence gradually earned me the status of an insider, especially as I sat in staff meetings and observed institutional deliberations. However, I sensed a subtle dissonance between their expectations of a CHRAJ representative (as an expert or authority figure) and my actual conduct: listening, observing, and at times occupying the stance of a 'novice' (Hammersley and Atkinson, 2007: 79), who sought local knowledge from officers and young people alike. This ambiguity gave rise to moments of suspicion; some lower-ranked officers were unsure of my identity and initially refrained from engaging in conversation. As familiarity and trust grew, this tension eased, though never entirely dissipated. Officers who were once reticent began speaking freely, sharing candid reflections on their work with youth, institutional frustrations, and even personal matters. My challenge shifted from soliciting dialogue to facilitating and moderating conversations aligned with their concerns.

During CHRAJ's monitoring visits, my positionality oscillated between insider and outsider. CHRAJ officers would often consult me about procedural nuances, recognizing my prior involvement in oversight roles, while correctional staff jokingly referred to me as 'one of their own' and even invited me to guide the CHRAJ team around. These same officers voiced complaints to me regarding CHRAJ's monitoring processes, noting that regular visits yielded few improvements in the material conditions of confinement.

At times, I questioned whether my prolonged immersion had blurred the boundaries of my practitioner self. For example, corporal punishment was rarely used at the SCC in the initial stages of fieldwork, but emerged later. I interpreted this as a sign that I had become a normalized presence, an acceptance that benefited my research. Yet I grappled with ethical concerns: Had I become desensitized? Was my human rights lens clouded? Had my pursuit of ethnographic detail outweighed my professional commitment to accountability? I found myself negotiating between personal values and professional imperatives, researcher priorities and practitioner ethics.

Negotiating access to officers was an ongoing and often complex process. At the SCC, regular staff transfers meant that I interacted with three different OICs over the course of two years. New arrivals often lacked awareness of my role, requiring strategic reintroduction. In such instances, I found it helpful, albeit contrary to conventional guidance, to employ leading questions that signalled insider familiarity and fluency with institutional discourse vocabulary (Rubin and Rubin, 1995, Brown, 2015). This approach helped situate me as a participant familiar with the setting, rather than a novice vulnerable to being denied social access.

Going beyond a mandate and legislation: negotiating power and consent

One critical consideration for institutions and individuals seeking access to detention centres is whether their entry is grounded in a clear legislative mandate. In Ghana, Section 42 of the Juvenile Justice Act (Act 653 of

2003) (GOG, 2003) explicitly authorizes the CHRAJ to visit and monitor all correctional centres housing juveniles and young offenders. My own access to research sites was facilitated through this provision, formalized in a notification letter signed by the head of my organization. In that letter, I clarified that I was conducting a practitioner-driven research initiative that would rely on informal methods distinct from CHRAJ's standard monitoring protocol.

However, despite this mandate, and the rapport I had cultivated with institutional actors over the years, I found myself confronting a set of ethical and epistemological questions as I prepared to begin fieldwork: did Section 42 truly authorize me to enter the intimate, subjective worlds of young offenders? Can any legislative instrument alone justify penetrating such personal terrain? What ethical grounds do I have to seek responses from children simply because access was granted by the OIC, who in effect acted as a proxy for parental consent? Have the children themselves granted me permission to engage with their lived experiences? Does gaining access to child 'Abena' necessarily imply access to child 'Kwabena'?

Through this reflective process, I came to recognize that, while legal mandates enabled institutional access, they did not substitute for the interpersonal and social negotiation required to engage meaningfully and respectfully with the children. I began to interrogate the power asymmetries embedded in my position: as a practitioner, a researcher, and an adult in relation to minors whose rights and agency demanded careful attention. Although I could schedule interviews, I felt compelled to ensure that participation remained voluntary and free from the authority of my institutional identity.

This reorientation forced me to confront the need to act not merely as a legally sanctioned agent, but as an ethically responsive one, guided by the principle of the child's best interests and the core tenets of a human rights-based approach to data gathering. Ethics in this context extended far beyond procedural compliance or the approval of an ethics committee. It demanded sensitivity to the emotional, perceptual, and social realities of children and other actors within the field.

Ultimately, I came to understand that 'access' involved far more than the formal granting or withholding of permission to conduct research, it required sustained relational negotiation and an unwavering commitment to ethical vigilance (Hammersley and Atkinson, 2007: 43).

Impression management

Partly aware of how I was perceived by both staff and youngsters, I made deliberate efforts to distinguish myself from institutional personnel and, at times, from my practitioner positioning. I had to consciously avoid projecting the inspector or monitor persona typically associated with CHRAJ officers visiting correctional centres, as such a stance could reinforce power imbalances and inhibit open dialogue. Yet, when necessary, I drew on my practitioner status to facilitate access. Initial negotiations with detaining authorities, for instance, would have been far more difficult without formal recognition of my affiliation and the letter of introduction from my employer. In high-level interactions, I maintained a formal demeanour that signalled professional legitimacy.

Social characteristics such as gender also shaped access dynamics. Senior officers, predominantly male, appeared more inclined to engage with me in my role as a female colleague. At the same time, with female officers, I often integrated seamlessly, joining in everyday interactions and participating in the familiar rhythms of 'women's talk'. My ability to speak two local languages further supported access, although an even greater asset was my grasp of conversational dynamics, for example, using rhetorical strategies such as dialoguing with oneself, or posing questions to oneself and providing responses as a means of maintaining the flow of conversations and narratives, was even more important.

Despite these efforts, some officers remained distant, and some youngsters hesitant to speak. Fieldwork also presented ethical dilemmas. At times, I felt drawn to intervene in particular situations by invoking my practitioner status, for example, when Afua, a young female resident, endured prolonged punishment after absconding. Torn between ethical obligations and the role I had assumed, I leaned on the relationships I had built to better understand the perspectives of young people, especially as these often contrasted with institutional representations of what constituted the 'best interest' of the child.

There were also moments when officers solicited my professional advice. In one instance, I was invited to serve on a committee established to consider reforms aligned with the Juvenile Justice Act, an opportunity I accepted. These encounters reflected the complex terrain I navigated, not only as a researcher embedded in an institutional setting, but also as a practitioner whose expertise was intermittently drawn upon, even as I sought to maintain a respectful and ethically grounded research posture.

Equity between the researcher and beneficiaries of the research

The sufficiency of formal mandate extended beyond mere access to include the use of research instruments. Although I had secured permission to use a voice recorder and a digital camera, tools not usually allowed even during CHRAJ monitoring visits, I soon observed that their presence provoked discomfort among the children. As a compromise, I opted for a small notepad, which I used cautiously, as I realized that even this seemingly innocuous tool sometimes disrupted the conversational flow. Each choice raised a deeper ethical tension: should I prioritize gathering data on my terms or centre the emotional safety and preferences of the children?

I had witnessed instances where professionals conducted interviews and children remained silent, opting instead to selectively share, or withhold, information. These patterns underscored the need for a more adaptive, child-sensitive approach to data collection.

While I remained attentive to issues of access, my prolonged presence in the field gradually fostered familiarity with both the children and the detention environment. This evolving embeddedness helped guide context-specific ethical decisions about what was acceptable or intrusive. Standardized guidelines may provide broad direction, but ethical decision-making in such settings demands continual reflection and reflexivity. For instance, negotiating social and emotional access was never a one-time achievement. Rather, it was a fluid process shaped by ongoing cues from the children, usually signalled through subtle or non-verbal gestures. Sometimes children say 'no' when their non-verbal expression depicts the opposite, which gave me a feeling of uneasiness to go ahead without a brief explanation or assurance of confidentiality. My research setting was a seemingly sensitive and structured one and youngsters needed assurance that they were not going to be victimized by the authorities after speaking with me, as some officers were in the know whenever I spoke with youngsters[3].

The question of whether it was right not to proceed with an interview also depended on the subject under discussion and indication by youngsters in the form of a pause, a break in articulation, or a faster way of speaking or shedding of tears, which were useful indications to pause an interview.

Similarly, I stepped in and out of my fieldwork, taking two shorts breaks of one month during the fieldwork period. These breaks offered a defined space for review and reflection on my fieldnotes, but they also provided an emotional rest from the sad and despondent stories and from a structured and monitored environment.

Institutional uncertainties and the limits of assumption: have the terms changed?

Detention environments may appear regimented and predictable, but beneath this appearance lie continual, often invisible shifts that outsiders rarely perceive. After pausing my field visits, I returned expecting to resume my usual routines, only to discover that institutional dynamics had shifted. During a brief visit, I greeted a senior officer and informed him of my intention to say hello to the children and staff in the classroom. I noticed a flicker of hesitation on his face but dismissed it. Moments later, he sent someone to recall me, explaining that he was convening a meeting with the teachers. I clarified that I merely wished to greet the children, having been away for some time. His change in demeanour was unexpected, until I later learned that he had been promoted to second-in-command. His altered stance likely reflected a need to align more closely with institutional expectations and oversight.

The boys' remand centre shares its grounds with the girls' correctional facility. Following a series of in-depth interviews, I sought access to the *remand boys*. To my surprise, the head demanded that I resubmit my introductory letter, despite having already shared it and discussed my intentions; eventually, access was granted.

Ethnographic research is inherently incremental. It resists fixed trajectories, making it difficult, if not impossible, to articulate a comprehensive agenda at the outset. Institutional actors, by contrast, often require predefined boundaries and explicit expectations. This mismatch creates a persistent tension from the very start: a gap between the openness required by ethnography and the control desired by institutions. Rather than seeing this gap as a flaw to be resolved, I argue for its recognition and open negotiation. One strategy I employed was to keep institutional actors informed and updated, though this demanded ongoing effort and relational labour.

Despite my efforts, the fieldwork process remained challenging. The misalignment between the iterative realities of ethnographic enquiry and the fixed expectations of institutional authorities, including ethical committees, can be deeply constraining. As Hammersley and Atkinson (2007) observe, such committees often operate from biomedical, psychological, or survey-based paradigms that do not accommodate the fluid, context-specific nature of ethnography.

Ethnography does not always fit within neat methodological frameworks, it is relational, emergent, and deeply attuned to particularities. Yet precisely this strength invites friction with bureaucratic structures designed for abstraction and standardization (Hammersley and Atkinson, 2007).

The strange and the familiar: traversing boundaries between home and field

The transition between home and the field was not merely logistical; it demanded a continual recalibration of self. Each shift meant moving from a space of comfort and familiarity to one marked by enclosure, volatility, and emotional intensity. The field was permeated by harsh language, resistance, confrontation, and traumatic stories – murder, defilement, assault – and even the sensory discomfort of unpleasant odours. Navigating this duality required ongoing reconditioning, socially, physically, emotionally, and psychologically.

Many rural detainees have spent their entire period of incarceration without and sometimes become unfamiliar with bearings within towns and cities resulting in some disorientation, upon release. During a conversation with one boy prior to his discharge, I learned that no relative was available to collect him. He lacked the money to return home and was without basic necessities. In response, I drove him to my home, provided food and supplies, and accompanied him to the lorry station. Upon returning home that day, I was met with an avalanche of security-related questions from my family. They viewed my actions as unusual, perhaps even risky. I struggled to reconcile their legitimate concerns with the familiarity and trust I had developed within the confinement environment. For me, the boundary between the 'strange' and the 'familiar' had blurred, creating both opportunities for deeper connection and potential consequences.

These two worlds are part of a continuous, entangled space and the slippage between them, between institutional strangeness and relational intimacy, highlights the psychological and ethical labour of fieldwork in carceral contexts. It also illustrates how the ethnographer may become enmeshed in both, often destabilizing normative ideas of distance, safety, and care.

From field notes to chapter outline: reflexivity and complexity in field documentation and analysis

At the outset of interviews, I noticed a palpable discomfort among the young participants in response to my note-taking and use of a digital voice recorder. Their reluctance manifested in hesitations, disjointed dialogue, repeated statements, and frequent darting glances, indicators of unease and perhaps surveillance-awareness. I had also overheard conversations in which some girls spoke openly about efforts to conceal certain information from professionals. In a confinement environment where both staff and young people are under continuous oversight, even minimal attempts to document interactions can arouse suspicion. In response, I adopted a low-profile approach to documentation while on-site, relying primarily on brief jottings and shorthand bullets. I also deliberately curtailed the number of hours I spent in the field each day, although at times the nature of unfolding events required a longer presence. When it became necessary to record specific details, such as names, figures, or striking statements, I would explicitly share with the interviewee why documentation was important in that moment and then quickly make a note.

Each day, either during lunch or upon returning from the field, I would expand upon these sparse notes, fleshing out key insights and contextual observations. I gradually developed cognitive techniques to enhance retention, using sequential mental mapping and visual imagery, to strengthen recall and narrative coherence. This process, though demanding and emotionally taxing, became an engaging and immersive ritual. Revisiting the day's encounters felt akin to re-living them. Over time, I cultivated note-taking as a reflective practice, beginning with raw 'free writing' and progressively refining the art of field documentation (Sunstein and Strater,

2007, Copland and Creese, 2015, Buscatto, 2018, Ziman et al., 2018, Hammersley, 2018a) to focused notes.

Engaging with the realities of fieldwork compelled me to confront the practice of reflexivity, not as a theoretical ideal but as an everyday necessity. This entailed being candid about my own biases, emotional responses, and evolving impressions of both staff and young participants. I found myself recording not just what I observed, but also the subtle taken-for-granted rhythms of institutional life, its ordinary routines, unexpected moments, emotions, tensions, and ethical quandaries.

One of the more complex challenges was attributing distinct voices to individual respondents, especially while differentiating my own reflections from theirs. The fluidity of insider language added another layer of complexity, terms like 'corner', for instance, carried context-specific meanings that required careful disaggregation. Documenting these nuances demanded ongoing attentiveness to voice, meaning, and positionality.

To support analysis, I structured my electronic notes to allow for both separation and dialogue between observation and interpretation. A double-entry format proved useful: one column for recorded observations, the other for reflexive commentary. Alongside these entries, I began annotating open codes, key words and phrases that captured thematic fragments from the field. These codes were not drawn from pre-set categories; rather, they emerged inductively, shaped by the data rather than any predefined framework. My intention was to generate as many codes as possible, leaving questions of relevance aside during this early stage.

From these initial codes, I identified recurring, divergent, and striking themes. This exercise illuminated areas that warranted deeper exploration and further dialogic engagement. Yet choosing which themes to pursue was far from straightforward. The sheer variety of themes presented an interpretive challenge.

While software like Atlas.ti offered technical efficiency in organizing and retrieving codes, the analytic process demanded far more than thematic aggregation. At this stage, I was no longer merely a researcher analysing content, I had become an interpretive instrument in the research itself (Hammersley and Atkinson, 2007) and had virtually become my own software. This is because, even when I had developed coded themes, the process of reflection and reflexivity required that I go back to read entire notes over and over again, noting contextual meanings and how youngsters and officers constructed various meanings diversely. For instance, merely dwelling on the literal meaning of a term such as 'corner' and grouping the various uses of this term on face value meanings could be misleading. While computer aided programmes can be useful, their use may suggest that the methods and data are separate entities. Yet, mine was an interpretative research process that drew not only on constructed and contextual meanings but was also laced with my own epistemological, ontological, and theoretical assumptions (Mauthner and Doucet, 2003).

Being mindful of the context within which meanings are constructed, I tried to do some selection and prioritization, noting both frequently and non-frequently occurring codes, looking out for commonalities, links, parallels, and contrasts out of which I constituted themes. Stemming from these themes, I developed analytical ideas. This process spanned the entire research process and was not limited only to the final writing stage of the manuscript. It was an 'ongoing critical and creative research process' (Hammersley and Atkinson, 2007: 159) that required that I regularly step in and out of my notes, identifying various viewpoints while distinguishing these from my own observations, my subjective feelings and impressions.

Thus, the analysis of field notes was not merely finding what data contains but a process of creating what is there by constantly thinking of the import of previously recorded events and meanings (Emerson et al., 1995). After the period of fieldwork, on the basis of these meanings and analytical ideas, I began to compose my ethnographic texts; this time making a gradual transition from the field to considering the disciplinary embeddedness of my research and revisiting the relevant theories that helped me to make sense of my ethnographic data.

In sum, the pathway for this research study has been predominantly inductive given that I have sought to derive interpretative frameworks from ethnographic field data rather than deduce at the outset a theory that explains certain phenomena in correctional centres. This ethnographic data is therefore not pure but laced with meanings underpinned by my own assumptions and theoretical perspectives. It is quite a distortion to refer to theory being discovered (Glasser and Strauss, 1967) as though data were pure and distinct from theory, since my prior analytic commitments are built into field notes (Emerson et al., 2001). I consider the entire process of my fieldwork and data analysis as reflexive; the fact that method and data are not separate entities but reflexively interconnected and interdependent (Mauthner and Doucet, 2003, Brown, 2015, Ziman et al., 2018).

Follow-up visits in 2019 and 2023

In both 2019 and 2023, I carried out brief follow-up visits to the same correctional centres, in line with my employer's standard visiting mechanism[4]. These visits mirrored the institutional rhythm of oversight, procedural, and often constrained in duration, yet offered a valuable opportunity to revisit spaces, routines, and relationships previously encountered (Ayete-Nyampong, 2019, 2023).

A central objective of my follow-up visits was to document institutional and experiential changes that had unfolded over the past decade, and to assess whether brief, formal visits, typical of the CHRAJ's monitoring framework, could nonetheless yield meaningful insider perspectives. As previously noted, CHRAJ, Ghana's national human rights institution and my employer, is legally mandated by the Juvenile Justice Act to inspect correctional centres housing juveniles and young offenders.

In alignment with this statutory mandate, and through formal letters of introduction to oversight bodies, followed by preparatory in-person engagements, I was granted access to correctional centres in 2019, and again in 2023. On each occasion, I remained attentive to ethical considerations around informed consent, ensuring that both staff and young people willingly agreed to speak with me.

The research adopted a non-probability sampling approach, with participants, both staff and youngsters, purposively selected based on predefined criteria and their relevance to the research questions employed[5]. Unlike the approach I had employed in 2009, the 2019 and 2023 visits were shaped by a clearer, more focused design, employing a combination of structured and semi-structured questions across one-on-one interviews and focus group discussions.

During these follow-up visits, I carefully introduced select leading questions to probe specific thematic areas, including the informal economies emerging within police cells and correctional centres, systems of inmate governance, and the initiation rites experienced by 'brannies', who were newly admitted youngsters. I deliberately employed select leading questions and insider terminology such as *brannies*, to signal continuity with my earlier fieldwork in 2009. By contrast, my initial 2009 visit involved minimal use of leading questions. I was acutely aware that such prompts could inadvertently steer young respondents towards rehearsed or externally shaped narratives, potentially distorting their authentic experiences, perceptions, and emotional truths. In that context, I prioritized open-ended enquiry to safeguard against introducing bias into the data.

Conclusion

Drawing on the preceding reflections, I have attempted to problematize the research reality that stems from my fieldwork experience, while critically examining my dual identity, as both practitioner and researcher. Although research was primarily conducted in the latter capacity, both roles informed the interpretive process. Despite the brevity of my follow-up visits in 2019 and 2023, they proved substantively informative and relevant. My prior engagement with the setting, and familiarity with insider terminology, positioned me less as an outsider. This afforded unique insights that might otherwise have remained inaccessible.

When practitioners and policy makers become genuinely interested in children's views, the potential for meaningful connection and resonant intervention is strengthened. Achieving this, however, calls for thoughtful reflection on the methods and approaches employed, specifically, those that centre children's perspectives, priorities, and lived realities. Methodologically, this chapter underscores the value of quasi-ethnographic approaches. These should not be overlooked by criminal justice and human rights professionals, monitors, and related actors seeking to better understand and respond to the complexity of the experiences of youngsters.

3

Who We Are, Where We Are From: Does It Matter to You?

Introduction

In this chapter, I present children's personal narratives of their growing-up experiences gathered through in-depth interviews conducted during my initial visit. By their narratives, youngsters are depicted as fearless, sharp-witted, resilient, and self-protective, yet simultaneously marked by trauma, timidity, uncertainty, and vulnerability. The narratives of children and their differentiated portrayals are central to the book's overarching analysis and thematic direction.

Whereas there is a growing effort to develop some consistent discourse on African children and youngsters in their own respect (Durham, 2000, Abbink and Van Kessel, 2005, Honwana and De Boeck, 2005, Richards, 2005, Christiansen et al., 2006, Anarfi and Kwankye, 2009, Kwarteng, 2012, Mizen and Ofosu-Kusi, 2013, Abebe and Ofosu-Kusi, 2016, Mumo, 2016, Abebe, 2019, de Castro, 2020, Holzscheiter, 2020, Kakuru, 2022, Koomson et al., 2022, Sabates-Wheeler and Sumberg, 2022, Abekah-Carter et al., 2024, Yeboah and Boafo, 2024), research on incarcerated children as social actors remains limited. One reason may be that children in legal custody are generally difficult for researchers to access and gathering interviews or personal narratives from detainees about their past, can be difficult.

Youngsters' accounts reveal both unique experiences and shared themes. The data shows that many children felt abandoned and rejected by their parents and families.[1] From the beginning, these children demonstrated an acute awareness of their circumstances, viewing themselves as victims of parental irresponsibility. They consistently described their parents' and relatives' failure to meet their needs as a matter of unwillingness rather than inability. This perception was echoed in focus group discussions, where children expressed feelings of anger and a desire for retaliation against their parents. Their awareness extended beyond family dynamics to include state actors such as the police, whom they criticized for arresting and detaining them, rather than their parents, for extended periods prior to formal committal.

Youngsters' narratives

This section begins with personal accounts from juvenile and young offenders. Of the eight individuals interviewed, only one was female. Most participants reported their ages as between 18 and 19, and some distinguished between their actual age and the age recorded officially. All but one had received some form of basic education.

The narratives were collected through one-on-one interviews, each lasting at least an hour. Prior to these sessions, I had established rapport with the participants through extended periods of participant observation, which informed the selection process. I explained to warders and staff the importance of conducting interviews in private, while also acknowledging their concerns about security. No objections were raised, likely due to the trust built during earlier interactions.

During fieldwork, I noticed that most state officials and professionals typically sought information about youngsters for administrative or legal purposes. Their focus was often on the nature of the offence, circumstances of arrest, evidence of abuse, punishment and torture, human rights of detainees, as well as material conditions in detention. In contrast, my interest lay in the youngsters' own perspectives on their upbringing, offering a different lens through which to understand their experiences. Many were initially surprised that the interviews did not centre on their criminal backgrounds. In several instances, participants became emotional, especially when discussing their families. As the interviews progressed, they grew more engaged and took ownership of their stories, sharing with enthusiasm and depth.

Apart from the data gathered through interviews and observation, I had no prior biographical information about the participants or their offences. I deliberately postponed consulting official records until the later stages of fieldwork to avoid framing them solely by their criminal histories.

The physical setting for female participants at the Juvenile Correctional Centre (JCC) was more open and resembled a school environment, unlike the more restrictive Senior Correctional Centre (SCC). However, the social atmosphere at the JCC was tense and marked by suspicion. The girls were often wary of staff and fellow inmates, making it difficult to obtain comprehensive personal narratives. It was easier to conduct conversational interviews and focus group discussions than formal one-on-one sessions. My involvement in classroom activities, vocational training, farm work, and church services provided valuable opportunities to observe, listen, and interact with the girls in more natural settings.

The stories shared by these youngsters, many of whom had never had the chance to tell them, reveal lives shaped by rejection, anger as well as varying degrees of resilience. These accounts laced with anger resonate with their expressions during focus group discussions that they would jail their fathers and jail the police. Some male and female youngsters did not hesitate to blurt out that they were wicked and bad, as reflected in Grace's account discussed below.

Despite facing neglect, powerlessness, and sometimes abuse, these young individuals still demonstrate remarkable agency within their limited spheres of influence.

Unpleasant beginnings

I begin this section with the story of a 16-year-old boy named Kwesi. His narrative reveals troubling experiences that many young people face while growing up within their families. During an institutional church service, Kwesi and other newly admitted boys were introduced through what resembled an initiation ceremony. Overcome with emotion, Kwesi wept as he attempted to share his story, though he never managed to tell it in full. His reaction piqued my interest, and I eventually interviewed him five months[2] after that initial introduction. Like many other young boys and girls who find themselves in conflict with the law, Kwesi described early life experiences that he viewed as deeply unpleasant from the very start of his upbringing:

> At the time I was born, my parents had already divorced and so I stayed with my paternal grandmother. I had a distasteful life before moving in to my grandma's end. My father never liked me and anytime I came late from playing football, I was beaten severely. He never took care of me. He beat me often and I never wanted to set eyes on him. Anytime I see his face my heart beats. That was why I moved to stay with my grandma. My father after the divorce remarried and now resides in Accra; he is now a storekeeper. My mother, I was informed, travelled somewhere after the divorce and she has never returned. (Ayete-Nyampong, 2013a: 39)[3]

Kwesi's account depicts rejection and maltreatment at the hands of his father. As a result of the beatings and rejection, Kwesi moved on to stay with his grandma. According to Kwesi, his stay with his grandma was not pleasant either:

> She said I was not smart enough and so she beat me often with her walking stick. I tried however to stay with her to attend school at least until primary two and when I could not bear it no longer, I stopped

> school. I left to stay with the sister of my maternal grandma and started primary one again and continued till primary school grade 6. Upon completing P6, I was taken to stay with my paternal grandmother where I continued my education till Junior High School[4] [JHS] form one. (40)

The frequent beatings Kwesi received obviously put him in a category of an abused child or one subjected to domestic violence and Kwesi's primary carers, including his grandmother, tended to be his abusers. While Kwesi detested the painful treatment he endured, and quit school as a result, his main concern was not the beatings per se but the rejection that such beatings symbolized for him, which was evidenced by the statement: 'My father never liked me.' Also, Kwesi said about his father, *wanhwɛ me* meaning the father never took care of him. In other words, his father could have provided for him but deliberately did not. In spite of these difficult situations, Kwesi managed to survive by engaging in some economic activity:

> I started collecting pieces of metal scraps and from the purchases I earned a minimum of GHS 2.50 [US$ 0.62].[5] Children like myself would go and collect these scraps and sell. One day, I went as usual to find some scraps, my grandma had gone to the farm and I was hungry and so I decided to make some money. The owner of the house caused my arrest when I collected some coal pot scraps in his compound. They asked about my family and as there was no one at the time, they thought I must have been a bad person and so I was taken to a police station. (40)

Kwesi's claims that his efforts to collect metal scraps coupled with the absence of his family at the time of arrest must have created the impression that he was a bad person. The turn of events was shocking for Kwesi who was arrested and kept under police custody for a month:

> I was surprised about the whole incident as I could not believe that collecting scraps of metal could end me in the police cell. (40)

Kwesi's situation was obviously a powerless one; he suffered beatings, neglect, and rejection from his own family. Yet in spite of his powerlessness, Kwesi managed to initiate certain moves such as changing location and engaging in the collection of scraps to earn some additional income. However, in attempts to make meaning of these difficult situations, Kwesi found himself in the custody of the state.

The second account is about William, 19 years of age, and an inmate teacher. I decided to speak with William when I observed him teach an elementary class. This is a class for inmates who according to the institution have the lowest educational background. William's active class and the confidence he demonstrated while he taught contrasted with Kwesi's timid outlook during the service. William is also senior to Kwesi in terms of age, educational attainment, and duration spent in committal.

> I am an Accra boy and stayed at Adabraka most of the time. My parents divorced when I was nine years and I have one sibling. My father is a mason and my mother is a trader. My father abandoned me, all he did was to smoke and it was my mother that took care of me. I got attracted to friends in and out of school when I turned twelve years. I was on drugs, drank alcohol and chased girls and had a lot of fun in night clubs and street jams during Christmas. [He paused and sighed and said that his mum had really suffered, taken him from one church to the other as his life was a mess.] I was part of a gang and we robbed people, almost all the members of the gang were older than me. I was very short and my height gave me a lot of advantage because people actually thought I was a child and did not suspect bad things about me. (41)

William though did not suffer beatings and physical abuse, yet, like Kwesi, suffered neglect from his father: 'My father abandoned me (*wanhwɛ me*), all he did was to smoke.'

William coped with his situation of neglect differently from Kwesi. The activities of the gang he was involved with provided him some source of livelihood. Besides, stemming from his reference to 'bad things' he tended, unlike Kwesi, to conceive the idea that he engaged in delinquent practices. His attraction to friends could not be attributed entirely to neglect as he admitted being cared for by his mother, of whom he spoke fondly.

Nana Bonsu is a 19-year-old boy who was preparing for discharge from the institution and looking forward to advancing his skills in welding and draughtsmanship, which he had acquired while in committal.

> I would not go to my mother's so as not to be tempted to offend again but would rather go to my father, who knows nothing about my offence or my committal. I was only three years when my parents divorced. My mother trades in yam and my father is a diamond dealer. My mother was most often in Accra to find work and had very little time for me. I stayed with my uncle who had four children. My uncle did not take good care of me and so I stole often from both my mum and uncle. (41)

Nana's account is yet another example of family dysfunctionality experienced at a young age. Nana admitted to committing an offence and attributed his involvement in theft to the neglect he suffered particularly from the mum who had little time for him. Neglect from Nana's viewpoint was not really deprivation, rather Nana was concerned that he was not worthy of the mother's time. Nana was, on the contrary, explicit that his maternal uncle deprived him of material needs. Thus, Nana construed neglect as both material deprivation and rejection from core family members. Like William, Nana depended on a gang to steal, but the latter, unlike William, stole from his own family in order to make a living.

The next narrative is from a female youngster. Grace, 18 years of age, is one of two girls I managed to speak to on a one-on-one basis at the JCC. The physical environment for female youngsters at the JCC was more open relative to the SCC; however, the social environment was quite restrictive. Thus, even though I had built quite some trust and acceptance, I could hardly obtain a full-length narrative from most of the girls. I depended mostly on conversational interviews as I participated in various activities such as vocational lessons, farm and grounds work, church services, and so on.

I realized through participant observation that Grace was most often by herself and interacted very little with others. Almost all the teachers had labelled her the laziest. According to the teachers, she could not acquire any skills or learn any vocation. I had observed that she was indeed not interested in any of the vocational lessons except hairdressing, which she did with some enthusiasm. On the day we spoke, I was with all the girls in the hall where they usually held their lessons. No teacher had turned up yet, except the caretaker, and the atmosphere was quite relaxing so I sought some private space to speak with Grace.

Grace was preparing and looking forward to being discharged and so it was a good starting point. Grace said she would like to be a hairdresser upon discharge though she was not really interested in any vocation taught at the girls' institution. She soliloquized mostly as she told her story, in fact at a certain point it seemed as though she was not very conscious of my physical presence as she spoke mostly to herself though she intermittently provided some eye contact. Grace, whose parents had also divorced, strikes an initial contrast in her narrative of like and dislike between her grandmother and the officer at the JCC:

> This place is a very difficult place. The woman sitting there always shouts at us and insults us. My grandma with whom I stayed never shouted at me, she liked me very much. My father[6] and mother divorced when I was very small and so I stayed with my grandmother. (42)

In the course of her narrative, Grace expressed dislike for her grandma:

> My grandma, though she liked me very much, was also the one who spoilt me (*ɔno na osei me*). [She paused for a while.] My grandmother

> is a witch; she asked me to change my father into a cat so I would ride on it and I said I would never do that. No one really wanted me nor cared for me. My grandmother gave me witchcraft and my father had to take me to a pastor and when the pastor saw me immediately he knew that I was one. The pastor told my father to go home and that he would deal with the case. The pastor asked me to bring a towel, sponge, a candle, and a fresh dress and said that what I wore previously I should not wear again. When the pastor prayed for me I became unconscious and very weak but later the next day, I felt strong and my father came to collect me. [She paused.] As for my grandma, she is the cause of all my bad behavior. (43)

Grace thus expressed ambivalent views about her grandma, while in some regard she was fond of her, in other respects, she was unhappy that the grandma had bewitched her and she attributed her bad behaviour, which she explains as stealing, and the use of drugs and alcohol, to her grandma:

> I started stealing when I was in the nursery and I would steal my father's coins. I also started going after boys at an early age because I was unhappy, felt unwanted and neglected and tried to find some happiness. I aborted only thrice and used cocaine for just a short while but I like Don *Simon*, the alcoholic one. I attended a party with a boy and while the party was in progress, I accompanied this boy who went to cut the window net of the woman in whose house the party was being held and stole five phones and he gave me one. Unfortunately, when someone dialed the *kasapa*[7] phone I responded. It did not occur to me to switch it off and so I was found out. I was then fifteen years old. As for me, [she sighs], no one knows my character; I am very bad and very wicked. (43)

Grace's account, like the others, depicts experiences of neglect and rejection and she attributes her involvement in stealing and other activities to her search for happiness. She however also attributes her present demise also to the doing of the grandma. By so doing, Grace tends to absolve herself from accepting responsibility for what she termed bad activities and positions herself as a victim of her grandma's influence and not a perpetrator. Yet, Grace's association with witchcraft may rather have reinforced her 'perpetrator' image, given that persons alleged to be witches in the Ghanaian and African context are regarded as bad, harmful, and dangerous, and as a result are stigmatized (Meyer, 1996, Onyinah, 1997, Honwana and De Boeck, 2005, Akoko, 2007, Adinkrah, 2011, Asamoah-Gyadu, 2015, Bauer, 2017, Iheme, 2020, Awortwe et al., 2025), thus explaining why Grace and the father made efforts to free the former of this spiritual label. Grace is one of few youngsters whose growing-up experiences with family depicted some involvement with spiritual powers, specifically, witchcraft.

Kojo, aged 19, was committed to the boys' institution on a charge of defilement[8] and was currently scheduled for discharge. This was the only interview carried out in the presence of an officer and the officer insisted to be present. Kojo looked partly dazed with weak eyes and spoke with little regard to the officer. While the interview was in progress, inmates kept calling out to him: '*rootman*'. When asked what that meant he said this was his nickname, which meant someone who smoked *marijuana* a lot. Kojo expressed no remorse for the offence that led to his arrest and conviction, defiling a young girl, the daughter of a pastor. He insisted that his time in the correctional centre had done nothing for him. Though he began learning auto mechanics, the constant shouting of some officers broke his resolve and pushed him to give up. He spoke bitterly of being locked away while other inmates roamed freely, a restriction that filled him with anger. In the end, he decided he would no longer attempt to learn any trade at all. He blurted out:

> I am no longer interested in anything here; all I am waiting for is to serve my sentence and leave this place. When I leave, I will find something to do. My childhood was not pleasant either. My father died when I was very small. My father used to sell second-hand items. My mother was just in the house and did not do anything, she did not trade, and she did nothing. I spent most of my time with my grandma and my paternal aunt. I got on well with my grandma than with any other relative including my own mother. After the death of my father, my mother abandoned me and I was not even breastfed. (44)

When I asked how he came to know all this, including the fact that he had not been breastfed, he explained that it was his grandmother who had told him the story. He continued:

> My mom had eight different children with different men and my father also had three children elsewhere but between my father and my mother were two of us and I am the oldest. My father took good care of me but after his death, my aunt [comes after the father] with whom I stayed overworked us on the farm. I therefore hardly had time for school. We farmed cocoa and food crops. My aunt was very quick tempered and beat us often. She kept making comments that her obligation was to take care of her own children. Her own children attended good schools and we were almost abandoned. On reaching JHS, I decided that enough was enough and I stopped school. (44)

Kojo, whose story depicts no record of divorce but rather the loss of a dear parent vents out anger and frustration against all adults he encountered with the exception of his father and grandmother. Like the other stories, his narrative features abandonment and rejection by the mother and other relatives. However, Kojo, despite his difficult circumstances, did not quit school early, but did so only at the JHS level.

Yaw, 18 years of age, and also due for discharge, was a recidivist or a repeat offender who experienced committal at the SCC twice. He claimed he had benefited from educational programmes at the boys' institution and that, even though he was 18, he would still like to go back to Basic School upon discharge as he realized the need to learn the names of his working tools. However, he dreaded going back to the family in the village from where he came:

> I look forward very much to going back though I would not go to the village as my grandpa and grandma always cursed me and said I would never succeed in life and this makes me feel unhappy and worried. I would rather stay with my brother who is ready to accommodate me and has always been advising me though he has no idea that I am at the correctional centre, I intend to inform him later. I have never known my mother as my aunt told me that my mother died after giving birth to me; I have never seen pictures of my mother … My father also died in a car accident – he was a taxi driver. I liked school but was mocked at school and accused of everything that got lost and went wrong even when I was not responsible. This made me dislike school very much. On account of my father's death and the fact that I lost interest in school, I was not doing well and so I decided to stop nursery school and that was at age of three years. (45)

Having lost both parents at an early age, Yaw did not experience rejection from them. Instead, he carried bitterness over the curses his grandparents directed at him. His story brings to the fore another source of rejection, the school. None of the youngsters in foregoing narratives made reference to the school as a source of rejection. Yaw attributed his action to discontinue school partly to the rejection he suffered at school.

John, 19 years, had played leadership roles throughout his period of detention and seemed popular among staff and youngsters. Because he managed to write his Senior High School (SHS) Certificate Examinations and had passed, he was held in high esteem by many. He seemed a quiet and gentle young man and resided in the last dorm, where youngsters enjoyed a good amount of freedom and were allowed to go on errands in town often. Though staff and warders were hesitant to vouch for youngsters' behaviour, a number of them said that John, in spite of his drinking habit, could be relied upon.

> I grew up with my parents and siblings at Mampong, in the Eastern Region. We had a large family; ten siblings, three of whom were female. I liked school and enjoyed my lessons and also had a lot of friends who kept me happy. On completing JHS, I wanted to continue school outside Mampong for a change as I had lived in Mampong all along, but my parents did not allow me. My parents said it would be difficult for them to know what was going on with me if I was not with them. I felt they wanted to monitor me and this angered me and so I decided to give myself some freedom and started hanging out with friends; I did that often and with time I realized my parents were no longer providing for me as they ought and this angered me further and kept me farther away from home.
>
> One day in January 2007, we held an athletic competition and I became very angry during meals time. You know when you do athletics at school, you have admirers, you are treated well, and you eat good food and have fun. It was meals time and the food was not forthcoming and so I confronted some of the guys whom I thought were causing the delay. I as well as some of the boys had drunk alcohol and we were intoxicated. In the course of the confrontation, two boys got infuriated and hit my face with the lid of a *waakye*[9] bowl. I was furious because we were very hungry and did not understand why the boys were keeping the food away from us. I picked up a knife in the kitchen and stabbed one of them. I regretted when I was arrested and put in police cells and I prayed to God that the boy should not die. [He sighed.] I'm glad I ended up here otherwise I would definitely have been worse. (46)

He kept repeating that it was good he was brought to the correctional centre otherwise he would have been worse. Unlike other youngsters interviewed, John lived with both parents until arrest and his account did not depict neglect.

The majority of youngsters demonstrate through their narratives as having suffered diverse degrees and forms of neglect and rejection, which was manifested in both material and non-material deprivation. Youngsters clearly indicated the unwillingness rather than inability of their parents and relatives to provide for their needs. Kwesi for instance lamented that there was no relative present in court and that, though he wished he was bailed, no one did. John, Kofi, and Yaw shared the same sentiments:

> My parents were not present and so the judge decided that I should be brought to the Borstal.[10] Sometimes when the judge realizes that you

> have responsible parents you can be put on probation to be supervised by a social worker or so. (47). Neither my mother nor any of my family was in court-maybe if they were, I would have been given fewer years. I stayed in police cells for a short period and then my case was heard. No family was present and so I was sent to the Borstal. (47)

Youngsters such as Kojo deliberately kept family out:

> When I attended court I was asked to bring my parents so they could settle the case at home but none of my relatives were available. In fact I did not want my family to be involved as they did not care about me. I said to the police officer that they should do whatever they wanted with me. (47)

Yet, parental and family involvement is considered central[11] to the decision of whether or not juveniles should be committed.

Rampant mobilities

Frequent movements from one social setting and occupation to another was typical of pre-detention lives of most youngsters. Kojo's narrative was replete with several such movements:

> Following the death of my father, I lived with my paternal aunt and later with my grandma and then went back to my aunt. While with my aunt I stopped school and got connected to a contractor. I went back to my mum after poor working conditions with the contractor when I realized I had nowhere to go. My mum provided no support and so I went back to my timber work and decided to rent my own house. Along the way, my grandma decided to put me in apprenticeship for three months to learn carpentry but I found it difficult working as an apprentice. My older brother tried to teach me how to drive; I did that for eight months and stopped and tried to learn masonry for two and could not continue that either. (51)

Following the death of his father, Kojo embarked on several movements within the family and as a result schooled at different locations. He also undertook several movements outside the family in order to earn a living and also to engage in some apprenticeship. In all, Kojo undertook approximately 12 different movements; the majority of these movements were on his own initiative and at one time, having encountered several frustrations for not being able to settle in a stable apprenticeship and occupation, he moved to a village unknown to him before:

> I moved to another town as I was informed that sawing business was thriving in the villages. I travelled to this village which was initially unfamiliar to me and managed to secure some sawing work later. However I was paid a very low wage and I got frustrated. It was in the process of considering what to do next that I committed the offence and got arrested. (51)

Thus, Kojo manoeuvred from one setting to the other, following the loss of his father and the rejection he suffered from his mother. In all these attempts, Kojo needed to survive and so embarked on several attempts to learn a trade and make some income. His movements were more like drifting from one family, career, and apprenticeship to the other; a kind of sporadic, but somehow purposeful, movement that initially seemed to go nowhere but always ended somewhere until he got arrested for defiling the daughter of a pastor. In his narration to me, there was no expression of remorse on his face. When I intentionally asked whether he felt sorry for his offence, he responded in the negative. Yaw also experienced frequent movements in varying situations:

> I stayed with my aunt following the death of my mother … I found it difficult to stay with my aunties as I farmed a lot and so I left to stay with friends at a lorry station in Accra. While with my friends, there was misunderstanding about sharing of booty after a robbery act, in the process, I got arrested. (51)

Yaw's movements depicted less family settings and family involvements as compared with Kojo. Nevertheless, the attempts of both youngsters to explore and exhaust residential options available to them are courageous, one dotted with uncertainty and characterized by 'trial and error' experiences, disappointments, and difficulties. In this respect, youngsters might not even have an idea what their next destination would be, yet, regardless of their challenging situations, youngsters always managed to find a place to perch.

Youngsters' social world and friendships in non-familial settings before committal

One commonality that runs through youngsters' narratives is their friendships and social lives before youngsters' committal to correctional centres. The social world outside the family setting with peers was probably one of the most pleasant times for youngsters relative to their experiences with parents and family. Friendships, which encompassed peers as well as older youngsters, constituted some source of social support for youngsters. Nana Bonsu shared his experience:

> My uncle did not take good care of me and so I stopped school at primary two and left to stay with my Mum in Accra. I was with friends who were between the ages of 15 and 55 and quarried for my friend's mum. We used to visit night clubs in the evenings to dance and I was very good at dancing. (55)

Besides sharing friendship with other boys of varying ages, Nana Bonsu also shared intimate relationships:

> One day, a girl who was in JHS, saw me dance and she became interested in me and we became friends. The girl came from a wealthy family and attended school for wealthy people. (55)

Nevertheless, youngsters such as Yaw admitted that their offences were linked to the activities they engaged in with their friends:

> I had many friends and was happy. I remember that one time there was a dance which I wanted to attend and I did go but was sent out as I did not pay the entrance fee. I felt sad as I did not have the money; I therefore went home and took my father's money … (55)

Some friendships, according to Yaw, carried unpleasant experiences:

> While at James Town, I made friends quickly but anytime we stole and shared the money I was cheated, possibly because I was very young. I decided to be by myself but once again and I found myself in the company of another person and we stole money to the tune of GHS 800Ghc [about US$ 471 [12]] and yet he gave me only GHS 2.00 [US$ 0.50]. I got very angry I thought that was so mean of him and decided to report my friend to the man whose money was stolen. My friend was caught and the money was taken from him but my friend did not know that I gave him away. Later both of us broke into the room of the same person again and stole GHS 3,400.00 [US$850.00] and then we left for the village. (55)

Friendships are therefore diverse; some intimate, desirable, others opportunistic. Mere associations with peers, such as in Yaw's case, are constituted based on resources at stake. Friendships are also laced with power and resistance, for while Yaw's friend exhibited control over the sharing of booty, Yaw, though younger, courageously defied the age gap and reported the latter, thus resulting in the arrest of the friend. This action however carried further repercussions and backlashes for Yaw:

> … My friend for some reason got to know that I reported him about the first case and so he told other people that I was a wizard and I was shunned as a result of this when I was admitted to the SCC in 2005. For the same reason, I was also seriously maltreated by inmates in the first dormitory … The isolation and the maltreatment was beyond me and so when we were asked on one occasion to go and weed, I seized the opportunity to run away and that was after four months of stay. (56)

Largely, youngsters relied heavily on friendships, which were constructed differently.

Youngsters, spiritual powers, and reformation

Yaw's association with witchcraft was within a friendship context rather than a family setting, different from Grace's situation. Relatedly, youngsters consult fetish priests, *Mallams* (Islamic prophets or spiritualists) and related supernatural powers outside family settings to settle scores, seek vengeance as well as seek protection and success in committing acts such as theft and robbery. In his narrative, Kofi and William stated their dependence on such powers:

> We do not usually sell items stolen immediately as we would like to listen in to hear what people say. Sometimes, victims of thefts and robbery acts contact fetish priests to find out culprits but what we do is we put the money we steal in water so the spell or curse does not affect us. (59)

> We rely on spiritual powers for our *operations*;[13] sometimes we are successful, other times we are not. As part of consultations, we sometimes have cuts on our body, are made to swallow concoctions and put talisman round our waist. Prior to being brought here, I visited a *Mallam* with my friends most of whom were older than me – I am very short and my height gives me a lot of advantage as people think that I am a child and so do not suspect bad things of me. The *Mallam* demanded GHS 50.00 [US$12.50] from my friends. The Mallam made some incantations on the money and then asked us to give the money out to people on the streets. The first operation was successful but the second one was not and this is what landed us here … These powers make us fearless, daring and confident. (59)

Seeking supernatural powers for protection, according to the narratives, is largely in connection with sources such as fetish priests and Malaams.[14]

Church pastors are consulted for exorcism purposes as shown in Grace's case or when youngsters feel the need for change. In most instances, these spiritual sources make certain economic demands on these youngsters. In Grace's situation for instance, the pastor asked that she brought a towel, sponge, a candle, and a fresh dress. In William's case, the Malaam demanded GHS 50.00 (US$12.50). Thus, an informal economy is nurtured as consultations with various spiritualists come at an economical cost incurred by youngsters who require some means of income. The relationship between youngsters and such spiritualists is therefore far from being unidirectional as the latter is also dependent on the former. In fact, the social and economic activities of spiritualists such as Malaams, fetish priests and pastors, thrive on the regular consultations by their customers including youngsters.

Other times, youngsters intentionally seek spiritual transformation based on their experiences in committal. For example, Yaw was accused of witchcraft by a friend who sought revenge while they were both in committal, allegedly because Yaw had previously exposed him in connection with a robbery. As a result, Yaw suffered maltreatment at the hands of fellow inmates, eventually absconding from the correctional centre, though staff were unaware of his reasons. He was later apprehended for another offence and re-arrested.

While awaiting trial, Yaw turned to spiritual resources that offered him space for reflection. He recalled:

> On return from escape, while at the remand home, many people visited to advise us. It was upon the advice of a black American that I reflected very much on my own life and decided to do a seven-day fasting to pray for repentance and then I was determined when I was admitted the second time that I would no longer run away. I took my church attendance very serious and would rally other youngsters round in the dorm to pray sometimes. I sing and play the school drum during church services and I have trained others who will take over from me. (59)

I observed that Yaw was indeed active in church activity while in committal and tended to conduct himself quite responsibly.

Scholarship on children's growing-up experiences has been largely silent on the ways in which children and young people themselves initiate engagement with spiritual and supernatural practices, including those that contribute to their reformation. This silence suggests that such practices are often interpreted through adult perspectives rather than understood from the standpoint of the children. The ways in which children draw upon the supernatural remain an important area for further research.

Life in police detention

Juvenile remand and detention practices under Act 653

According to the Juvenile Justice Act 653 of 2003, section 23 (GOG, 2003), juveniles who are arrested and not released on bail must receive a court order either committing them to the care of parents, a close relative, or another willing guardian, or remanding them into state custody. Section 14 further stipulates that juveniles must be sent to a place of safety or a remand home within 48 hours of arrest (GOG, 2003, section 14). A remand warrant may last for a maximum of seven days and must be renewed at each court appearance. The total remand period cannot exceed three months, except in cases involving offences punishable by death, where the limit is six months (GOG, 2003). Section 15 requires that juveniles in police custody be placed under the care of an adult of the same sex, whether in a police station or during transport to a remand home or place of safety. While detained, juveniles are entitled to adequate food, medical treatment when necessary, reasonable visits from parents, guardians, lawyers, or close relatives, and other conditions essential to their welfare.

In practice, police cells and remand homes serve as temporary sites of confinement for juveniles awaiting trial. Young offenders may remain in police detention during trial proceedings or after trial while awaiting transfer to correctional centres. Police officers, as part of their law enforcement role, maintain control over juveniles temporarily in their custody. In Accra, male and female juveniles on trial are often remanded within the same premises as the girls' correctional centre, overseen by the same director under the Social Welfare Department. Other juveniles are held in police cells under the Ghana Police Service.

For females, remand is typically a single multi-purpose room that houses those awaiting trial, newly committed youngsters, and those isolated for misconduct as punishment. Authorities note that no state provision is made for education or skills training during remand, as this period is considered temporary. Male juveniles, however, may access educational lessons sponsored by NGOs in remand homes, while female juveniles sometimes participate in educational or vocational activities organized by the girls' correctional centre. No educational opportunities exist for juveniles held in police cells.

Upon arrest, the Juvenile Justice Act imputes to the state officer the responsibility of care and in ensuring conditions reasonably required for the welfare of juveniles. Notwithstanding the above provisions, youngsters' accounts during the period of fieldwork point to the fact that some youngsters are unduly detained in police detention for a period exceeding one year, in contravention of the provisions of the Juvenile Justice Act. Visits by CHRAJ's monitors[15] reveal that most police cells are overcrowded with barely any space to stand, or sit. In some police cells, inmates take turns to sleep on card boxes spread out on the bare floor due to the lack of space. Not so with remand homes situated within correctional centres.

Represented below are interviews with youngsters about their practical experiences in police cells during the initial field visit from 2009 to 2011. John (19 years), Kofi (20 years), and Kwesi (16 years) share their initial experiences:

> It was difficult life in the cells, there was little food and we defecated in the same cells. (67)

> It was filthy and smelly; we did the toilet in the cells and also ate in the same cells. (68)

> It was hard life as I was the only youngster in the cell, all the others were adults and I stayed for a long time in the cells. We did everything in the cells, we ate, urinated and eased ourselves in the cells and sometimes it took days before we were able to dispose of our excrement. (68)

Police cells, according to youngsters, housed both youngsters and adults and served an all-in-one function of toilets, dining rooms, and sleeping places. There was no official provision of food in cells and youngsters devised their own means of survival sometimes through the payment of cell fees; other times, police officers were relied upon for food[16] as stated by Kojo: 'I did not have to pay cell fees. There were only three persons at the time but the number increased later on. The police officer gave me food regularly' (69).

Philanthropists, charity organizations and churches, who provide material and non-material support to prisons, orphanages, and remand homes, rarely visit police cells. Besides, only a few religious organizations visit[17]. Kwesi was the only youngster interviewed who received regular visits from a pastor: 'When I was first remanded, I received visits from a pastor who provided us with food; I was then 16 years of age' (69). At the time of arrest, youngsters do not have much contact with family either. Kwesi narrates how one of his family relations chanced upon him while in police cells:

> One day while in the cells, to my surprise, I saw the sister of my grandma [with whom I stayed] passing and I asked someone to call her. She was surprised to see me in police cells and cried a lot and said she had only one Ghana cedi [US$0.25] and that I should take 50 pesewas [US$0.12] to buy some food and I declined and said she should keep it and that I would manage to find some food in the cells. (69)

Youngsters such as Yaw also spoke about long periods in police custody before committal. In fact, besides the period of committal, the next longest stay in detention encountered was in police custody. Yaw, for instance, narrated that he spent almost two years in police and remand custody before being committed finally to the correctional centre:

> I was in cells for four months prior to being arraigned before court and it took the intervention of one of the chief officers who visited the cells one day. When the chief officer saw me he asked the other officers why I was still in the cells. He quickly arranged that I be brought before court. The judge remanded me to a remand home as he said none of my relatives were forthcoming. I spent one and a half years in the remand home and it took the intervention of one of the teachers namely Mr Asiedu to send me to the police station. The police officer prepared relevant papers and also went to court to collect a social enquiry report and I was admitted at the Borstal. (69)

Contact with the police and subsequent detention in police cells for several months tend to evoke feelings of ambivalence and confusion where youngsters do not understand their encounters and processes in police custody. Kwesi, who was reportedly arrested for collecting scraps of metal, also expressed surprise for being arrested and yet at the same time considered himself deserving of such treatment. Similarly, Yaw, who had spent a considerable amount of time in police custody, said he did not question the length of stay in the cells. He stated: 'I did not question why I was in the cells for that length of period. I thought that maybe I deserved it. One day, a police officer visited and commented that I had kept so long in the cells and asked that I should be sent to the Borstal' (70). In other words, Yaw's trial process was completed and yet he was still kept in police custody and Yaw tended to accept his fate without question.

Life in police cells apart from being long also induces suspense as youngsters never know when they would be picked up. Yaw, for instance, would not have been discovered if the chief police officer had not visited.

Youngsters' narratives also reveal that police officers[18] sometimes depend on youngsters' parents and relatives for transportation money to execute official duty as was the case with Kwesi: 'One day, a police officer visited and commented that I had kept so long in the cells and asked the CID to send me to the Borstal. The police depended on my family for money to transport me to the Borstal' (70). Yaw stated the same, that the police took money from his family in order to convey him to the Borstal.

First experiences in police custody on the basis of the above narratives depict youngsters who hold differentiated perspectives of themselves and state officers. Some conceive of themselves as being dumped in police cells and forgotten about until other police officers chance upon them. Others portray state officers as persons who switch from being powerful and wicked to seemingly kind officers who feed them (youngsters). Yet, the same officers forget that youngsters are in their custody and should be conveyed for trial or to correctional centres. Also manifest is a poorly resourced state that has barely enough resources to cater for children under its care and whose officers depend on the resources of youngsters' relatives to execute official duty. The ramification for youngsters who seldom have contact with relatives to resource the state may be a lengthy stay in police cells without court attendance or conveyance to correctional centres. State officers may have their own reasons for keeping youngsters in police custody for unduly long periods as police custody may be less expensive for the state than keeping youngsters in correctional centres.

My empirical evidence, drawing on follow-up visits in 2019 and 2023, establish that, while the problem of pre-sentence detention persisted, fewer children were detained in police cells and remand homes and the duration of detention had also reduced (Ayete-Nyampong, 2019, 2023, CHRAJ, 2021a).

Final thoughts

This chapter presents stories and accounts of children that constitute the foundation of the discussions in this book. Youngsters' accounts, perspectives, and lived experiences often stand in stark contrast to those of criminal justice or human rights professionals, who tend to perceive and label young people as delinquent, criminal, or in conflict with the law, subjects to be corrected or managed by total institutions. The vengeful responses voiced by male participants in focus group discussions, 'We shall jail our fathers'; 'We shall jail the police' (70), illustrate how both boys and girls reject the notion that they are in need of correction. This defiant stance helps explain their everyday cynicism towards institutional efforts at reform. Yet, during fieldwork, I observed that criminal justice and human rights professionals, along with reformers such as religious leaders, showed little interest in the formative experiences of these young people. By overlooking such experiences, these formal and local practitioners remain unaware of the persistent neglect and rejection children often endure from their parents and families, factors that contribute significantly to their arrest, eventual committal and their everyday relational dynamics in correctional centres.

Reflecting on Kojo's unapologetic attitude towards defilement, together with its frequent occurrence, suggests that some boys may be using harm, anger, and vengeance as weapons in response to long-term neglect by families or the state. My empirical evidence establishes that, for more than a decade, theft and defilement have been the most common offences at the SCC, leading to the arrest and confinement of male juveniles. The persistence of defilement points to a systemic behavioural challenge among boys. When coupled with the violent acts increasingly evident among young males in contemporary society, particularly within Senior High Schools[19], this pattern may reflect a troubling form of retaliatory justice. Such dynamics underscore the urgent need for strategic support directed towards the boy child.

Generally, youngsters' experiences do not necessarily reflect their conscious alignment with normative conceptions of human rights. Yet children lay implicit and differentiated claims to human rights through the narratives they share and the strategies they employ. In particular, their eagerness to tell their stories resonates with the spirit of Article 12 of the UNCRC (1989), which guarantees children the right to express views and have those views taken seriously. Respecting children as rights holders requires honouring their narratives, even those that conflict with adult expectations or human rights norms. When a child asserts 'I am very bad, no one knows how bad I am' or declares 'I will jail my father, I will jail the police,' these expressions offer profound insights into their constructed understandings of justice and morality, grounded in their lived realities. Rather than allowing neglect to fester into retaliatory justice, systems must prioritize nurturing boys' sense of belonging, accountability, and empathy. This also entails strengthening family and intergenerational bonding and support, while ensuring correctional centres are places of rehabilitation rather than cycles of harm.

Practitioners and allied actors, such as pastors, play a crucial role in either attributing meaning to, or silencing, these perspectives. When they refrain from essentializing the child and instead commit to careful listening, their interventions gain greater meaning and resonance within the children's specific contexts. Many of the children I engaged with exhibit acute awareness that practitioners often lack genuine interest in hearing their perspectives. As a result, children develop coping mechanisms to disengage, from clinical psychologists, pastors, and other actors, as shared in Chapter 7 on escapes.

Children's reliance on peer relationships outside the family emerges as a vital coping strategy. These connections embody not only emotional strength but also aligns with Article 31 of the UNCRC (1989), which affirms the right to play and recreational activity. Likewise, children's efforts to pursue income-generating ventures and flee hostile home environments highlight their enactment of rights to survival and development, as articulated in Article 6 of the UNCRC (1989).

An aspect of youngsters' accounts that remains underexplored is the caregiving role often assumed by grandparents, most frequently grandmothers, who, paradoxically, may also engage in abusive behaviours as portrayed in the accounts of Grace and Yaw. Older adults, particularly grandmothers, frequently shoulder the responsibility of raising grandchildren while simultaneously grappling with their own vulnerability, social isolation, and neglect (Van der Geest, 2002, Van der Geest, 2008, Van der Geest, 2016). This situation creates a double bind: grandparents who serve as primary caregivers may themselves be denied care, subjected to abuse, or even stigmatized as witches (CHRAJ, 2022, Ayete-Nyampong et al., 2025) within the very networks of care they sustain. Lacking adequate resources and facing mistreatment from those they nurture, some grandparents may channel their frustration into abusive behaviour towards the children in their care. Efforts to address this phenomenon have been limited, and little has been done to intentionally foster inter- and multi-generational approaches that provide support across the generations. Lacking adequate resources and facing mistreatment from those they nurture, some grandparents may channel their frustration into abusive behaviour towards the children in their care.

These personal accounts underscore the need for preventive and responsive interventions for both boys and girls whose adverse childhood experiences can reverberate across their lifespan. The narratives call for multi- and intergenerational programming that link parents, grandparents, and extended families to both material, psychosocial, faith-based, and related supports. Policies must prioritize family wellbeing, including expanded paid parental leave, accessible mental health services, constructive parenting education, and measures to reduce the financial burden of child-rearing.

Conclusion

Discussions in this chapter, which largely underpin those in subsequent chapters, have examined youngsters who have encountered trauma, adversity, and systemic neglect, yet they rarely remain tethered to positions of helplessness or powerlessness. Despite these challenges, many demonstrate agency in navigating the harsh realities of their daily lives, engaging in actions such as dropping out of school, relocating, forging or renegotiating relationships, pursuing informal livelihoods, or seeking recourse through spiritual or supernatural means. Such agency, however, coexists with persistent vulnerability and exposure to abuse, often inflicted by parents, grandparents, extended families, peers, and the state. The narratives reveal a profound inversion: youth frequently construct the family and the state not as sources of care or accountability, but as themselves delinquent, abusive, or criminal. This runs counter to dominant justice and rights-based discourses, which tend to frame youth as transgressive subjects in need of correction.

I do not seek to glorify or romanticize bad activities or being bad, it is important to appreciate the differentiated meanings that children attribute to what they say and do. For instance, if children say 'illicit' economic activities serve as a coping mechanism and social fulfilment, they may be expressing the fulfilment of genuine needs that must not be ignored. Further, what meanings do children associate with statements such as 'I am very bad and wicked', or 'I will jail my parents and the police'? When actions that seek to reform or correct do not accord significance to the meanings that children attach to what they say and do, such correction may be devoid of realistic contexts.

Importantly, children's stories complicate simplified causal links between neglect and structural precarity. While poverty, bereavement, and separation certainly contribute, many youngsters interpret their abandonment as intentional, imbued with emotional weight and moral judgement. Their accounts express varied interpretations of exclusion, each shaping their strategies to reclaim agency, redefine belonging, and reconfigure their social worlds.

My ethno-inductive approach proves indispensable not only as a method of listening and meaning-making, but also as an orientation that centres the lived experiences of detainees and creates space for practical insight. Researchers, practitioners, and reform advocates must take seriously these diverse epistemologies, which enrich our understanding of childhood and correction in holistic ways.

4

Views from Literature on Children's Growing-Up Experiences

Introduction

In this chapter, I place scholarly perspectives alongside the lived narratives of child detainees. These perspectives reveal how the experiences and viewpoints of detained children often receive little attention from adults, resulting in a dominance of adult-centred accounts of child-rearing practices and a silencing of children's own voices.

Although prison ethnography in Africa has seen a modest rise, literature remains limited in two crucial respects: first, in tracing the life trajectories of juveniles and young offenders prior to their incarceration; and second, in documenting their lived realities while in state custody. This gap reflects a broader neglect of children's perspectives, as scholarship tends to privilege adult interpretations over the voices of the young people themselves. The chapter underscores the need for research that not only situates children within familial and societal structures but also takes seriously their own accounts of friendships, survival, and meaning making.

Child mobility between and betwixt the family

Most literature on experiences and practices of Ghanaian children as they grow up is either located within the family context, or in other contexts such as practices on the street, child labour and its worst forms, as well as child fosterage, which situates child mobility between and betwixt the family. According to various authors, both local and in the diaspora, whereas parents bring forth children, child upbringing is a shared responsibility for all adults within the extended family. Child mobility and child fosterage, from one relative to the other, as part of shared parenting is therefore a common practice in Ghana and Africa (Isiugo-Abanihe, 1985, Ardayfio-Schandorf and Amissah, 1996, Nukunya, 2003, Honwana and De Boeck, 2005, Owusu and Adjei, 2009, Twum Danso, 2009, Boakye Boaten, 2010, Kassa and Abebe, 2016, Abdullah et al., 2020, Cotton, 2021, Bentum and Manful, 2022, Kyei, 2024). A key process by which children leave home to reside elsewhere is fostering, a practice that is widespread and well researched in Ghana. Reasons for child fostering may include death, illness of parent, or the need to receive formal education or skilled training from adult mentors. Parents may also give their children to relatives or even non-relatives as companions for elderly people, or for domestic or marketing assistants (Pilon, 2003, Kielland and Maurizia, 2006). Thus, from birth to adulthood, a child may pass through the nurturing hand of numerous adult members of the family. As far back as 1982, Oppong and Bleek (1982) had documented mobilities of children. Such movements, which were at the initiative of adult family members, are contrasted with the movements of youngsters, where mobility was sporadic, uncertain and usually at the instance of youngsters and not adult members of the family. Generally, portrayals of literature about child mobility are at variance with the narratives of youngsters. Mobility from the viewpoint of youngsters is usually triggered by the rejection and abandonment that youngsters encounter (Ayete-Nyampong, 2010, 2013a, 2017b, 2024). Such frequent mobilities constituted more or less an escape as well as a coping measure.

Literature portrayals tend to associate such non-familial settings with criminal practices and yet, for most youngsters, the initial effort to engage in some activity that yields some economic gain is a desperate endeavour of youngsters to escape familial hostilities and also to survive, besides the opportunity to forge friendships and have fun (Abekah-Carter et al., 2024, Chikoko, 2025). The emphasis on the economic motivation for child mobility by scholars such as Anarfi and Kwankye (2005) tends to overlook such non-material livelihood supports that youngsters' narratives emphasize within non-familial settings.

What adults, whether scholars or practitioners, often classify as criminal or delinquent behaviour is, for many youngsters, simply an attempt to meet both material and non-material needs. Young people interpret these activities differently, viewing them not as acts of deviance but as part of their livelihood strategies and peer associations. Within their narratives, such practices are embedded in efforts to survive and to secure companionship, in contexts where familial support is minimal or absent. This divergence in interpretation underscores a critical gap: adult perspectives tend to criminalize survival strategies, while children themselves frame them as necessary responses to neglect, hostility, or exclusion. Recognizing this distinction is essential, as it reveals how youngsters construct meaning around their actions and highlights the importance of situating 'delinquent' practices within broader social and emotional realities rather than reducing them to legal infractions.

Children and a family support network

Literature committed to practices such as child labour, the street, and migration assume that African children have some family support network or that children or youngsters always keep some contact with the family (Aptekar, 1994, Schimmel, 2006, Orme and Seipel, 2007, Okafor, 2010, Archambault et al., 2012, Abdullah et al., 2022, Gatsinzi and Hilson, 2022, Abekah-Carter et al., 2024, Chikoko, 2025). For instance, based on his study *Street Children in Harare*, Bourdillon recommends that attention should be directed at policies that seek to improve the lot of children along with their families rather than policies that move children out of their communities. In the first place, Bourdillon's generalized usage of the term community may suggest that the child's community is assumed to be the family and yet youngsters who participated in my research may construe their community differently; the latter may refer to their peers, occupational, or religious associates. A familial support system is virtually minimal for the children that engaged my attention. Such presumptions may tend to overlook the fact that some children and youngsters may have no such familial support as demonstrated by narratives of youngsters.

Drawing binary connections between the home and practices of child labour, the street and migration may also result in analytic limitations. For instance, certain practices of children on the street are construed as involving both the street and the home, that is, children make a living on the street and retire to the home at the end of the working day. Similarly, there is some connection established by literature, between the home and other non-familial settings (Aderinto, 2000, Boakye-Boaten, 2008, Hassen and Mañus, 2018, Ayete-Nyampong, 2019, Okafor, 2010, CHRAJ, 2021, Ayete-Nyampong, 2023, Abekah-Carter et al., 2024, Julien, 2024, Chikoko, 2025), such as children who migrate and who make efforts to maintain contacts with the home. The binary relationship between such contexts and the home, however, imposes a dichotomous limitation. This limitation overlooks dynamic and complex relational aspects involved in the diverse processes of growing up within multiple settings and sometimes oscillating between and betwixt diverse settings as depicted for instance in narratives of Kojo and Yaw's frequent mobilities. The narratives of Kojo and Yaw depict pathways that are far from linear; they crisscross from one setting to the other and also from one actor to another.

Views of literature on youngsters' social life

Youngsters' experiences and friendships outside the family setting featured prominently in their narratives, and yet it remains underrepresented in Ghanaian and African scholarly work on children (Boakye Boaten, 2009,

Twum Danso, 2009, Porter et al., 2011, Mukasa, 2021, Yusuf et al., 2021). Scholars within the Ghanaian and African context rarely discuss the social world of children outside the familial context. Scholars who attempt to advance discussions in diverse non-familial contexts, such as practices related to the street, labour, and migration restrict the motivation for such practices of child mobility mostly to reasons of economic survival, thereby narrowing the motivations behind such practices (Boakye Boaten, 2009, Twum Danso, 2009, Porter et al., 2011, Bonsu, 2021, Koomson et al., 2021, Ogunkan et al., 2024).

Whereas most Ghanaian scholars as discussed above tend to situate the growing-up experiences of children within the family, these scholars rarely discussed friendships and peer associations of children labelled delinquent, outside their familial context. Bosiakoh and Andoh (2010) examined the activities and friendships of children and their linkage to delinquency but did not focus on the relevance of such friendships to youngsters' fulfilment of material and non-material needs. When these and other scholars advance discussions in diverse non-familial settings, such practices are usually related to the street, labour, migration, crime and so on, which restrict the motivation for such practices to economic, criminal, and related reasons. The empirical evidence of my research, however, establishes that youngsters' friendships outside of the family were diverse, desirable, fun and experimenting with new environments. In other respects, such friendships were ambiguous, episodic, and opportunistic. Simplistically reducing the survival efforts of youngsters drawing on material resources to 'bad' activities misses out on non-material resources associated with their lived realities.

Views of literature on youngsters and the supernatural

Generally, views of literature on spiritual powers and the supernatural tend to attribute to the child an adult-imposed status as in the case of Grace who was accused of practices such as witchcraft (Adinkrah, 2011, Jindra, 2020, Onyinah, 2020, Yoder et al., 2021). This stance gives little regard to how children and youngsters utilize magic and other supernatural powers, as well as religious observances such as prayer, in their everyday practice. Whereas Christiansen's paper on 'Youth, Religiosity and the AIDS Pandemic' (Christiansen, 2006) is relevant in terms of how youth perceive their agency in religious terms, generally few scholars focus on how youngsters construct their own forms of religiosity or spiritual practices (Yushawu and Jaishankar, 2025) different from the formal religious practices in which their faith is embedded (De Boek, 2005, Adinkrah, 2011, Boyatzis, 2011, Knoetze, 2015, Mhaka-Mutepfa and Maundeni, 2019, Alhassan and Ridwan, 2023).

Yet most youngsters interviewed claimed some involvement with spiritual powers or the supernatural during the period they had grown out of their families and resided by themselves or with friends. These practices were on children's own initiative, for instance, embarking on prayer and fasting privately for reformation purposes, or engaging in occultic practices as a resource for thefts and robberies.

Views of literature on youngsters in pre- and post-sentence detention

Scholarship on pre-sentence and post-sentence detention in police cells and remand homes in Ghana remains skeletal. While valuable studies have emerged since my initial research, focusing on juvenile justice and children in correctional centres (Boakye, 2012, Golo, 2018, Ame, 2019, Baffour et al., 2021, Boakye and Akoensi, 2021, Dako-Gyeke et al., 2022), only a few of these works give sustained attention to children's own accounts of their lived experiences in police detention.

Philanthropic support, including that from faith-based organizations, often concentrates on adult prisons and formal juvenile correctional centres, leaving police cells largely overlooked. Yet juveniles held in police custody face acute hardship, as family visits are rare and support is minimal. Kwesi's account underscores this neglect, during his time in police detention. He recalls only occasional visits from philanthropic groups or family members while detained in police custody (see Chapter 3).

There is virtually no scholarly work exploring how youngsters survive in these spaces, including the role of informal economies and peer networks in sustaining daily life within police cells or remand homes. This silence obscures the realities of children who navigate detention environments with minimal external support, and it highlights the need for research that foregrounds their voices, strategies, and social worlds rather than reducing their experiences to institutional categories.

Conclusion

Scholarship and legal frameworks, whether international, regional, or local, tend to overemphasize familial contexts when discussing children and young people. This narrow focus obscures the realities of rejection and abandonment that often define the pre-custodial lives of children in conflict with the law.

The literature reviewed rarely acknowledges the differentiated ways in which children construct their growing-up experiences. Their relational worlds, peer associations, frequent mobilities, spiritual engagements, and diverse accounts of pre-custodial life remain largely hidden. This absence is not necessarily because children are unwilling to share their stories, but probably because researchers, practitioners, and professionals often overlook them or rely predominantly on adult-centric interpretations.

By privileging adult perspectives, scholarship risks silencing children's voices and misrepresenting their realities. Recognizing and documenting these lived experiences is crucial, not only for a fuller understanding of childhood in Ghana but also for designing interventions that respond to the actual conditions of neglect, mobility, and peer-driven survival strategies that shape children's lives before, during and after custody as these worlds are interrelated.

5

Everyday Correctional Practice: Mortification Processes and Non-Compliance

Introduction

This chapter initiates a series of discussions on the everyday practices within correctional centres. Drawing on Goffman's concept of *total institutions* (Goffman, 1968), it explores how daily routines and structural dynamics function as mechanisms of mortification, designed to reshape inmates into conformity with institutional norms. Yet the authority of correctional institutional norms is never absolute; compliance with rules is uneven, and governance often relies on the very individuals it seeks to control.

Discussions in this chapter begin with an overview of the Junior Correctional Centre (JCC) and the Senior Correctional Centre (SCC), before examining routines that often disregard the personal histories of the youths. Against this backdrop, discrepancies between official and actual ages, alongside acts of non-compliance, highlight the discrepancy between institutional rules and youngsters' agency. The analysis then turns to Scott's notion of the *hidden transcript*, uncovering backstage negotiations, as well as revealing how correctional centres express human rights in complex, often contradictory ways. Within this framework, human rights are feminized and marginalized, while toughness is masculinized and upheld as the legitimate form of authority.

In sum, the lived realities of confinement portrayed in this chapter unsettle neat, binary distinctions between staff and inmates, governor and governed, revealing instead a social world defined by entangled relations and mutual dependence.

The JCC and SCC

The JCC and the SCC are both located in Accra, the capital city of Ghana, and hold most children in conflict with the law in Ghana. The SCC, the only one in Ghana, holds young male offenders, whereas the JCC holds female juvenile offenders, also the only correctional centre for female juvenile offenders in Ghana (see Chapter 1). These centres have their differences in terms of architectural layout and are manned by different oversight authorities. The Ghana Prisons Service, under the auspices of the Ministry of Interior, has direct oversight of the SCC. The JCC is manned by the Social Work Department under the Ministry of Employment and Social Welfare. The JCC and the SCC are popularly known as *mmmofra bonne sukuu*. This literally translates as schools for bad children.

The SCC or the boys' institution presents a more stringent security setup compared to the JCC. At its checkpoint stands a massive crossbar supported by two large pillars, prominently inscribed with 'SCC'. Despite this imposing entrance, the facility's security does not reach the level of maximum confinement seen in adult central prisons, which are characterized by towering walls. Still, the atmosphere of incarceration is unmistakable at the SCC, reinforced by the visible presence of numerous uniformed prison officers, nearly as noticeable as the inmates themselves. During my visit in 2009, the institution housed six dormitories; a decade later, I observed that additional dormitories had been constructed. The Head of the SCC is usually a Deputy Director of Prisons who doubles as the Regional Commander of Prisons in charge of the Greater Accra Region. The Head is supported by senior officers that occupy various hierarchical ranks: Assistant Director of Prisons, Chief Superintendent of Prisons, Deputy Superintendent of Prisons and Assistant Superintendent of Prisons. The Head and the senior officers constitute the management of the SCC, who oversee other staff such as teachers and workshop instructors and nurses. Yard officers also assist the management to supervise staff in the yard such as clerks, drivers, dorm wardens, kitchen staff, store keepers, among other staff. The SCC experiences frequent transfers of staff and, at the time of fieldwork, I regularly encountered new faces. Within the two years, I encountered three different Heads or officers-in-charge (OICs).

The number of youngsters in committal at the SCC changes daily as admissions and discharges are done on a daily basis. Official records[1] of the Ghana Prisons Service show that the average daily lock-up of male youngsters at the SCC from 2001 to 2006 did not follow any trend of increase or decrease. However, years 2007, 2008, and 2009 realized an increasing trend from an average lock-up of 108 through 118 to 122 respectively. During follow-up visits, the number of inmates committed to the SCC increased from 114 youngsters in 2014 to 263 youngsters in 2018, though this number decreased slightly to 260 in 2019 and again decreased in 2020 from 260 to 251 in 2022. At the time of visit in March 2023, which was within the first quarter of the year, 32 inmates had been committed.

The SCC assumed its present name after the passage of the Juvenile Justice Act in 2003, yet the former name 'Borstal' is commonly referred to by staff and youngsters. The Borstal, according to youngsters, is a prison for bad boys. An assistant Officer-in-Charge, however, maintains in an interview that the philosophy of the institution is different from that of an adult prison. The Borstal Institute gives emphasis to vocational, technical training and moral correction. The motto of the institution 'I shall rise again' (Ayete-Nyampong, 2013a)[2] according to the officer, encourages inmates to avoid criminal tendencies that do not promote peaceful co-existence. In spite of this assertion, I observed that, in practice, the SCC was largely administered by prison officers who lacked specialized training in working with children and young people. In effect, the institution operated more like a prison than a correctional facility. As one assistant officer reflected: 'This institution was governed by rules formulated by the Ghana Prisons Service, yet these inmates are children. Almost all of us were transferred from adult prisons, and we have no particular training to prepare us for working with them' (67).

During focus group discussions, eight out of ten reported that, prior to committal, they had heard of the Borstal only as a prison for 'bad boys'. Kojo, for instance, explained in an interview: 'Before committal I had heard about the Borstal, and that it was a place for bad boys' (67). Others, like Kofi, offered metaphorical descriptions – he likened the Borstal to fetching water with a basket, suggesting it was a place of impossible tasks where troublesome youngsters were compelled to attempt the unattainable.

The JCC does not have the appearance of a prison but portrays a school-like atmosphere under the oversight of the Social Welfare Department. The rooms and dormitories at the JCC, relative to the SCC, are less congested and accommodate less than half its capacity. Notwithstanding its school-like appearance, the JCC is not without regimentation. Whereas the general architecture of both institutions does not compare with that of an adult prison, yet monitoring mechanisms that are usually associated with Jeremy Bentham's panopticon (Foucault, 1977) are not absent. Frequent verbal reminders from the all-female staff about rules and routines, coupled with the sense of being constantly watched, created a strong feeling of surveillance. In this context, control and authority were exercised more through people than through the physical design of the facility. The atmosphere at the JCC fostered a pervasive sense of suspicion, making interactions between staff and the girls challenging at first. Over time, however, this tension gradually diminished, allowing communication to become easier.

There is no presence of prison officers at the JCC and, similar to the SCC, walls are slightly lower. There is no security bar or checkpoint and anyone can come in and exit at will during the daytime through a gate, which is not locked. Apart from a signboard that points to the correctional centre, there is little indication from the general outlook that it is one. Military-like parades, marches, and salutes, are absent at the JCC. The management of the JCC comprises a director who is assisted by an assistant, both of whom are social workers. The director, assistant, a social worker, and a caretaker reside on the premises. The JCC is supported by other non-resident staff who provide instruction in vocational skills. At the time of fieldwork, an average of eight girls whose ages ranged from 12–17 were in committal.

Unlike conventional prisons, the SCC and JCC are not surrounded by imposing high-security walls; instead, their modest boundaries were intended to embody the correctional philosophy guiding these institutions. In practice, however, the prison identity remained pervasive. As several youngsters observed, the very presence of the low walls paradoxically reinforced the impression that the centres were prisons (see Chapter 7 on escapes).

Enforcing compliance through mortification procedures

In this section I exemplify correctional centres as Goffman's total institutions (Goffman, 1968), characterized by a clear boundary line between staff and inmates. According to Goffman, tasks in total institutions tend to be executed without regard to persons, and pervaded by a spirit of formalistic impersonality: 'Social mobility between the two strata is grossly restricted' (Goffman, 1968: 19), and an inmate–staff split is conspicuous. There appears a marked boundary between the official and the unofficial, the public and the private, with officers perceived as executing their roles perfectly and inmates disciplined to be compliant.

I begin with an institutional ceremony, which is an initiation rite that welcomes male youngsters who are keen to narrate their diversified experiences. This usually happens at the SCC on Fridays, when the institution holds a prolonged service commonly referred to as 'Padre hour'. Initiation ceremonies are rites of passage, which according to (Goffman, 1968: 27), are elaborated forms of admission procedures called 'the welcome' and constitute socializing moments that seek to indicate to the inmate that he is merely an inmate. By obtaining initial cooperativeness from the inmate right from the outset, that which Goffman (1968: 26) describes as 'obedience tests', inmates learn not to challenge orders and learn to conform to the homogenizing and programming demands of a Goffmanian total institution.

I observed youngsters who are eager to narrate their stories and yet their audience do not give much attention to their distinct and differentiated stories. With the passage of time, inmate roles are enforced and stories are quietly tucked away, possibly never to be told.

Welcome to the group

> Today was one of the routine church services usually organized on Friday mornings and which sees the attendance of both staff and youngsters. Having listened to the sermon and danced round for the offertory, the Officer-in-Charge (OIC) invited newly admitted inmates to line up in front of the gathering. The OIC asked them to introduce themselves and to state what crimes had brought them to the institution.
>
> One after the other they did their narrations with each taking about three or four minutes. Their offenses run the gamut from petty pilfering, through defilement to armed robbery and other offenses. Those who had committed robberies were asked to state the specific amount of money involved and the specific items stolen.
>
> New arrivals told their stories amidst various interjections from staff and giggles and mumblings from youngsters seated. Some shouted: 'stop telling tales and go straight to the point'; 'the story is too long, not necessary, cut it short'. The narrators, who seemed absorbed in their stories and oblivious to the reactions, showed little sign of shyness; they did not stutter. Most youngsters spoke as though they were in a dialogue with themselves, and this sustained interest amidst the seeming distractions.
>
> In the course of narrations, my attention was drawn to Kwesi, a sixteen-year-old boy who was equally adept at narrating his experience yet seemed to lack the courage to carry through with his story; he broke down in the process and cried. He said he could not believe that collecting metal scraps that earned him two Ghana cedis [less than a dollar and fifty cents] would contribute to his present demise. My curiosity and interest were whipped by his sense of innocuousness, innocence and naivety, yet Kwesi had little opportunity to tell his story. (72)

I was moved by Kwesi's compelling story, yet equally struck by the apparent lack of interest from his listeners. The audience's interjections suggested that the youngsters had already been convicted and that their identity and distinctness should therefore remain in the past. In effect, entry into these centres meant that young people were immediately stripped of personal attachments and stable social ties from their home lives. What followed was a series of routinization and mortification procedures through which the self was gradually diminished, until it seemed almost dead.

Routines and procedures, according to Goffman (1968), constitute processes of mortification in total institutions, aimed at shaping youngsters to fit within the structure of these institutions. Goffman (1968) explains mortification as processes by which inmates, upon entrance into total institutions, become stripped of stable social arrangements associated with their homes and growing up as well as pre-custodial experiences. These procedures create a barrier between inmates and the outside world and enforce dispossession of role and identity through undressing, bathing, hair cutting, wearing of uniforms; admission and related procedures such as counting, listing, assigning numbers and categorization of dormitories (Goffman, 1968: 24–26). Goffman (1968: 26) refers to these procedures as 'trimming or programming' because the new arrival or inmate is shaped and coded and fed into 'an administrative machinery' of correctional institutions.

Staff, inmates, criminal justice, and related professionals including human rights monitors tend to give recognition to new identities of detainees as juvenile offenders, with little reference to their pre-custodial, growing-up or home-related experiences as being worthy in their own respect. Under section 24 of the Juvenile Justice Act (Act 653) of 2003, Social Enquiry Reports (SERs) are intended to be detailed assessments prepared by social workers, drawing on investigations into the juvenile's family, school, and broader environment, as well as other factors contributing to the offence. In practice, social officers face logistical constraints that limit their ability to produce comprehensive reports. Moreover, even when Social Enquiry Reports (SERs) and related documents are relatively detailed, their accounts of upbringing or pre-custodial experiences, prepared by criminal justice and allied professionals, tend to reflect the offender's newly constructed identity within the judicial system's administrative framework. By contrast, personal narratives often illuminate the social, emotional, and structural factors shaping the trajectory from childhood through arrest to committal.

Homogenized identities enforced by mortification processes

Upon committal, youngsters do not only tuck away their past and varied growing up experiences, but are made to put away their personal belongings and are clothed in identical uniforms and shoes and sometimes bear the same name. One boy quickly retorted when I addressed him as '*Kweku*' (having heard one of the officers address him by that name), that this was not his real name and that the officer in question addresses all of them as '*Kweku*'; thus, even their names are homogenized.

Daily, one observes a large number of like-situated individuals of young people and children engaging in activities that are repetitive and regimental. A typical day for a young male offender is a 12-hour day, well packed with tasks. The day's chores commence at approximately 6 am and run an array of activities ranging from fetching water, morning preparations, breakfast, and morning assembly through classrooms lessons, vocational and technical workshops, religious discussions, and counselling sessions.

Counting, which is referred to as *shooting* (a slang used by warders and understood by youngsters), is a regular activity undertaken by staff and youngsters from morning till the end of the day. Counting is done by both captains (inmates in charge of dormitories) and officers when exiting or entering the dormitory, the classroom, workshop, dining hall, and church services; in fact, counting is done virtually everywhere. It is a monitoring mechanism and one can easily tell during counting whether or not a youngster is absent or has escaped.

Often a warder would shout out '*Shoot*' and then counting begins. Whereas staff manage to do such counting without missing any number, there is the reliance on leaders of dorms, namely captains and their assistants, to undertake this task. On one occasion when youngsters were almost done with their counting and about to leave, the warder who was seated by me shouted to the last youngster to say: '*Last 15*', meaning he is the last person and also the 15th. This reduces the burden of the officer having to always remember the total number.

Marching is usually paired up with counting. In the process of changing shifts, marching follows once numbers are checked, in other words, youngsters usually march away once they are counted. From morning onward, activities are largely overseen by staff, captains, inmate leaders, and inmate teachers. These continue throughout the day until 6 pm, when the youngsters take supper and prepare to be locked in until the following morning. Within their dormitories, captains, inmate leaders, and their assistants maintain responsibility for supervision.

Largely, while youngsters become objects of mortification processes, they are also enlisted by staff to participate in the supervision and, for that matter, governance of these institutions. Such routines tend to be beneficial in the sense that they allay anxieties evoked by the unpredictability that can characterize daily encounters (Carrabine, 2004, Midtlyng, 2022, Routley, 2023, Annamma et al., 2024). In other words, these routines assist youngsters to adhere to certain disciplines, they know that at a certain time they will eat, hold lessons, or be in their dorms. Correctional centres hold the expectation that such procedures will result in the production of disciplined inmates.

Are staff mortified too?

Goffman's mortification processes are directed at inmates on whom the total institution, likened to a forcing house, acts. However, discussions that follow demonstrate that this forcing house does not only act on inmates, but acts on staff too, in other words staff as well as youngsters appear mortified.

On entering the SCC, one is usually struck by an overbearing number of officers, all neatly dressed in their uniforms. The SCC at the time of the initial visit had an average staff strength of 30 prison support officers, 202 subordinate staff and 10 senior staff. The main shift, which runs from 7 am to 4 pm, has an average of 80 staff. It was difficult at the very outset to distinguish between officers and youngsters as they were all dressed in uniform. Superior officers issue commands powerfully while officers in the yard go about their duties, taking orders promptly with their salutes. A brief parade is held three times daily to mark the change of shifts. In total, there are about four shifts, some overlapping, including a night shift that runs from 8 pm to 7 am and four daytime rotations. The longest and principal shift extends from 7:30 am to 4 pm, staffed by roughly 80 officers. Lighter shifts, such as 6 am to 2 pm and 2 pm to 8 pm, are covered by fewer personnel – about 20 officers each – and these shifts overlap.

During one such change-of-shift parade, I observed seven officers lined up opposite two others: the yard master and a senior officer. The senior officer carried a writing board from which he read aloud the names, ranks, and duty posts of officers – for example, 'Sergeant A, House Master, Dorm 2.' Each officer responded to their name and exchanged salutes. These parades are brief, lasting about five minutes, and serve primarily to record attendance and assign officers to specific duties.

During parades, commands and salutes are exchanged in strict sequence, and interruptions are not permitted. Such commands, and salutes, occur regularly throughout the day, reinforcing authority and hierarchy. While I was in a small office near the gate speaking with one of the officers, another officer stationed at the gate stepped out to greet a senior officer who had just driven through the security barrier. Standing before the vehicle, she saluted and declared: '*Good morning madam, 200 in custody, permission to carry on.*' This recital is common at the gate and whenever a subordinate officer reports to a superior. The figure announced, such as '200', includes both staff and inmates. By contrast, in the yard, officers report only the number of youngsters under their charge. In this way, senior officers immediately gain a general overview of total persons present and can monitor or regulate staff and inmate movements. A detailed breakdown of staff and inmate numbers is displayed openly on a board in front of the administration office.

Homogeneity in dressing, uniforms, routines, and the uniformity of issuing and carrying orders gives an appearance of officers who are unilateral with one voice. Officers have a well-respected hierarchy observed strictly by superiors and subordinates by the way they take their salutes, and their promptness in carrying out orders, not challenging authority. Officers attribute this to a well-disciplined force and are proud to talk about their discipline and training. Some two senior officers commented that, though they appear disciplined, the present discipline is nothing compared to the past:

> Change of shifts used to be longer with emphasis on small details such as inspection of handkerchiefs and boots and when you were found without these, you were sanctioned to perform extra duty. When we were recruits, our training was thorough; we were not entitled to visitors for the initial six weeks and were put on a very modest feeding ration. We got up as early as 3 am for jogging and thereafter engaged in many other activities. By the time classes started in the morning, we were already tired and would usually doze off during lessons and yet we were expected to write competitive exams and pass; anyway, our tutors also went through the same training. (78)

Officers also show a strong adherence to ranks and designations. A few weeks into my fieldwork, one of the officers did not hesitate to assign to me a trainee rank – cadet officer. Generally, confinement space for staff is structured, orderly, and dotted with daily routines, coupled with staff who show a strong adherence to hierarchy, ranks, and designations; characteristics that are in keeping with the structure of total institutions (Goffman, 1968).

In sum, institutional processes such as attendance of parades, wearing of uniforms, monitoring of staff attendance, and adherence to commands are all ways by which a prison officer is shaped and coded into an 'object that can be fed into an administrative machinery' of correctional institutions, to be 'worked on smoothly by routine operations' (Goffman, 1968: 26).

The structuredness and repetitiveness of everyday routines

The structured and repetitive nature of daily routines, such as shift changes, marching, and headcounts, leaves little space to question their relevance or legitimacy. Tasks are performed with diligence, whether or not they are strictly necessary. For example, officer nurses routinely call out for medicine at designated times, not always because inmates are ill or are in need of such medication. I observed regularly that whenever painkillers such as paracetamol were announced, youngsters responded promptly and in expected fashion 'The officer shouted to them that those who needed some medicine should let her know. She specifically mentioned paracetamol – soon two boys passed in front of me to register complaints' (75).

In practice, youngsters respond immediately to calls from officer nurses. During focus group discussions about health, youngsters almost unanimously joked that the institution is saturated with pain relief medication, remarking that they are 'tired of taking medicines' – *yeanom abre* – and weary of them. While some may suffer from serious health conditions requiring care beyond paracetamol, the constant and generous supply of painkillers sustains the appearance that medical needs are adequately met and that institutions provide sufficient health care.

Moreover, the routine distribution of painkillers keeps officer nurses visibly occupied; without such duties, they risk appearing idle and, in turn, susceptible to dismissal. Thus, when youngsters adopt the 'sick role' and officers fulfil their duty of dispensing pain relief at set times, the practice not only reflects the structured nature of daily routines but also safeguards employability. In other words, if youngsters remain consistently healthy and do not require medication, the role of officer nurses may be perceived as less necessary, potentially threatening their job security.

Relatedly, mealtimes are equally orderly and regimental; a large number of youngsters are observed matching in a file from their respective dorms with their bowls and dishes to collect their meals from the kitchen. Sometimes youngsters collect food for others but, in most cases, each youngster collects his own food. The server ensures that the same amount is dished out to each person. During breakfast, a standard cup is utilized to fetch the porridge from the bowl for them. Boys and girls use cups, bowls, plastic containers, and all sorts of containers to collect food for themselves and others. In an interview with a kitchen woman who served the food, she said she ensured that each youngster got a serving without anyone cheating the other, she said usually she knew the exact number and so there was little chance for them to cheat, though some still attempted to cheat. Boys and girls wait until the serving is done and then they take their breakfast. Thus, similar to the relationship between job security and medicalization, there is the expectation that youngsters must eat once meals are served even if one wishes not to eat.

On the whole, therefore, the repetitiveness of routines does not only aim at rendering youngsters compliant but also fulfils institutional interests of keeping appearances thereby providing the justification for the functioning of these institutions.

The next couple of sections unveil a parallel confinement world in which inmates do not seem to be entirely mortified and compliant.

Non-compliance: are youngsters really mortified?

Officers strive to maintain control over young people and ensure adherence to institutional rules, yet in practice enforcing compliance proves difficult. This section opens by exploring inconsistencies in reported ages, highlighting how youngsters often cite ages that are different from documented ages in official records. I was initially struck by this practice during my preliminary research, having previously relied solely on their official documented ages as a practitioner during monitoring visits.

Inconsistencies in age determination

At both the SCC and the JCC, children and young people frequently cite different ages depending on the context and the expectations at play. The 'official' age is typically used for administrative records and in interactions with social workers, psychologists, and other professionals within the criminal justice and human rights systems. In contrast, the 'unofficial' age, what youngsters refer to as their real age, is shared informally among peers and used in everyday social exchanges. These discrepancies extend beyond age; similar inconsistencies were noted in the names they provided. Later, during extended fieldwork, I gained a deeper appreciation of the prevalence and complexity of age inconsistencies, an insight that challenged my prior assumptions as a practitioner and human rights monitor accustomed to relying solely on official age records.

As a practitioner, my work relied primarily on official records, as I was well aware that age played a key role in defining who qualifies as a juvenile or young offender, making it a critical factor for magistrates and social workers adjudicating such cases. According to Sections 46 and 60 of Ghana's Juvenile Justice Act (Act 653 of 2003), a juvenile offender is defined as a child under 18 years who has been convicted of an offence. A young offender, by contrast, is someone aged 18 or above but below 21 years who has also been convicted. In cases where birth or medical certificates are unavailable, the Act stipulates that age must be determined through medical assessment:

> In the absence of a birth certificate or baptismal certificate signed by a medical officer as to the age of a person below 18 years of age shall be evidence of that age of the juvenile without proof of signature unless the court directs otherwise. … Where it appears to the court that the person brought before it has attained the age of 18 years, the person shall for the purposes of this part, be deemed not to be a juvenile … (Juvenile Justice Act 653: 2, 3)

Medically determined age raises important questions about accuracy, as such assessments yield approximations rather than definitive chronological ages. In an interview with the OIC of the female correctional institution, she acknowledged that verifying the ages of juvenile and young offenders can be challenging. Medical professionals, she noted, typically provide an age range rather than a precise figure. Despite this ambiguity, the OIC expressed little concern about age accuracy, explaining that the institution operates based on the age stated in the detention order. Nonetheless, she admitted that, in certain cases, staff deemed it necessary to verify the age listed, particularly when it influenced decisions about appropriate treatment or placement.

More broadly, difficulties in age determination stem from systemic factors such as the absence of birth registration, limited public awareness of documentation processes, and the lack of reliable technological tools for assessing chronological age. Ethnographic evidence from my fieldwork reveals that, at the point of arrest, many male juvenile and young offenders had already lost contact with family members. Approximately eight out of ten had experienced early abandonment and had discontinued schooling long before their arrest. For many, birth registration was unfamiliar or inaccessible, rendering age verification especially problematic. Medical age assessments also required payment of fees (UNICEF, 2005), which most young people could not afford.

According to monitoring reports by the Commission on Human Rights and Administrative Justice (CHRAJ), some juveniles are reportedly advised by police officers to inflate their ages. This strategy allows them to be processed as adults, thereby avoiding the mandatory three-year term in juvenile correctional institutions and serving shorter sentences in adult prisons[3]. A Regional Commander stated in an annual report on Inspection of Prisons and Police Cells '… the procedure at juvenile courts is cumbersome and that accounts for the inflation of ages of juveniles on the recommendation of the police so as to avoid going through the process' (CHRAJ, 2001: 37).

During further interview sessions with prison officers during the time of my research, they attested to the fact that the process of committing and conveying juveniles to correctional centres was more cumbersome than if juveniles were sentenced to adult prisons.

Following their arrest, many juvenile and young offenders were effectively abandoned by their families, left to navigate the justice system with minimal support and at the mercy of state authorities. With limited understanding of legal procedures and little to no guidance from parents or relatives, these children often felt compelled to follow the advice given by police officers. Prior to the passage of the Juvenile Justice Act, juvenile and young offenders were in most cases committed to correctional institutions for a mandatory three years. The passage of the Juvenile Justice Act in 2003, however, provides for shorter periods of detention, in which case the argument of avoiding longer sentences by inflating one's age becomes invalid. By the age of 21, in keeping with the Juvenile Justice Act, young offenders in committal are expected to have completed their term in the state's SCC. This is however not always the case as youngsters held in committal sometimes claim unofficially to be older than 21 years.

Encountering these age discrepancies was therefore a new discovery for me, which subsequently shaped my decision to seek official data only after engaging in interviews and interactions with the youngsters. This contrasted with my earlier practitioner practice, where requests for official data always preceded any direct observations or interactions. As a researcher, however, I adopted the reverse sequence, an inductive or inside-out approach that allowed me to ensure official statistics did not predetermine or constrain the meanings I attributed to the ambiguities arising from my firsthand observations and field interactions.

Hidden transcript

In formal correctional practice, officers appear to exercise full authority in enforcing institutional rules in public or formal settings, yet they privately acknowledge challenges behind the scenes. Ensuing discussions centre on the concept of offstage or hidden transcript (Scott, 1990), exploring how both staff and young people express themselves differently from how they carry themselves officially or on stage. Scott (1990: 2) introduced the concepts of public transcript and hidden transcript in his book *Domination and the Arts of Resistance*. Public transcript refers to an action that is openly avowed to the other party in a power relationship, and transcript as a complete record of what is said, which includes non-speech acts, gestures, and expressions. In other words, public transcript is the official, outward-facing interactions between the dominant and subordinate groups. It consists of the carefully controlled and often deferential communication that takes place in public settings, where subordinates conform to the expectations set by those in power.

The offstage transcript of elites is like its counterpart among subordinates and consists in those gestures and words that inflect, contradict, or confirm what appears in public (Scott, 1990: 10). In other words, the hidden transcript represents the private, offstage expressions of the youngsters and sometimes staff, depicting their critiques, resistance, and subversive narratives, often conveyed through indirect means, away from the public eye.

The section discusses institutional admissions of some challenges involved in producing disciplined, compliant inmates and in asserting the authority deemed necessary for effective control.

Reproducing compliant inmates – an illusion?

Most officers admit to difficulty in adequately keeping youngsters under control and rendering them compliant to institutional rules. Officers at these centres execute their duties officially commanding authority and compliance on stage, and yet they admit behind the formal scenes the difficulties and frustrations they encounter in enforcing compliance (Scott, 1990: 2). Officers complain that working with youngsters is difficult relative to adult prisoners. According to officers in the yard, youngsters do not yield to discipline; they do not take orders promptly. One officer shared his frustration:

> I was transferred from my former station following its closure and I find working with these children difficult. They are difficult to manage. In

> adult prisons, very strict shifts are run, from 6 am to 2 pm, from 2 pm to 8 pm and then from 8 pm to 6 am. The administration runs from 7.30 am with a short break in between and then they close at 4.30 pm. Because of these shifts, inmates are tuned to waking up at early and working according to a strict timetable. Adult prisoners have little comfort, the cells are crowded, and there are no toilets or water closets and so they have to get up early and empty their pans. Here, young offenders take life easy and sometimes at 7 am some are still not out of their dormitories. Sometimes I think the boys are pampered and so they behave anyhow they like. (79)

At the SCC, a female officer had to virtually beg youngsters for about ten minutes to attend lessons, against lots of excuses by the boys that they were unwell and tired. Finally, the boys followed her and she complained to me that almost all the boys feigned illness and yet they were preparing to write their major exams soon in April. Another officer who supervises the everyday running of the yard observed that adult prisoners are not as defiant as young offenders:

> Adults who have experienced life and its difficulties quickly submit to instruction and so they are easy to control. The prefectorial system for adults is very effective and their leaders can be trusted to maintain order and this gives some freedom to us. Adult inmates have various levels that they can rise to – stars, rose and other ranks and they have their own court sittings where they have their lawyers, judges and secretaries, among other roles. If a judge pronounces a sentence and you do not comply, you are subjected to punishment and in fact you dare not exhibit non-compliance. (80)

At times, officers employ repressive measures and coercion in an attempt to secure compliance. However, even such force offers no assurance that inmates will obey. Moreover, staff members face structural limitations and challenging working conditions, which compound the difficulty of enforcing rules. Some officers acknowledge the boundaries of their official authority, leading them to depend, in part, on the cooperation of the youths themselves.

Employing compromises amid structural constraints

Staff at correctional centres are fraught with poor working conditions, low salaries, and deplorable housing conditions. A senior officer lamented to me that the salaries of police, army, and fire service personnel were better than theirs. Offstage frustrations of officers also reveal antipathy and contempt about discrepancies in the social status of youngsters and officers.

In an interview with one of the assistants in charge at the SCC, she lamented about the housing situation of officers, which I had also observed during a visit to their living quarters. She said: 'officers sleep on the veranda and have to unpack their furniture each night to make space for their beds; their fridges and freezers are all kept outside' (86). On a visit to the living quarters of staff, one senior officer said to me: 'Look we are more overcrowded in our homes than the boys and yet you do not speak about our rights being violated?' (83).

An officer candidly expressed his desperation coupled with other structural challenges encountered:

> … Look, a whole place like this, there is no water; a tanker supplies water every other day but you know there are 113 inmates and the water is used for cooking, bathing, and everything. Look at this huge compound, it is not fenced. Last week, one of the boys said he was going to use the toilet and he never returned, so you see … when it happens like that then you are queried. [While I was with him, one of the senior officers asked him to send one of the youngsters studying under him to run an errand.] You see, these are some of the challenges, now if the boy runs away then you are in trouble … . (86)

Apart from structural frustrations cited above, officers also harbour a feeling of envy, rancour, and frustrations against fellow staff.

> One of the inmates we trained became a successful person and was later taken to Australia – look, he earns United States dollars while I earn Ghana cedi. We are trying our best and it is a lot of work here but people do not recognize our work. Another boy became a police officer and I could not recognize him. One also passed out of dormitory two and is a journalist now with TV3. Look at us, we train the people, they earn big money and look at what happens to us. Here, I am the only one, the work is slow and yet we have many orders and I cannot meet all the orders. (86)

Thus, officers face severe hardships, from overcrowded housing and lack of water to insecure facilities that undermine their authority. They also feel undervalued despite their central role in rehabilitation. Many express frustration and envy as some former inmates achieve success while their own efforts remain overlooked, leaving them burdened by structural challenges and emotional discontent. The following discussions highlight how correctional staff are frequently stereotyped along gender lines, with female officers perceived as 'soft' and male officers as 'tough'.

Gender, authority, and institutional context

At the SCC, a regular complaint by male officers concerns the overbearing presence of women[4], which according to male officers promotes insubordination and compromises compliance with institutional rules. Official data on staff puts the total number of female subordinate staff at 100, two less than the total number of male subordinate staff, thus there is not much difference between the population of male and female staff. Most women are deployed in the yard to oversee youngsters. Male officers sometimes remark that female officers are not tough enough. According to such officers, female officers pamper youngsters and spoil them: 'These children [he paused], they need to be subjected to discipline otherwise they will never be serious. You know, sometimes the women here also pamper the youngsters and that is why they misbehave, in fact this is a big problem for us' (81).

Others are of the view that this defect would be corrected if female officers were trained to be tough like male officers or replaced entirely. The officer maintained that, when officers get tough with youngsters, they sit up and comply:

> There was this other student who after writing his examinations, decided he would not do anything. He sat up and became serious only after suffering a lock-up by one of the male officers. Now, he participates actively in general electrical workshop and has been active since. So, you see, you spoil them when you pamper them. (82)

Female officers are sometimes perceived as too lenient in their disciplinary approach, criticized for lacking firmness. They themselves often lament that youngsters show them little respect, expressing it in the phrase *wommu yen o*, meaning, 'these youngsters do not respect us'. Female staff often blend authority with everyday responsibilities – such as cooking for the boys, using these practical tasks as a means of fostering compliance with institutional rules through encouragement and enticement. The officer explained that, even when staff extend such kind gestures in exchange for conformity to institutional rules, youngsters often breach these compromises and still abscond.

> One of the lady officers took such good care of one of the boys, she cooked for him regularly just to encourage the boy to stick to the rules and not abscond. But this boy absconded while this same lady was at post. When the boy was questioned he said he knew that the kind lady with her big buttocks could not run after him so he decided to

> run away while she was on duty. So you see, this is what you get for being good to the boys. (81)

One officer explained that she frequently escorts seven male juveniles at a time in search of water, a situation she described as risky, since the boys could attempt escape or even turn against her. At times, she resorts to humour or gentle persuasion to maintain cooperation: 'An inmate once escaped under my command, but what do you do when there is no water? I just do my best – coax them or joke with them, so they cooperate with me' (87). Such circumstances highlight the vulnerability of officers, who face both the threat of possible attack and the consequences of sanction should an escape occur. The risk described, escorting groups of boys outside the compound, highlights the porous nature of institutional boundaries, where staff must rely on persuasion and practical support to secure compliance.

Authority in correctional institutions is however not inherently determined by gender. Instead, it is shaped by individual disposition, situational context, and the broader institutional culture. At times, female officers demonstrated authority with striking clarity, commanding parades with strong voices and firm, piercing eye contact that conveyed confidence and control. Conversely, some male officers appeared hesitant when faced with inmates labelled as 'dangerous', lowering their voices and speaking in whispers.

Thus, *toughness* or *softness* is negotiated through relational dynamics rather than being fixed to biological sex. The tendency to generalize staff behaviour based on gender obscures the complexity of institutional authority. Both male and female officers can embody strength or vulnerability depending on circumstances; their effectiveness often depends on how they navigate the expectations of the institution and the realities of working with young offenders. Recognizing this nuance encourages a more complex understanding of authority and relational dynamics within these centres.

Toughness, gender, and human rights in correctional context

The concern of 'not being tough' or an attitude of softness was also extended to human rights. In a meeting with some senior staff, one OIC of an adults' prison located within the same premises forcefully opened the door to the room in which a meeting was being held. He went direct to speak to the chair about a youngster who was being kept in one of his cells for punishment. In the course of their discussion, this OIC was informed that we were in a meeting and that I was part of the meeting and he retorted: 'Okay but I really mean business and I am here to talk about man's rights and not woman's rights' (Ayete-Nyampong, 2013a: 82). I understood this as implying these are men's issues, tough issues that matter and should be addressed with urgency. In other words, the prison had no place for *softie*, woman-like issues such as human rights. Relatedly, human rights officers or the CHRAJ (my employer) were sometimes considered by staff of correctional centres as weak advocates, as they could not represent the needs of prisons and correctional centres adequately. During one of CHRAJ's monitoring visits, while I was already in the field, the OIC of the correctional centre spoke passionately about some of their challenges. He stated:

> When we wear this uniform, we are expected to behave in certain ways, we cannot just say anything even when we are unhappy about a particular situation; in fact, our hands are tied. Often ministers of state classify young people as criminals and yet most of them seldom visit and have little idea what pertains inside these centres. He continued: that is why we count on you [CHRAJ] to speak on our behalf; while we are glad that certain conditions have improved, we feel that you can do better. It looks like now, you are becoming more or less toothless, and you cannot bite. (82)

Correctional centres often perceive CHRAJ as a weak advocate, incapable of adequately defending their rights. During a visit to the SCC's mechanical workshop, one of six officers lamented poor staff conditions, questioning whether CHRAJ cared about issues such as inadequate housing or denied promotions. Similarly, a senior officer at the staff quarters remarked, 'We are more overcrowded in our homes than the boys, yet no one speaks of our rights being violated' (83). On another occasion, while descending the administrative office staircase, a superior officer jokingly said, 'Pass before we commit our human rights abuse' (83), implying that respect for rights exists only in appearance, not in practice. In staff meetings, when harsher punishments were discussed, the chair would sometimes glance at me as if to assert, 'This is our domain, not that of human rights, leave us to act as we wish.'

The research of Ugandan prisons (Martin, 2010) illustrates the polyvalence of human rights: management invoked rights discourse to secure funding and support, yet simultaneously administered corporal punishment. Officers labelled this 'reasonable caning', distinguishing it from torture and thereby circumventing inconsistency with rights principles. Englund's ethnography of Malawi also highlights the contradiction between rights rhetoric and lived realities (Englund, 2006: 9). Merry (2006) similarly argues that programmes often retain normative codes despite the need for translation and indigenization, while her later work stresses the importance of local particularities and contextual meanings (Merry, 2011, 2016, Merry and Levitt, 2019).

These examples resonate with what pertains in Ghanaian correctional centres, where staff may profess the usefulness of human rights but dismiss them as impractical for everyday detention challenges. Thus, human rights in correctional contexts may assume diverse and polyvalent meanings. While central to institutional legitimacy, their translation into practice remains uneven, contested, and shaped by gendered notions of authority.

Conclusion

Correctional centres embody what Goffman describes as *total institutions*, governed by routines and procedures that portray processes of mortification. Yet the authority of these institutions is never absolute, compliance with rules is uneven, and institutional governance often depends on the very individuals it seeks to govern. Daily life behind bars resists simple binaries of staff versus inmates, instead it unfolds through fluid negotiations and permeable boundaries, in which the supposedly powerful staff and powerless youngsters are entangled. Scott's notion of the *hidden transcript* illuminates this offstage social world not as mere subversion, but as a functional counterpart to the public transcript, revealing how actors navigate and adapt to institutional constraints. To grasp the realities of confinement, one must attend to the multiplicity of meanings produced both onstage and offstage, and to the disjuncture between formal representations, such as human rights standards, and the practices that actually shape institutional life.

6

We Have Carved Our Own Space: The Social Underlife

Introduction

Drawing still on Goffman's total institutions, I discuss in this chapter yet another implicit and 'behind the scenes' perspective of the relational life of the total institution, 'underlife' (Goffman, 1968: 161–2). In the face of mortification procedures of the total institution resulting in dispossession of role, name, and identity of inmates, Goffman's inmates adopt a system of techniques, namely secondary adjustments. Secondary adjustments describe ' … habitual arrangements by which a member of an organization employs unauthorized means or obtains unauthorized ends … ' (Goffman, 1968). These unauthorized means, which do not pose direct resistance or confrontation to staff management but allow inmates some level of satisfaction, is what Goffman refers to as the underlife. The underlife, or the social relational life of correctional centres, has received less attention from researchers and human rights monitors given that it is usually concealed from the public eye and yet it is well patronized not only by youngsters but also sometimes in cooperation with staff.

In this chapter, I examine how predominantly agentic male juveniles and young offenders position themselves to carve out their own social spaces within the underlife, within the grip of total institutions. The creation of social spaces often functions as a coping mechanism in challenging circumstances, especially when young people perceive that responsibility or punishment should fall on the state or their parents rather than themselves. Within these social and relational contexts, their ability to navigate experiences of confinement, shaped by earlier encounters with trauma, anger, and rejection, becomes evident and the dynamics of this underlife, structured by rituals and hierarchies, come to the fore. Hierarchy plays a central role in inmate relationships, partially formalized through roles such as captains, seniors, inmates, and *brannies*. The chapter also explores how privacy is constructed through designated 'corners', the operation of patronage networks, and the use of supernatural practices as a means of settling scores among inmates.

I do not equate the underlife (Goffman, 1968) in correctional centres with an inmate subculture that is entirely homogenous (Hensley et al., 2003, Agozino and Dastile, 2022, Dvoryanskov and Sika, 2022, Higgins et al., 2022, Petrus et al., 2022). The social underlife in correctional centres is a complex one, and to some degree is also shared by staff. This underlife reveals boundaries that are permeable and fluid – such boundaries are negotiated and renegotiated through everyday practices.

The underlife

The concept of underlife stems from Goffman's discussions on primary and secondary adjustments in public institutions in his book *Asylums* (Goffman, 1968). Underlife, according to Goffman (1968: 172), comprises all 'practices' of an individual employed in an organization to obtain 'unauthorized ends'. It is to an institution 'what an underworld is to a city' (Goffman 1968: 180).

Goffman's underlife is applicable to staff and inmates, which he describes in fine detail under 'The Underlife of a Public Institution' and 'Hospital Underlife' respectively. Given that Goffman conceives secondary adjustments within the context of total institutions, he establishes a clear boundary line between staff and inmates thereby categorizing them differently. According to Goffman (1968), tasks in total institutions tend to be executed without regard to persons and pervaded by a spirit of formalistic impersonality. Thus, correctional centres often present a clear divide between official and unofficial life, with officers viewed as performing their duties seamlessly and inmates trained to comply. Yet relational dynamics at the heart of confinement is complex, where institutional power is negotiated rather than imposed, and the boundaries between the governed and those who govern are continually blurred, permeable, and fluid.

Underlife in police detention cells

This section briefly documents certain aspects of an informal economy that thrives in police cells, prior to the committal of youngsters.

Narratives of youngsters bring to the fore difficult and harsh conditions in police detention characterized by overcrowded cells as well as a mixture of pervasive pungent smells of urine, human excreta, and disinfectant as frequently reported by CHRAJ (2001, 2021a) and have received extensive media attention in the past decades. At the mercy of difficult conditions of detention, youngsters manifest an informal life characterized by hierarchy and an informal economy driven by cell leaders, inmates, new arrivals, and sometimes police officers. In this context, police officers become part of a broader network of relational support.

The social life functions as a differentiated space, within which youngsters can draw on material and non-material resources, as shared respectively by Yaw and Kwesi:

> Life in cells is difficult, the cells are dirty and smelly and there is no food to eat. We pay cell fees to the cell leader who is the longest staying person. The cell leader is a kind person and always makes sure that there is some food to eat. He also ensures the cell is kept neat though he keeps some of the money to himself. (92)

> … there were about sixty people in police cells when I arrived. They were all asleep when I arrived and so I also found some place to sleep. When I woke up in the morning, I am sure it must have been difficult to locate the new face and so they did not take cell fees from me. … cell fees range from GHS8.00 to GHS15.00. Sometimes the cell captain uses the money to buy *Omo* [washing soap], food etc. for the common good of all of us. Some cell leaders however would keep the money and when they are transferred elsewhere they take it along. …
>
> … the cell leader spent about 4 years in the cell; this was because of his condition of physical disability and so he could not be taken to prison. He always protected me and gave me food. He could sometimes collect about 30.00 Ghana cedis a day as each newly admitted person had to pay about 5.00 Ghana cedis, this money was usually kept with one of the police officers. Anytime I was hungry the cell leader would provide me some food. (93)

Leadership within police cells is typically determined by the length of time an individual has spent in custody; the longest-serving suspect or inmate often assumes the role of cell leader or captain. However, this status is fluid. Transfers between cells can result in a former leader being reclassified as a newcomer, thereby relinquishing their previous authority and becoming subject to the rules and directives of another captain. This shift tends to underscore the precarious nature of social hierarchies within custodial settings, where one may temporarily enjoy the privileges and economic benefits associated with leadership, only to be repositioned within a different social order elsewhere.

Cell leaders routinely impose 'cell fees' on new arrivals, charges that vary across cells but generally range from three to ten US dollars at the time. These fees, collected almost daily due to the constant intake of suspects, sustain an informal economy within the cell. The funds are used to procure disinfectants, food, and other necessities, with captains exercising discretion over their allocation. This economy is built on the contributions of newcomers and the resourcefulness of cell leaders, who manage both the collection and distribution of goods. Young detainees, such as Yaw, describe cell leaders as occasionally benevolent but also capable of exploiting their position for personal gain.

Police officers, too, play a role in this informal system. As Kwesi recounts, officers sometimes safeguard the collected funds, and they may also facilitate the purchase of food, given that detainees are restricted in their movements. Distribution of food is typically handled by cell leaders, reinforcing their central role in both material and social provisioning.

The social world that emerges within these cells is marked by a complex underlife, an informal system of hierarchy and exchange involving cell leaders, inmates, newcomers, and occasionally state actors. This underlife extends beyond meeting basic needs; it serves as a platform through which young detainees, particularly those in leadership roles, reclaim agency and construct domains of influence. As Yaw notes, power is not solely economic, it is also expressed through acts of care and civility, such as maintaining cleanliness and hygiene within the cell.

Relatedly, a parallel underlife is evident in correctional institutions, despite the formal boundaries and mortification procedures designed to institutionalize and discipline young people. These spaces, too, host unofficial economies and social structures that subtly resist the intended effects of mortification. In both settings, the interplay between formal authority and informal agency reveals the agency and adaptability of incarcerated youth.

Underlife at correctional institutions

An active parallel underlife thrives within correctional institutions, defined by shifting hierarchies, rituals, private spaces, informal economies, and systems of patronage.

Hierarchy: captains, seniors, boys, and brannies

During my initial visit to the Senior Correctional Centre (SCC) in 2009, male juveniles were accommodated across six dormitories (dorms), numbered one through six. By the time of my subsequent visits in 2019 and 2023, two additional dorms had been added to the SCC, reflecting a rise in the number of committed inmates. In contrast, the dormitory structure at the Junior Correctional Centre (JCC) remained unchanged.

At the SCC, progression through the dormitories is typically determined by length of stay and demonstrated good behaviour. Discharge often coincides with reaching the final dorm. Placement may also be influenced by factors such as educational background. Youngsters who adhere to institutional rules tend to advance more quickly, while those who violate them may face demotion. Movement through the dorms is not merely symbolic; it comes with tangible benefits, including increased autonomy, privacy, and spatial freedom. Dorm six occupants, considered the most senior, enjoy greater liberties and may be permitted supervised excursions into the city[1]. In contrast, those in dorm one experience the most restrictions, often remaining locked in for extended periods with minimal privacy.

Each dorm houses between 15 and 30 inmates and is overseen by a dorm captain and assistant captain,[2] both appointed by staff to enforce rules and maintain order. These dorm-level leaders support the warders in managing daily routines and ensuring compliance. Within the inmate hierarchy, leadership flows from the overall captain to individual dorm captains, and then through a stratified structure of seniors and newcomers. At the dorm level, this hierarchy is clearly delineated: captain, assistant captain, seniors, and finally new arrivals, commonly referred to as '*brannies*'. Hierarchies change due to a number of factors, for instance, as one moves from one dorm to another. The term *brannie*, derived from 'brand-new', denotes newly admitted inmates. While the term may be used informally across dorms, its most prominent and institutionalized usage refers to those placed under mandatory observation upon admission, typically housed in dorm one. This formal designation is the focus of the discussion that follows.

For *brannies*, daily life diverges significantly from that of other inmates. While a typical day for a young offender spans 12 structured hours, from 6 am to 6 pm, *brannies* experience a more confined and monotonous routine. The physical environment, marked by rows of bunk beds, stale air, and unpleasant odours from in-dorm bathrooms, can be unbearable[3]. The mandatory observation period, usually six months but sometimes extending to a year, further isolates them. *Brannies* are generally excluded from technical and vocational training, which constitutes a major part of the daily schedule. Some report feeling physically unwell, attributing their discomfort to prolonged confinement and lack of sunlight. These challenges compound the vulnerability of new arrivals, shaping their early experiences of institutional life, according to a former captain of dorm one:

> … Most brannies arrive empty handed with little money and do not receive visitors, it is a big problem for them. I, therefore, as a captain collect gifts from those who receive visitors. We refer to these gifts as 'apparatus' and then I would in turn distribute to those who have none. Many brannies, when they arrive, seem lost and confused and what worsens the situation is that they do not receive visitors. (95)

Rituals (ammamre)

Brannies have much to contend with in the first dorm besides receiving virtually no visitors. Away from the public glare, their fellow inmates take them through a series of initiation rituals, which they term *ammamre*: 'My stay at dorm one was difficult and I nearly absconded. You do not go out, you are maltreated by other inmates; you are told to salute the TV, they pomp your cheek until blood comes out and you tend to think about bad things' (96).

These rituals are numerous and range from one degree to the other. Examples of rituals of lesser severity, as rated by youngsters, are '*Bro Issa*', which requires that you look constantly outside while bowing your head to greet an imaginable person. '*Think for Yourself*' demands that you stand on one leg for a long period of time, while another entails saluting the television as in the above quote. More severe rituals include *Abodwe Down*: you squat and rise continuously with your elbows on your lap and hands crossed over your ears. By the continuous gaze outside, repetitive salutes, and standing still on one leg, youngsters employ rituals to exemplify the repetitiveness of everyday detention routines but also the stillness of time and boredom that characterize their occupation of dorm one. Youngsters have admitted in various focus discussions that this period of observation is an emotionally and physically traumatic period. Youngsters who prior to detention have been extremely active all of a sudden are grounded to a life of stillness where active time passes them by (Medlicott, 1999). Bowing and saluting as depicted in rituals such as '*Bro Issa*' and '*Think for Yourself*' manifest as forms of deference to a superior, which represent an interplay between ritual, authority, and imagination in correctional settings. Yet the 'superior' in these practices is not always a tangible figure. At times, authority is imagined, projected onto an abstract presence; at other times, it is camouflaged in objects of pleasure, such as the television. This deflection shifts the locus of authority and the painfulness of the ritual away from fellow youngsters and onto something external, but it does not diminish the severity of the ritual itself. In this sense, the rituals operate as metaphorical representations of authority from the youngsters' perspective, authority that is simultaneously real and imagined, never fixed in one figure and cannot be directly visualized. The imagined oppressor becomes embedded in the ritual, making the act both a lived experience of subordination and a symbolic enactment of institutional control. What emerges here is a complex understanding of authority: it is dispersed, and sometimes displaced, yet always felt.

Further, the ritual of saluting the television illustrates how correctional centres are not sealed off from wider society but remain porous spaces (Martin and Jefferson, 2019, Cunha, 2020, Weegels et al., 2020, Ellis, 2021), where cultural flows penetrate institutional boundaries. The presence of the television situates youngsters as consumers of global trends, fashion, music, theatre, even narratives of crime and terrorism. Correctional life is thus marked by a paradox: while youngsters are confined, they remain active participants in broader social processes, blurring the line between inside and outside. Thus, correctional space is permeable and fluid – part confinement, part society – where boundaries are constantly renegotiated through everyday practices.

Youngsters interpret rituals in varied ways. For them, rituals serve both as initiation rites for *brannies* entering dorm life and as punitive measures for those who defy insider rules. Refusal to comply with a ritual often results in harsher sanctions, reinforcing the authority of peer-imposed discipline. Several youngsters acknowledge that these peer-driven rituals can be more severe than formal institutional punishments. Yaw's experience is telling: branded a 'wizard' in the first dorm, he endured intense emotional and physical trauma from ritual sanctions, trauma so unbearable that it compelled him to escape. In this sense, rituals operate as powerful mechanisms of social control among inmates.

Apart from a few rituals that are known to warders, most rituals are unknown, and constitute a secret code among youngsters. Prison argot (Sykes, 1958), slang or special type of language, is employed to confine real meanings of such rituals to youngsters, thus evoking uniqueness, sense of belonging, and privacy against a context subjected to continuous surveillance. This secrecy not only sustains their autonomy but also underscores the fluid interplay between institutional oversight and inmate agency. Rituals also function as informal systems of governance that both reinforce hierarchy and foster belonging. While staff may not directly oversee these practices, they benefit from the order maintained by inmate leaders, such as captains.

Privacy and ownership: dorms and corners

The term 'corner' is coined by youngsters and connotes different meanings such as private space. This is similar to Goffman's 'personal territory' (Goffman, 1968: 216) where the individual makes a private claim on space and 'develops some comfort, control, and tacit rights' that he shares with no other except by his own invitation. A corner also denotes physically bounded space where two sides of a wall meet; or a shared space to some, while excluding others.

A corner boy within the context of a shared space is one who has legitimate access to someone else's private space. Corner, as employed in ensuing discussions, denotes private space that is owned rather than a physically bounded space where two sides of a wall meet as shared by a *brannie*:

> Life initially was very hard and I cried when I was introduced because I thought about my family that I had no one to care for me and the fact that I was here to spend 2 years. Dorm one is a difficult place but

> when I am in the dorm, I try not to invite trouble, I keep to myself in my corner and I am fine. (98)

> … I took my church attendance and activities very serious and also prayed in my corner often and would also rally other inmates round in my corner to pray. (98)

The sense of ownership and privacy means so much to young people in an environment where everything belongs to everyone and commonness and sameness is pervasive and imposed. In this context, a *corner* is understood as a private space, yet its meanings extend beyond simple privacy. Much like Goffman's notion of personal territory, where objects play a crucial role in shaping boundaries and identity role (Goffman, 1968: 218), corners are defined and enriched by the presence of objects. In dorm one, these markers include beds and personal belongings such as towels or underwear, which delineate individual space. As youngsters move into other dorms, boundaries become more elaborate, marked by flowers, pictures, and mosquito nets. The mosquito net, for instance, carries significance beyond its practical use; seniors employ it to construct enclaves that symbolize hierarchical distinction between themselves and newcomers. Corners, and the objects that constitute them, thus become imbued with power.

Yet these boundary markers are not fixed. During one visit to dorm one, flowers and mosquito nets were absent, while on a later visit they were prominently displayed, underscoring the fluidity of meanings attached to private spaces. Corners are continually redefined, serving at times as social spaces where youngsters laugh, chat, and bond, and at other times as spiritual spaces for prayer; their associations shift depending on circumstance.

The notion of a *corner* therefore carries ambivalent meanings. While it can symbolize privacy and personal fulfilment, it also evokes restriction, powerlessness, and the deprivation of freedom when youngsters are confined there by senior inmates or captains as punishment. What functions as a space of autonomy can just as easily become a site of coercion, where confinement transforms the corner into an abhorrent place of punishment. Within this setting of punishment, corners denote a physically bounded space where two walls meet and which is not a necessarily designated private space, to which one can be confined as a form of punishment as shared by one of the youngsters: 'I was made to sleep in the bathroom area most of the time in the corner where the boys used to smoke Indian hemp [*wee*] and I could not stand the smell. The isolation and the maltreatment were beyond me …' (98).

In such underlife, power to command punishment and compliance with rituals or insider rules, such as consigning a *brannie* to a corner or subjecting him to a ritual, portrays that inmate hierarchies are not necessarily constructed on the basis of identity positions or institutionally defined statuses such as race, ethnicity, class, or sex. Even those at the lowest rung, like *brannies*, assert agency and privacy through practices such as creating 'corners'. Statuses and hierarchies are far from fixed but are negotiated through practices that result in interdependence and the sharing of resources.

An informal economy

Correctional centres operate within the limits of state budgetary allocations, yet authorities readily acknowledge that these resources are insufficient for daily management and inmate feeding (Ayete-Nyampong, 2019, 2023, CHRAJ, 2021a). Monitoring reports by CHRAJ have consistently recommended increases in feeding rates, which have remained stagnant for over a decade (CHRAJ, 2021a). Youngsters themselves complain of monotonous menus and meagre portions. Despite these inadequacies, institutional rules prohibit juveniles from freely managing their finances: all money must be deposited with the administration.

Nevertheless, youngsters creatively construct an informal economy to meet their needs, whether for food, communication with friends and relatives, or even facilitating escape. Afua, for example, concealed money in her underclothes to purchase food, enlisting another youngster to transact on her behalf (see Chapter 7, on escapes). Their ability to conceal such exchanges from certain officers, while conducting them openly before others, reveals the fluidity of staff–inmate relations.

Money often circulates outside official channels. Many youngsters prefer entrusting funds to warders rather than the administration, citing easier access and the absence of commissions. At the SCC, formal withdrawal requires written requests, forcing youngsters with low literacy to pay peers to draft letters; thus ironically one needs money to access their own money. Officers who safeguard funds benefit in return, receiving errands or commissions, while youngsters earn cash or in-kind rewards by serving staff.

At the JCC, the informal economy extends to mobile phones, secretly used to contact friends and solicit money. In one escape attempt, youngsters reportedly paid to use an officer's phone to coordinate with outsiders. In another case, a new arrival was beaten for revealing that the captain possessed a phone shared among peers. These practices show how prohibited items circulate through informal networks, with staff and captains often taking commissions. Through access to phones – and potentially social media – the boundaries of confinement become porous, offering youths an unregulated link to the outside world. This informal economy exposes the permeability of correctional centres, where official structures seek to restrict resources, yet youngsters continually negotiate alternative pathways that blur distinctions between inmates and staff, as well as between confinement and free society.

In the underlife's informal economy, youngsters devise creative ways to earn and use money, often channelling it towards survival needs or escape plans. Female inmates at the JCC, for instance, engaged in cobbler work to save small amounts for necessities, including implements for escape. At the SCC, Kwabena, who enjoyed relative freedom in the last dorm, borrowed money from peers to purchase a hacksaw blade, a common tool used to cut through metal barriers, keeping part of the funds for himself. These practices reveal how financial exchanges among youngsters are embedded in networks of trust and desperation.

While the informal economy sustains daily life, it also has its repercussions. During CHRAJ's 2019 monitoring visits, I helped introduce, for the first time, questions on unofficial practices such as informal economies. The findings, later included in CHRAJ's report (2021a), revealed new insights. In adult prisons, inmates sustained an informal economy where beds and spaces between beds were sold at a price. This local knowledge illustrates how inmates and staff devise ways to cope with challenges like overcrowding, while also exposing the risks faced by those unable to afford such arrangements. These practical strategies and informal norms (Olivier de Sardan, 2008) should not be overlooked by professionals and policymakers, as they provide valuable guidance for designing realistic interventions and policies.

In the next section, I discuss certain relationships that mimic Goffman's 'patron relationships', which he describes as 'semi-official indulgences' (Goffman, 1968: 253). These relationships are marked by semi-official economic and social exchanges of gifts and acts of kindness between staff and patients.

Patronage relations and inmate hierarchy

Relations within the prison underlife are structured around unequal hierarchies among inmates, such as dorm captains, newcomers, or *brannies*. This dynamic mirrors Goffman's account of the patient (Goffman, 1968: 253), who is not simply a passive recipient but actively makes demands and expectations that compel patrons or staff to provide additional indulgences. Similarly, in correctional centres, *brannies* are not merely passive dependents; rather, they participate in patron–client exchanges that involve both material and non-material resources, offering services in return for economic or social benefits.

Within these patronage networks, *brannies* often assume the role of 'corner boys'. Dorm captains adopt them into their social space, sharing physical and social space while assigning tasks such as fetching food from the kitchen. In return, corner boys receive protection and, at times, exemption from harsh initiation rituals, highlighting the reciprocal nature of these relationships:

> I was maltreated by my fellow-inmates in dormitory one. My fellow inmates pulled my nose and did *pump* to me. Kojo was the captain then and was a very quiet person and could not protect me all the time. Kojo later took me as a corner boy and so that helped me; I would go and collect his food for him and run errands for him. (102)

Patronage practices are not only limited to inmates, but staff are also beneficiaries. Captains or other inmates provide services beside their usual obligations. Such services include being sent by staff to the kitchen to collect food or watch over an officer's house when the officer attends to some other duty outside the premises. Youngsters, in return, are rewarded in kind or cash.

Sometimes, patron–client relations depict emotional attachments. An officer at the female centre lamented about how she would miss the services of a female captain upon discharge:

> I am really going to miss Yaa, the girls' captain. She was almost like a daughter to me. She could freely enter my kitchen and never touched anything and would not even ask of anything. I do not worry about the possibility of a theft when I go to town as she watches over the house. There is no replacement for her! (102)

Thus, youngsters and staff benefit from both material (such as food, money, gifts) and non-material (such as kindness, care, protection, love) resources through patronage practices and carve out social, economic, private spaces in order meet their everyday needs.

While trust and reciprocity are crucial elements of such patronage relationships, these elements fade easily, rendering relations sometimes transitory, to the disappointment of one party or the other. For instance, youngsters abscond regardless of however kind officers are to them. A female officer spoke about a female youngster whom she had taken as her daughter but later got disappointed: 'I took Tina as my daughter, she ate in my house and did almost everything as my daughter and then she betrayed my trust and absconded' (104).

Thus, certain compromises are sometimes made, as staff and inmates tend to go outside their acceptable boundaries and, in the process, gains are yielded to both inmates and staff.

Warders often assume that acts of kindness, such as cooking for youngsters or offering them gifts, will be reciprocated with good behaviour and loyalty, particularly by refraining from escape. Yet this expectation is not always fulfilled, and trust is at times betrayed. Such dynamics reveal that patronage practices within correctional centres are far more complex and entangled than the clear-cut dichotomies described by Goffman (1968) and Scott (1990). Relatedly, Mechlinski (2007) observed in his study of transportation in West Africa that patron–client relationships frequently extend beyond simple dyadic exchanges into loose relational networks where roles can shift, and patrons themselves may become clients. Within correctional life, these interdependencies complicate the notion of a unified inmate culture defined by solidarity against staff. Instead, they highlight fluid and negotiated relationships, where power, trust, and reciprocity are on the move.

Underlife and shallow friendships

Narratives from youngsters reveal that the majority, nearly eight out of ten, had lived independently of parents or relatives before detention, with familial support remaining minimal both at arrest and during confinement. In this context, peer relationships within the underlife become vital, even if they are shallow, as shared by John:

> I have friends I talk and laugh with, but I cannot talk about personal matters. It is good to have friends around, I had a good friend though I did not share intimate matters but later he was released. We however continued to chat on the phone. The problem here is that, this place you cannot trust anyone not even a friend, you say something deep to someone and next time you hear it elsewhere and you face punishment because of that. Here, friendship is shallow but you cannot do without someone to talk to and laugh with. It also helps if you have something like food to share as friendship is usually give and take. When you receive visitors and they bring you things and you have a friend, you do not keep the things to yourself. In the same way, they also share gifts from visitors with you. (106)

Relationships, which take the form of peer linkages rather than friendships, such as in the case of John, constitute a lifeline for youngsters. These links, though treasured, are short lived. Similar to the observations of Mathiesen (2006), peer links in confinement are transitory, they form, un-form, and reform depending on resources at stake. In fact, at the time of arrest, most links including peer contacts are loosened. Yet contacts and links are seldom entirely exhausted; youngsters sustain links while in committal and others also re-form new links. In the process of searching for new links, youngsters forge new friendships.

Friendships and associations are mostly opportunistic and thrive more on reciprocity than trust, though some proportion of trust is required for such associations and contacts. This possibly implies that anyone who does not have anything to offer in terms of resources may end up being *ankonam* or a loner, in the sense that the person does not enjoy benefits of material and non-material resources from others. Loners however are rare as youngsters seem to make every effort to forge links, even when such links are opportunistic and characterized by betrayals (Ayete-Nyampong, 2011, 2013a). Yaw in an interview narrated how a friend who was committed ahead of him made life exceptionally unbearable for him due to a betrayal on his side. In fact, it would have been difficult to appreciate Yaw's narrative if I had not been aware of his growing-up experiences, which provided an interconnection between his pre-detention and custodial world.

According to Yaw, this friend, who felt betrayed, decided to retaliate by spreading rumours that he was an *anyen* or a wizard and as a result he was isolated and very lonely at the initial stages to the point that he contemplated escape and actually escaped. Thus, peer links and friendships constitute lifelines for youngsters, yet are episodic, opportunistic, and can be dotted by lack of trust and betrayals.

Supernatural practices and culprit identification

In the social underlife, youngsters draw on formalized religious observances such as church services, reading the Bible, praying and so on, to appropriate their own diverse forms of spirituality. Amid formalized religious observances youngsters also resort to some supernatural powers such as using the Bible to solve disputes and settle scores among themselves. Given youngsters' traumatized pre-committal experiences, coupled with the fact that such youngsters seldom receive visitors from relatives, youngsters tend to thrive on few resources such as food items, soap, dental cream, and bathing towels. They jealously guard these personal possessions by punishing those who seek to deprive them of such resources as Yaw explained:

> … we use the Bible to determine wrongdoers and thieves in their dormitory, but this practice is unknown to staff and inmates in other dormitories. Culprits, who are identified using the Bible, face harsh consequences and are not let to go free. After we use the Bible to catch the thief in the dorm it sometimes results in a fight and some people hurt themselves, one person for instance was bleeding when he came to the parade that day. (107)

By beatings and other harsh treatments, supposed wrongdoers and culprits who are found out by the Bible are severely punished.

Largely, the underlife is vital to the everyday life of inmates whose past growing-up experiences are characterized by trauma, rejection, anger, and vengeance. Within such underlife, youngsters' capacity to process social experience and devise ways of coping under difficult situations of confinement is clearly evident and staff and inmates mutually depend on each other as they access material and non-material resources.

Goffman's underlife or secondary adjustments (Goffman, 1968) should not be envisioned merely as a weapon aimed at the oppressor or officers (Scott, 1985). It is not a two-way, binary dichotomous relationship between staff and inmates, nor can it be reduced to a homogenous subculture of inmates positioned against a dominant total institution. Neither should it be equated with a prison subculture of inmates as suggested by Hensley et al (2003: 290). The underlife is therefore not analogous to a homogenous inmate culture. Neither does the underlife evoke a bleak image of young, hopeless and despairing criminals isolated from broader processes of change who are at the mercy of a unitary life that the forcing house of a total institution imposes on them.

On the contrary, the underlife is marked by ambiguity, multiple realities, and relational entanglements between staff and inmates. It is further defined by permeable boundaries, as young people remain connected to the outside world – legitimately through television and illicitly through cell phones.

Conclusion

The social underlife of correctional centres reveals that everyday correctional life is not fully defined by formal rules and staff authority. Youngsters continually negotiate spaces of autonomy and belonging through rituals, corners, peer linkages, and informal economies. These practices, while often hidden from staff, serve as mechanisms of social control, reciprocity, and survival. Hierarchies among inmates are characterized by everyday negotiations and constructed less by institutional and structural categories. Objects such as mosquito nets, televisions, or hacksaw blades become charged with symbolic and practical power, mediating both friendships and coercion. Peer linkages, though fragile and opportunistic, provide lifelines in contexts of limited familial support, even as they remain vulnerable to betrayal. Similarly, informal economies sustain daily needs and portray informal exchange that can complicate governance of these centres.

Taken together, the foregoing dynamics highlight correctional centres as spaces where official, unofficial, and external relational worlds intersect and overlap, and where youngsters actively construct meaning and devise strategies of survival amid conditions of deprivation. Recognizing this complexity challenges simplistic notions of inmate culture and inmate–staff relationships.

7

The Everyday Relational Dynamics that Surround Escapes

Introduction

This chapter examines escape incidents within correctional centres. Young people cite diverse motivations for attempting escape, but most often their actions stem from a deep sense of displacement shaped by histories of rejection and trauma at the hands of both family and state. In seeking to resist these structures, they frequently view the correctional institution as fundamentally misaligned with their needs and seize any opportunity to break free from its hold. The discussions here suggest that, even within confinement, youngsters, through acts of defiance and apparent violence, may already be asserting control and symbolically taking the law into their own hands. The preoccupation of correctional authorities is to deploy a range of educational, religious, psychological, and related programmes, purported to reform, but to also ensure that youngsters do not abscond and pose danger to society. Everyday life in correctional centres is fundamentally organized around the imperative of custody. Despite concerted efforts by correctional centres to use education, religion, surveillance, and disciplinary procedures to retain young people in custody, escapes persist. In some cases, the very stringency of these measures inadvertently provokes the desire to escape, becoming catalysts for the very outcomes they seek to prevent. While educational programmes are intended to foster reform and reduce the likelihood of escape, the occurrence of escapes frequently leads to the suspension of such activities.

The anticipation of escape, and its actual occurrence, provokes an escalation of strict controls, from tightened movement restrictions to the suspension of educational programmes and liberties, effectively constricting the detention environment. Yet, paradoxically, escapes also expand the space of confinement, sparking spontaneous narratives and gossip among insiders. I seized this moment to observe and record these unprompted accounts, which would otherwise have been difficult to capture, particularly within the Junior Correctional Centre (JCC) for girls. Generally, escape events illuminate the everyday relational fabric of detention life, yet they are often reduced within criminal justice discourse to matters of security, risk, and recapture. Such reductionism obscures the deeper social dimensions of escape, which demand a more nuanced and reflective engagement from those working within the justice system.

Correctional centres and escapes

Escape data as reported by the Ghana Prisons Service is not disaggregated on the basis of age, thus no separate official data on escapes existed for the SCC at the time of my visits. In an interview with the officer-in-charge (OIC) of the boys' institution who had newly assumed post, he quoted the daily lock-up as 131 with one escape[1]. However, I observed that a number of escapes occurred during the period of fieldwork. For instance, James, one of the youngsters, had escaped thrice, three other youngsters escaped at the same time and there were additional escapes of two other youngsters. Thus, approximately, an average of four escapes occurred annually within the period of fieldwork.

The JCC has a small lock-up population relative to the SCC. Yet, the JCC experiences escapes more frequently than the SCC. The escape rate[2] based on my observations was about 50 per cent during the period of fieldwork with four out of eight girls absconding more than once during the period of committal. Akua, who is a female juvenile, absconded four times and was recaptured, but the fifth time she escaped she could not be recaptured. Generally, official records on escapes, both at the JCC and the SCC, do not adequately reflect the frequency of escapes observed in practice, probably on account of its sensitive nature and partly that youngsters that escape are usually recaptured or brought back to the institutions.

In view of the frequency of escapes and the importance that correction institutions attach to the prevention of escapes, these institutions employ programmes such as educational training and religious activity, which are purported as crucial means to correct and reform, but also to keep youngsters in custody. A senior officer states: 'Over the years the rate of escapes has reduced remarkably as we organize a lot of educational programmes to engage their attention. Even now, we have started the West African Senior School Certificate Examination [WASCE] …' (112).

By participating in educational activities, youngsters are kept busy, and the tendency of escapes is reduced. Thus, the promotion of various educational activities is interlinked with the promotion of the custody of inmates.

However, the anticipation of escapes and event of an actual escape incident induces an opposite effect; outdoor activities such as formal and non-formal lessons and workshops and even religious activity come to a halt and young people are kept behind doors longer than usual. Other times, special arrangements are put in place so as to prevent a re-occurrence of escapes. At the JCC, I observed that young girls worked in two groups and these groups alternated their participation in vocational activity such as dressmaking and hairdressing. Given that two vocational lessons were conducted concurrently, the arrangement afforded girls the opportunity to participate in other activities. However, following an escape incident, the institution would tighten security and monitoring measures and youngsters were made to participate in only one type of skills training at a time. This arrangement was to facilitate monitoring of the movements of youngsters by the few available staff.

Staff meetings are also conducted to discuss stringent measures. In one such meeting at the SCC, one senior officer who chaired the meeting gave the following directives:

> The wearing of long sleeves by boys is banned – as they can hide *asor*[3] blades underneath. If the boys misbehave, report them and we shall punish them … [She continued.] You must intensify searches as the boys tie all sorts of things to their knees and bodies, even if you need to check their buttocks, do so. (115)

A subordinate officer, in response to this directive, said that youngsters deliberately did not listen to them, and so the staff would continue to employ more repressive and stringent measures to ensure they were compliant. Escapes evoke stringent measures for youngsters as well as staff. At the same meeting by staff, the chair further said:

> This time I leave the office late and I realize that some of you are not at post at the time I leave. Sometime when I get to the dormitory, I honk but no one comes out and I do not see anyone. You remember the last time James said that he and the other boys absconded when no officer was around. So, you see that we have ourselves to blame. (116)

Upon saying this, the meeting became rowdy with officers talking out loud and blaming one another for various reasons. In ending the meeting, the chair said: 'I will stringently enforce my measures. I warn you to be regular and punctual at services; I would start taking note of latecomers.'

One officer prior to this meeting had shared with me his frustrations that officers encounter when inmates, who are put in their charge, escape: 'When you supervise a youngster and he absconds, there is trouble for you. Your rank is reduced or you forfeit your increment for about six months' (116). Largely, while inmates are monitored, officers themselves are also monitored and, while inmates are punished, officers are also punished. Relatedly, Martin (2010) described escapes in Ugandan prisons as most dramatic and potentially harmful professional experiences for the prison staff. According to Martin

(2010), escapes directly challenge staff's professional survival, and the latter have traditionally responded with brute, if not lethal, force, if an escapee is recaptured. Similarly, Bandyopadhyay and Jefferson (2010) observed that escapes symbolically reassert an imagined total institution where warders assert authority and prisoners play a submissive role. Bandyopadhyay (2010) further noted that escapes do not only evoke stringent measures and close detention space but also close research space and restrict access to researchers. She observed that, whenever there was a jail break within the period of her fieldwork in India, she was requested by prison authorities to avoid being around for about a week.

My observations quite differently revealed that, whereas escape events result in the disruption of institutional and the tightening of totalistic measures, they also serve to open up the social and relational dimensions of confinement life. Behind the scenes and offstage, escapes elicit a cascade of spontaneous narratives and gossip from a wide array of internal actors. From senior officers to junior staff and detained youngsters, nearly everyone has something to contribute, whether directly or indirectly, about the escape.

Despite these openings, correctional centres tend to manage escape information with caution in their formal, onstage representations. They often handle such incidents internally and are reluctant to disclose details publicly. Youngsters are acutely aware of these dynamics. Those who know that escape incidents are rarely made public and who perceive a lower risk of severe punishment upon recapture may be more inclined to escape. In contrast, those whose escapes are publicly acknowledged by the electronic media, such as radio and television, typically face harsher consequences. The diligence of the severity of sanctions that youngsters who are recovered by the institution are subjected to is the sort of diligence described by Goffman (Goffman, 1968: 62) as breaking the intransigent inmate or showing '*as much special devotion to the rebel as he has shown to it*'.

One senior officer explicitly endorsed the non-disclosure of escape information, framing it as being in the best interest of the youngsters, though the implications of such a stance remain operationally complex:

> Inmates who abscond are usually sent to the adult prison and locked up and then on their return, are demoted and sent to the first or second dorm. Sometimes we calculate the days they stayed away and add it to their sentence. We do not report them to the police, if we did, they would be taken to court and given an additional sentence and so we try to handle it ourselves. (113)

At a staff meeting, a senior staff member reiterated to other staff that escape disclosure can also have repercussions for staff, it could mean that staff have been negligent of their responsibility. In a meeting with senior staff, I indicated to them that youngsters reportedly escape because their stay in the first dorm is unbearable for them. After this indication to staff, a number of measures were immediately put in place, which gave the indication that staff were discharging their duties effectively. Regular meetings were arranged for inmates of dorm one to discuss their peculiar problems and additionally the institution began to consider the possibility of promoting activities for youngsters, so they did not have to stay in lock-up, under observation for too long a period.[4]

Why do youngsters escape?

As discussed in earlier chapters, many youngsters do not perceive themselves as deserving of the punishment of legal custody. Instead, they often view their parents, families, and the state as the rightful targets of blame or retribution. When asked why they choose to escape, their responses reveal a range of other motivations, each rooted in personal experience, institutional dynamics, and broader relational tensions.

During focus group discussions, most girls expressed that they absconded primarily because they feared and loathed the experience of confinement. For instance, Yaa escaped to avoid having her hair cut, a requirement imposed by institutional rules. Grace, in a one-on-one interview, explained that her escape was a form of protest directed at her father, who rarely visited due to outstanding debts owed to the centre. She feared that these debts would delay her discharge, even after her sentence had ended.

James described his escape as a reaction to multiple grievances: a demotion from dorm five to dorm four, being labelled 'notorious' by staff, and the psychological toll of isolation. He also referenced another boy who fled under similar circumstances following a demotion. Yaw's escape was prompted by maltreatment in dorm one, where he was stigmatized as a 'wizard' by a peer who accused him of betrayal during their pre-custodial lives.

These narratives underscore that escapes are not merely acts of defiance or delinquency; they are embedded in the emotional, relational, and institutional contexts of detention. Each escape reflects a complex interplay of resistance, identity, and perceived injustice, often directed not just at the institution, but at the broader systems and relationships that shape young people's lives.

High fencing liberates us and low fencing imprisons us

All correctional centres for young and juvenile offenders in Ghana seeking to project an image of correction are devoid of high walls. They do so by not erecting high walls around their compounds. Low walls, however, pose a security challenge for staff as shared by some officers:

> The walls are so low; some time ago, Yaa and some other girls jumped the wall at the side of the plantation … In fact, the walls are too low

> and this does not help us at all. The compound is not fenced and the walls are very low. One of the boys last week said he was going to use the toilet and he never returned, so you see … when it happens like that then you are queried. You see, one of the senior officers has sent this boy to collect something from me and the boy is by himself, now if something happens, then I am to blame. (114)

Low fencing walls, though a security concern, convey openness, signaling correctional centres as spaces where youth remain connected to society rather than isolated behind barriers. Youngsters, however, interpret the existence of low walls differently. In fact, low walls according to youngsters induce an opposite effect and give them a feeling of being imprisoned. Youngsters shared their opinion when they were interviewed in a focus group discussion about their views on the fenceless nature of correction centres: 'The place should be fenced so that we can move freely. Now, we are locked up for so many hours and followed everywhere because there is no fencing and officers fear that we might abscond' (114–15).

For most youngsters, constant surveillance and restrictions on movement imposed by low fencing walls evoke a sense of imprisonment, undermining the very objectives of correction and rehabilitation. Thus, the physical structure of correctional centres is in itself an invitation to abscond and tends to defeat not only the goals of penal intervention but also the functionality of prison officers, who seek to ensure that youngsters do not abscond.

As earlier indicated, escapes can be generative for researchers, providing rare entry points into the social fabric and inner workings of confinement. I therefore used these moments to observe and document the relational dynamics surrounding the escapes of three youngsters.

Three escape cases

Below, I present three cases that demonstrate the centrality of escapes to confinement life, to inmates and officers, as well as correctional institutions as a whole. On the basis of escape incidents involving Afua, Theresa, and James, I illustrate everyday complexities that characterize escape occurrences and how these intricacies unfold through multiple narrations dotted with violence, anger, revenge, intimidation and sometimes emotional outbursts.

Afua's case

This elaborate case, based on 18 months of participant observation, draws on spontaneous narrations surrounding an escape incident involving Afua, a young female offender. Her case demonstrates that escape incidents are not simply breaches of institutional control; they are contested sites that expose how everyday correctional life is saturated with violence, anger, trauma, and vengeance. Afua at the age of 15 was pregnant when committed to the JCC and eventually gave birth while in committal. She nursed the baby for some time after which, to her dismay, the baby was transferred to a children's home. One morning while the girls were holding their morning lessons, I noticed that three out of eight girls, including Afua, were missing. Upon enquiry, the girls said these girls had absconded. I could not speak further with them on the issue as lessons were in progress, so I went to the office of the headmistress where I met her and other officers in a meeting. They asked whether I had heard what had happened and the Head went ahead to narrate to me what had ensued:

> It was in the evening and the girls were watching television. Theresa, one of the girls, with a special case and the oldest among the girls was invited by the other girls to join them watch a TV programme in the dorm. Upon joining them, she changed the TV channel to a different programme to the dismay of the other girls. A squabble arose amongst them as a result and the girls began to beat up Theresa. Afua and Akua, [Akua was regarded by staff as a 'notorious girl'], bit Theresa leaving marks on her body. Even while Theresa was weak and crying in her room, Akua, still followed again and pulled her hair … (117)

The headmistress called Theresa in and showed the scars to me and said that she was receiving treatment at the hospital. Two weeks after the incident when Theresa was feeling better, I spoke with her. Theresa narrated her side of the incident:

> We were all watching television and I wanted the channel changed. Three of the girls by name Afua, Akua and Akpene got angry and did not allow me, but I insisted and Afua and Akua jumped on me and started beating me. Before this incident I had been beaten several times [many a time the other girls just looked on]. All the girls with the exception of two had beaten me before. I usually get infuriated by comments that they make such as 'who is your father?' and 'who is your mother?' and so I also insult them. Sometimes an officer looks on while I am being beaten. This officer was the one to whom I was entrusted when I first arrived at the centre and so I visited her often and liked her very much. However, she leaked confidential information from the doctor about me and that made me very angry. (118)

Theresa's story shows that escapes are rarely just acts of absconding; they grow out of the everyday realities of confinement, a space marked by conflict, competition, and recurring violence, including aggression among inmates.

She also revealed some additional information about her relationship with other staff, which I discuss later in this chapter.

I observed that girls such as Afua, Akua, Akpene, and Theresa often quarrel for various reasons, such as which television channel to watch. Theresa, being the oldest, typically asserts her preference based on age. However, Afua and Akua, who are physically stronger than the others, often command compliance through force and they are known for their overt defiance. Akua, older than Afua, frequently displays rudeness through shouting, insults, and even invoking curses against officers, often in collaboration with others. Her posture, hands on hips, walking deliberately in front of staff, is interpreted by officers as a provocative and disrespectful gesture. She has a reputation for physically assaulting other girls and occasionally threatening staff.

Afua, though she presents an innocent demeanour, is also verbally aggressive. Together, Afua and Akua leverage their physical strength and reputational boldness to assert dominance, often escaping consequences, though not always. When reported, they risk disciplinary sanctions.

Theresa's role within the centre further complicates these dynamics. She is frequently assigned cleaning duties by management, which leads other girls to associate her with institutional authority. This perceived affiliation, combined with her age, grants her a degree of power, even when she is physically overpowered. Her connection to staff instils fear in Afua and Akua, who worry about being sanctioned or placed in isolation, commonly referred to as 'remand'.

While many girls carry histories of violence prior to their committal, confinement life itself fosters conditions where conflict and aggression easily erupt, especially when interests and power collide. Confinement does not only provoke violence among peers; it can also manifest in harm towards one's own child. During a staff meeting, I enquired why Afua, who was caring for a three-month-old baby, had chosen to escape. An officer responded: 'Afua had already begun neglecting the baby, she wasn't feeding her regularly, she shouted at her to stop crying, and recently locked her in a cupboard and put her in hot water' (119). The Head interjected: 'I had initiated processes to send the baby to the children's home' (119).

Further discussion revealed deeper emotional undercurrents. When I asked why Afua might have behaved this way, the Head recalled: 'Once, Afua said the baby would rather die than be taken to a children's home' (119). It appears that the threat of separation triggered Afua's violent actions, acts that may have been expressions of fear, desperation, and protest against the looming severance from her child.

Afua was eventually recaptured. Two weeks after the meeting, I requested to visit her in the remand room. The officer with the keys asked one of the youngsters to accompany her, citing safety concerns. The officer explained that during a previous attempt to open the remand door, a girl had pushed her aside and tried to escape. Youngsters in the remand cell are considered by staff as being potentially violent and aggressive as depicted in the indication by the officer that it was not safe to enter the remand cell alone. Ironically, while officers anticipate violence from youngsters, they also rely on the same youngsters for protection.

We managed to enter safely, and I spoke briefly with Afua. She said:

> I put the blame on Akua, who absconded with me as she advised me to do so. But I also decided to escape on account of previous happenings as I did not want to be in the remand cell after the quarrel that arose in the dorm and so I boarded a taxi and left, I did not pay the taxi driver … (119)

Two days later, I visited Afua again and she spoke further about the escape incident: 'I absconded because I feared to be on remand after the incident involving Theresa. I remember when I came newly, I was put on remand for seven months and I decided I was not going back there again' (120). Afua had possibly anticipated the repercussions of the incident and, considering the punishment the incident was likely to attract, she decided to escape – the anticipation of totalistic measures tends to invite escapes – though the bait for Afua must have been the company Akua offered. However, a crucial issue for Afua seemed to be that her baby was to be sent to the children's home:

> I was unhappy when I heard that the baby was to be sent to the children's home as I wanted to keep my baby … I actually had not planned to return. I hear that babies sent to the home were usually sold and I did not want that.

The girls' institution, according to the Head, sometimes makes arrangements at the children's home for fosterage[5] of babies of youngsters who are unable to provide the required care for their children, though with their mothers' consent. Afua in anticipation of being put in a remand cell and her child being sent to the children's home, began to exhibit aggressive and violent behaviour. I have observed in my daily interaction with youngsters that, despite the exhibition of certain violent acts, they also manifest pleasant and kind gestures. Afua has on a number of occasions held her baby tenderly, sang to the baby, and fed the baby.

Management's consideration to send Afua's baby to the children's home clearly clashed with Afua's interest, depicting varying levels of interest and power clashes that are evident also in staff–inmate interface. In the remand room, Afua shared her frustrations regarding certain structural needs:

> My father does not visit often; he has visited only once. Every month my father is expected to pay GHS20.00 [US$ 5.00] monthly to the

> centre, which he does not do. My boyfriend was also asked to clear hospital bills when I delivered but he has not done that. (120–1)

Thus, besides the fear of being put in a remand cell, Afua must have been needing visits from home. While everyday detention life incites certain behaviour in young offenders, structural factors are equally contributive, as Afua's closest relatives, the father and boyfriend, were negligent of their responsibilities. Starved of the support from both the family and the father of her child coupled with youngster's violent behaviour, Afua seemed to have had enough encouragement for her actions, which must have accounted for the physical abuse she meted out to her own baby.

At the same meeting with staff, the Head also considered another option besides sending Afua's baby to the children' s home: 'I was considering probation because having spent six months at the centre, Afua could be released on license under the supervision of a social worker and so earlier this month I and some staff went to look for Afua's father, in efforts to explore this option' (121).

The Head, at the meeting, shared some frustrations the institution had encountered in ensuring that Afua's father assumed some responsibility for Afua's stay when the possibility of probation was considered:

> Upon consideration of a probation option, we decided to trace Afua's father. It was a tiring search; the father had defaulted in certain payments to the centre and so he had tried to avoid any contact with Afua and the home. We left in the morning at about 9 am and finally managed to bring to the centre some of Afua's relations including her father at about 4.30 pm. Afua had previously not received any visits from anyone apart from the boyfriend who is also a young man of about eighteen years but with no employment. (121)

Another officer confirmed that, because Afua's father had defaulted in payments, he was unwilling to cooperate with the institution to trace Afua's whereabouts:

> I'm sure the father of Afua was concealing some information purposively as the correctional centre had demanded payment of GHS 300.00 [US$ 75.00][6] from the family towards the upkeep of Afua and the baby and which the father seemed unwilling to pay. (121)

Besides attempts by Afua's father to avoid contact with the institution, other issues according to the Head made it impossible to pursue the probation option.

> On the day Afua's relations and father were brought to the centre, Afua's auntie stayed with her for a while and the auntie even bathed the baby. The father before departure gave Afua GHS 2.00Ghc [US$ 0.50]. Afua apparently got angered because the money was too small and as a result, threw the money at her father and directed insults at him. The father became furious and told us to give the baby up for adoption. The father said to us not to waste our time to trace Afua's mother as the mother gave up on Afua long ago. (122)

According to the Head, the aunt also said that, when Afua absconded and came home, she left the baby with her (the aunt) and went somewhere else unknown to the aunt. The aunt indicated that, though she was willing to assist Afua, she did not want anything to do with her because of her rude behaviour. The Head concluded that probation was not a viable option, as no relative was willing to assume responsibility for Afua upon release. This reflects a central challenge discussed in Chapter 3 and in a recent writing (Ayete-Nyampong, 2025a) about the absence of parental presence throughout youngsters' formative years, extending from arrest to committal, which complicates the implementation of diversionary measures.

Afua's baby was finally taken to the children's home. While participating in a dressmaking lesson, I overheard the girls and the teacher speaking about Afua's baby. Afua then was still under punishment and kept in the isolation room. They said: 'The baby is not feeling well; he has diarrhoea and not eating well and so he has been admitted to the hospital … ' (122). I asked one of the teachers when she would be released. She responded: 'I do not really know, you need to find out from the Head' (122).

Regularly, I arranged a meeting with the Head and the assistant to discuss issues that had come up during my observations and interviews, and I sought an opportunity to discuss Afua's release from the remand cell as she had spent two months in isolation. In response to the question about the duration of time Afua had spent in isolation, and whether or not the institution was considering releasing Afua, the Head said: 'Not immediately' (122). I asked why they still wanted to keep her in the remand cell and she said:

> Afua's presence in the remand cell served as a check on newly admitted girls as newly admitted girls were often unstable. Currently there are two newcomers and they have already started tampering with the windows and have even broken the ball in the cistern and so the toilet can no longer flush. Afua's presence therefore acts as a positive impact on newly admitted girls. Afua partakes of all activities organized for the other girls and only comes to sleep in the cell in the evening. The presence of an older one always helps them to settle. (122–3)

Whereas Afua must have construed her isolation as punishment for absconding and expected a release from the remand, the institution's attention had however shifted from punishment to a positive function. Afua's presence was now being supposedly employed as a positive influence to demotivate newly admitted inmates to escape; this new intention was however unknown to Afua.

When youngsters escape and staff are not able to recover them, as was the case with Akua, youngsters tend to position themselves as having overridden the authority of the institutions. This tends to provide justification for institutions creating the impression or appearance that they make every effort to retrieve youngsters, even when escape incidents are kept internal to these institutions. In practice, however, there is not much success in recapturing youngsters.

Akua and the other girl who absconded were never recovered. While Akua managed to escape with impunity, Afua was recaptured and subjected to severe punishment. Also, for fear that recaptured inmates may have negative influence on the other girls in custody, minimal efforts are undertaken to recapture them. As depicted above, when youngsters are finally brought back, they are severely sanctioned, put on remand for unduly long periods as was the case with Afua and, by so doing, power is repositioned in the hands of institutions, a demonstration that the latter is in control.

Afua's behaviour continued to worsen as some staff had begun to complain to one another that they were not pleased with some utterances of Afua. One officer said to me: 'I would like you to counsel Afua as she has been talking a lot of late and saying so many unnecessary things' (124). About one month after, I had also observed that Afua acted quite violently while working on the farm one evening with the girls:

> Afua wore a frown while she weeded. The girls whispered to themselves something which I did not hear and then the captain acted as though she was teasing Afua and the latter got really angry. She picked up a big stick so I said to her to be careful and then the captain said to me that she dared not hit her. Soon one of the senior officers joined us with her granddaughter; the latter was playing with a stick. Afua immediately lifted the little girl, took the stick from her and forcefully held her tight in the presence of the grandmother and another teacher who was also with us on the farm. The little girl cried out loud but Afua continued to hold on to her; eventually she let go. (124)

Midway through the year, Afua was finally released from 'remand' to join the other girls in their dormitory, and she was replaced by another girl, who also absconded and was sent to the remand cell. Following her release from remand, Afua had become generally uninterested in most activities and seldom participated in lessons. When she did participate, it was with little enthusiasm:

> I was with the girls in their hall with two officers. All the girls were busy with their sewing. They all seemed to be doing their work quietly. Afua was not with them; I came out and saw Afua lying on the bench. I asked why she was not with the girls in the hall and she said she did not feel like being with them. I asked about her baby and she said that she had visited the baby in August and the baby was doing well. (125)

Three months later, Afua escaped again. Like the other girls, Afua seemed to have escaped for good as she had not been recaptured at the time of my last visit. By escaping and not returning, Akua appears freed from the confines of a correctional institution as well as being kept in isolation.

Theresa's case

The entanglements and ambiguities between the official and the private

This case which concerns Theresa, illustrates blurred boundaries, betrayals, and emotional entanglements that characterize everyday relational life in correctional centres. As previously noted, she endured mistreatment at the hands of Afua and other young girls Her outburst and insults arose during a quarrel with Afua and Akua, after they provoked her by raising a sensitive issue related to her parents. As noted in Chapter 3, matters relating to family often strike a deep chord with youngsters, who may become highly emotional when such topics arise. Moreover, Theresa revealed that equally sensitive and confidential information had been leaked by a staff member entrusted with her care, compounding her sense of betrayal. In her story, Theresa alleged that this staff member usually looked on while she was being beaten.

On the same day that I spoke to Theresa, I also spoke to this officer. I asked about Theresa's background and why she was admitted to the centre as her case was usually referred to by staff as a special case. The officer in question responded:

> Theresa was a special case recommended to the centre. She had a bad temper probably because of a surgical operation she had undergone. The doctor spoke to me upon her arrival and asked that I should ensure she was well taken care of. I tried to provide as much support as possible for her. She got a job in a nearby chop bar and usually brought some food along to my children in the evening. She tried to entice my children with food anytime she returned from work and the door was locked so that the children would open the door for her. (126)

The officer's intention to protect Theresa was, however, short lived. She continued:

> One evening when I was about to enter the girl's dorm, I realized that the dorm keys were not being handled properly and so I warned my children not to take food from Theresa any longer as this will stop her from coming to demand the key. I also warned Theresa not to provide the children with food any longer. This however did not go down well with Theresa and so one evening she came to the door with a bowl of food and one of my children told her to go back. When I questioned why she should still bring food to the children, she said she offered them food because they begged for it. While I spoke with her, she became very angry and hurled insults at me. She dared me to draw closer if indeed I was a lady. On hearing this, I no longer could control myself and I beat her up mercilessly. (126)

Thus, a relationship that was initiated on the basis of safeguarding the welfare of Theresa rather ended in an assault case. The officer further continued her story:

> Theresa reported the case to the Head and she was advised to report the case to the Domestic Violence and Victims Support Unit of the Police Service, which she did. I therefore was summoned to provide explanations as to why I behaved in that manner. They sent some of their officers to carry out investigations but it looked as though they had been prejudiced against me and were unwilling to listen to my side of the case. I was asked to apologize to Theresa as the latter requested I do. I said I would never apologize as I suspected that this was a plot by the management of the centre who intentionally incited Theresa to infuriate me and get me into trouble. I was certain that my action was justified and I was ready to go any length to pursue the case further. (126)

This case, according to the officer, was further referred to their regional head office to handle. The officers along with other officers were summoned to give their respective views. The officer continued:

> I stood my grounds amidst various squabbles that arose in the process and the threat to have me transferred. Finally, we were only advised to learn to live amicably and this ended the case. I have however decided that I would keep a distance from these young girls. I used to counsel and advise them but I realized that they were adept at playing one teacher against the other. (126–7)

The same officer who had been involved in Theresa's case also reflected on her experience with Akua, a girl frequently labelled as 'notorious'. Initially, the officer had embraced Akua as a daughter, offering her care within her household. However, this relationship later unravelled. She recounted:

> I would no longer go beyond my official relationship with these girls, as I have learnt so many lessons. I took Akua as my daughter, she ate in my house and did almost everything a daughter would, but then she betrayed my trust and blamed me for her escape. (127)

As with Theresa, the officer resolved to maintain a firmer boundary between her official duties and personal involvement. Similar dynamics are evident in the boys' institution, where relationships frequently blur the lines between the official and the personal, often in connection with escape incidents. In one interview, a male officer described how a youngster exploited such a relationship with a particular staff member to facilitate his absconding:

> A male youngster who absconded along with three other boys enjoyed so many favours from a female officer. The officer was kind to this boy, cooked for him regularly and treated him as a son. Yet it was the same lady who was at post when the boy absconded. When questioned, the boy said that he knew that the lady had big buttocks and could not run after him. This was the lady's reward for being good to the boy. (127)

Another female officer shared a similar sense of disappointment. She had treated a young boy as her own son, cooking for him, offering care, and providing guidance. Yet, he absconded with a peer who allegedly introduced him to a gang of armed robbers. Reflecting on the experience, she stated: 'I took one of the boys as a son; cooked for him, cared for him and advised him. This boy however absconded with a friend who reportedly took him to a gang of armed robbers … I decided to have nothing to do with him' (127).

Such moments of betrayal often prompt officers to withdraw emotionally and reinforce professional boundaries. Yet, maintaining a strict separation between official duties and personal involvement is not always feasible. As discussed in the previous chapter (Chapter 6), everyday confinement practices are marked by reciprocal exchanges, material and non-material, between staff and inmates. Officers frequently extend acts of kindness, treating some youngsters as their own children. In return, they expect compliance and loyalty. However, these expectations are not always met, and when trust is broken the consequences reverberate across both staff and youth.

Theresa's case, like Afua's, illustrates how gestures of care can be met with betrayal. These examples reveal that detention life is not only structured by institutional violence but also by the emotional toll it exacts on both staff and residents. They also expose the blurred boundaries between formal roles and personal relationships, underscoring the entanglement of social lives within carceral spaces.

James' case

James, is a male youngster, known for his notoriety and repeated escape attempts and as a result, was regularly confined to an isolation cell by a senior officer. His case reflects how staff manage notoriety through everyday informal compromises. The conditions were harsh, poor ventilation and intense heat made the cell nearly unbearable. In response, a junior officer supervising James negotiated a compromise: James would spend brief daily periods with other boys in a nearby dormitory. This informal arrangement, built on mutual trust, offered relief to both parties. James gained some freedom, social interaction, and access to television, while the officer was spared the burden of constant surveillance.

This arrangement was known to other dormitory staff and to James' peers, but it remained hidden from senior management. James had effectively negotiated and leveraged trust with junior staff to circumvent the rules imposed by senior officers. However, the arrangement was short lived. During an unannounced inspection, a senior officer discovered James outside his isolation cell and immediately reinstated stricter sanctions. Furious, James declared that, regardless of the punishment, the choice to escape was his alone. In an angry outburst, he exclaimed that no one realized how bad he was.

During an educational session, a male officer nervously escorted James into the dormitory where I was seated. When I asked who the boy was, though I already recognized him, the officer whispered: 'He is a very bad boy and we're monitoring him closely. He was the one who used the asor blade in the recent escape. He has only a few months left, so we're trying to be careful so he can finish his term and leave' (128). When I asked if the boy was James, the officer replied, 'Very good,' visibly surprised that I knew his name. James was frequently the subject of offstage conversations among staff. At the security gate, one officer described him as 'a very notorious boy and an expert in crime. He doesn't sleep at night and disturbs the others. I'm fearful of him and very cautious' (129). Another officer blamed staff for James' behaviour, suggesting that keeping the lights on at night prevented sleep: 'Once the lights go off, the boys will be compelled to sleep. James uses juju, or fetish power, a kind of spiritual protection, and this deprives him of sleep. Armed robbers who use such powers do not sleep at night' (129). A female officer added:

> James recently threatened me. He said if I came near him to punish him, he would knife me. He told me not to compare my meagre salary to his income, he works with big people. A junior male officer

> responded: 'James smokes marijuana. That explains his behaviour, this has probably affected his mind. I just hope he finishes his term and leaves.' (129)

James clearly generated unease among staff. He was a recurring topic at staff meetings, where officers debated how to manage him. Eventually, he was transferred to an isolation cell within the adult prison on the same premises. Even there, he attempted another escape before being recaptured. Staff appeared to be counting down the days until his discharge.

Yet not all officers were intimidated by James. During another educational session, I sat beside a female officer while James was having his hair cut by another boy. When I asked why he was not in class, she explained: 'James had a haircut that wasn't allowed by the authorities, so he had to re-barber' (130). After the haircut, James greeted me and the officer with a broad smile, strikingly different from his demeanour with male staff the previous day. She let him into the dorm and locked the door. I asked her about James, and she replied: 'I do not consider James stubborn as others thought; James enjoyed a high standard life and he was always compelled to steal in order to keep this standard' (130). While sitting by her, she shouted to James and asked how many times he bathed in a day and James muttered something I did not understand, to which the officer responded jokingly that he was telling lies. The officer turned to me and said: 'I like him and he is very neat; he keeps himself very neat' (130).

Another female officer shared a viewpoint about James:

> You need to talk with the officers because sometimes they also contribute to boys acting the way they do. James said to me that even though he is known to have made several escape attempts, he tries to reform but officers do not recognize his effort to change and always brand him as a bad boy. For instance some time ago, certain items were stolen and although officers suspected James, he was not responsible. He was taken to a senior officer and the latter upon seeing him, shouted out: 'You again?' This hurt James so much that he decided to abscond that week. Sometimes, officers brand inmates and stick to their brand even when there is change. (130)

Prior to James' discharge, I held an interview with him. He said his actual age was 21 though his official record stated 20: the officers insisted that I stay with him in one of the offices rather than in the open. I requested that they leave the office to us so we could have some private space to hold our discussions; this was a couple of days before his discharge:

> My father is from France and mother, Ghanaian. I never got to see my father and my mother; they never took good care of me. No one really was ready to care for me when I moved from one relation to the

> other. I felt content with friends, most of whom were older than me. I attended night clubs, stole from people, hanged out with girl friends and I enjoyed it but it was also a tough world. My outside world is tougher and even though I went through a lot of tough times I am tough enough to face them. I decided to embark on numerous escape attempts because of the way staff treated me. For instance, one of the officers demoted me from the 5th dorm to the 4th without giving me a reason and so I was very angry and said to myself that at all cost I would escape and it was the following day that I escaped. (130–1)

While James narrated his story, he seemed well composed and calm. There was little indication that this was the same youngster that exhibited such violent and aggressive behaviour and intimidated other officers, in fact I would have doubted James' violent behaviour if I was a cursory visitor, or a human rights monitor. Following a later visit, I was informed that James upon discharge had re-offended and is now in a maximum-security prison for adults.

Final thoughts

The cases of Afua, Theresa, and James demonstrate how correctional centres operate as repositories of violence, not only by confining individuals shaped by anger, trauma, and vengeance, but also through the everyday dynamics of confinement (Papadopoulos et al., 2008, Martin, 2015, Ayete-Nyampong, 2017b, Martin and Chantraine, 2018). The lived realities within these institutions are marked by complex relationships between staff and inmates, punctuated by moments of compromise, defiance, and tension, and can themselves generate and intensify violent dispositions.

Institutional responses to escape incidents often reflect a totalizing assertion of power, aligning with Michel Foucault's conceptualization of disciplinary authority as top-down and omnipresent, exemplified by Jeremy Bentham's panopticon (Foucault, 1977). However, the three escape cases discussed here challenge this centralized view. Rather than disciplinary authority being monolithic and unidirectional, it emerges as diffuse and relational, embedded in the everyday interactions and negotiations of confinement life.

The architectural features of Foucault's conceptualization of power, drawing on Jeremy Bentham's panopticon, may not necessarily be present within Ghana's correctional centres, but the panopticon is still exemplified. By the constant reminders verbally by staff, of rules routines and the fact that one is being constantly watched, this gives the feeling of being observed and monitored. In this regard, control and power is more defined by people, than by the architectural layout.

Empirical evidence from these cases reveals that escape incidents are not merely breaches of institutional control; they are sites of contestation, resistance, and relational entanglement. Acts of violence, defiance, and aggression by young inmates may reflect deeper, often unspoken, expressions of anger and vengeance, directed subtly towards both familial structures and the state.

For example, James, at one point, positioned himself as a figure of influence and control, so much so that some officers privately admitted feeling intimidated by him. Similarly, Theresa's bold challenge to an officer to beat her, and Akua's confrontational demeanour and verbal curses, illustrate how young people under institutional supervision can assert defiance in differentiated and strategic ways. These moments underscore that while staff retain formal authority, such authority is constantly negotiated, resisted, and reconfigured through everyday interactions.

Escape incidents illuminate how violence, aggression, defiance, and conflict are not only present but actively produced and reproduced within correctional centres. The experiences of James, Theresa, and Afua reflect broader patterns among young people who are frequently labelled as 'bad' by staff, criminal justice professionals, and even religious figures (see Chapter 8). These labels often shape how youngsters are perceived and treated, and in turn how they come to see themselves. Some come to accept the 'bad' identity, living up to it; others attempt to project a more compliant image in line with institutional expectations.

As previously discussed, recognizing children as rights holders entails respecting their views, even when those views challenge adult norms or moral frameworks. Listening to a child who says, 'I am very bad, no one knows how bad I am,' offers insight into how children construct and understand notions of 'badness', rooted in their lived realities. When practitioners and institutional actors engage with children in conflict with the law as rights-bearing individuals, taking time to listen, understand the roots of defiance, and interpret acts such as cursing, insulting officers, or attempting escape, this relational engagement can begin to bridge the disconnect. In doing so, the messages conveyed by adults may become more meaningful and resonant for both parties.

The everyday dynamics of violence, provocation, and resistance linked to escapes are not limited to the physical confines of detention. They are continually reproduced across porous boundaries (Martin and Jefferson, 2019, Cunha, 2020, Weegels et al., 2020, Ellis, 2021), as young people, through absconding and occasional recapture, move back and forth between the worlds of confinement and freedom. These dynamics risk negatively shaping youth experiences in wider society. Many of these youngsters, often connected to criminal gangs outside detention, influence peers within confinement, and as the two spheres overlap the cycle of violence persists.

Although my study is small-scale and not intended for broad generalization, it is significant that recent years have witnessed escalating violent incidents among young people. In 2025, for example, confrontations among senior high school students culminated in stabbings[7]. The following year began with a disturbing wave of assaults, as secondary students attacked teachers with sticks and clubs[8]. And, in February 2026, while this book was being finalized, reports emerged of secondary school students being injured and assaulted by peers during a District Schools Athletics Game, an event meant to celebrate youth talent and sportsmanship, that instead descended into violence[9]. The everyday interplay of violence, provocation, and resistance are constantly reproduced across the permeable boundary between confinement and freedom, as young people move back and forth through acts of absconding and recapture. Such cycles risk fostering violent tendencies among youth in free society.

These patterns underscore how the circulation of violence between confinement and free society contributes to broader societal instability. The escalation of youth violence in Ghana and beyond highlights the urgent need for interventions that address not only the immediate acts of escapes but also the broader and everyday situations that perpetuate them.

Conclusion

From the moment of committal, many young people carry with them a deep sense of displacement shaped by histories of trauma. Their resistance to both familial and state structures reflects not simply defiance, but a profound critique of institutions they perceive as misaligned with their needs. Within confinement, their acts – often read as violent or unlawful – can be understood as attempts to reclaim agency in spaces where they feel silenced. This chapter underscores that such responses are not merely challenges to authority, but expressions of lived realities that demand recognition. Respecting the perspectives of young people is therefore not optional; it is essential for any meaningful reform. Without listening to their voices, institutions risk perpetuating cycles of violence and resistance rather than fostering pathways towards rehabilitation and justice.

When young people's voices are not respected, they inevitably search for belonging elsewhere. In the context of Ghana's growing youth prison population, this silence risks breeding frustration and alienation. Correctional centres, rather than serving as spaces of rehabilitation, may slowly transform into reservoirs of violence, places where suppressed identities and unmet needs erupt in destructive ways. Respecting and amplifying the perspectives of these youngsters is therefore not only a moral imperative but also a practical safeguard against institutions becoming sites of harm and violence rather than rehabilitation. Recognizing the relational fabric of confinement and the everyday dynamics surrounding escape incidents opens up possibilities for constructive engagement. Such recognition can help foster young people's capacity to communicate and relate in non-violent, non-confrontational ways. Conversely, when these informal and relational practices are treated solely as disciplinary breaches, they may instead reinforce cycles of violence, defiance, and aggression.

Ultimately, this chapter has highlighted that escapes are integral to the lived experience of confinement. Reducing escapes to mere infractions to be prevented and punished overlooks the deeper relational signals and everyday realities that young people express through these acts.

8

Appropriation of Educational and Religious Goals in Correctional Centres

Introduction

Education holds a central place in correctional centres and is highly valued by both staff and young people. On average, about 80 per cent of each weekday – excluding Fridays and weekends – is devoted to educational activities. Accounts from youngsters reveal that even before entering these centres, they are aware of the educational purpose tied to their sentences, which often specify that they are committed in order to gain vocational training or practical skills. Alongside education, correctional centres frequently employ religious practices – such as church services, prayer, and Bible study – as instruments of correction and reform. This chapter focuses primarily on these two core provisions – education and religion – within both the Junior Correctional Centre (JCC) and the Senior Correctional Centre (SCC). They not only serve as the foundation of institutional reform but also shape the wider socio-cultural environment of these facilities. The discussions highlight the perspectives of the youngsters themselves, exploring their participation in educational programmes and religious services.

Findings suggest that while institutions often employ structured educational and religious programmes as pathways to reform, youngsters tend to reinterpret or adapt them in ways that reflect their personal search for meaning and belonging. Within this framework, correctional centres can be understood as development projects, where youngsters sidetrack from and appropriate institutional goals. Drawing on Olivier de Sardan (2005), this process of 'sidetracking' refers to how target groups deviate from the formal objectives of a project in order to appropriate it. Appropriation involves reshaping or redefining a project in ways that may differ from – or even appear to contradict – its official aims and methods.

The chapter exposes a paradox evident in observations of formal lessons within correctional centres. Although youngsters value certificates, they often disengage from rigid, lecture-based teaching that lacks interaction and relevance. In contrast, peer-led lessons built on appropriated methods generate strong engagement and meaningful outcomes. William, an inmate teacher, drew on custodial experiences and familiar practices to capture attention, enforce discipline, and achieve rapid literacy gains, during a non-formal lesson. His sensitivity to subtle learner cues and insistence on participation ensured steady progress, from mastering alphabets in English and Twi to reading and reciting short words. Though unconventional, William's appropriated approach connected deeply with learners' lived realities and advanced institutional goals more effectively than staff-led sessions.

Yet appropriations themselves present a paradox: while often at odds with institutional norms, they are not consistently resisted. On the contrary, they may inadvertently support correctional centres in sustaining operational effectiveness, underscoring the value of peer learning and contextual pedagogies in these settings.

Educational provisions: a status symbol for institutions and youngsters

Correctional centres pride themselves in their educational attainments and do not hesitate to conduct visitors round their classrooms and educational workshops to observe lessons and to exhibit their latest equipment. Equipment such as books, furniture, and machines for use in vocational and technical workshops are provided by philanthropists, religious organizations, financial institutions, and sometimes the state.

Youngsters who perform well in educational lessons and those who pass their national examinations are usually cited when reference is made to the achievements of the institutions. Such youngsters are also commended as evidence of change by their teachers to their fellow youngsters but also to other practitioners, philanthropists, and charity groups who visit. Educational achievement therefore provides a sense of pride for youngsters.

Possessing a Basic Education Certificate Examination (BECE) or a West Africa Senior School Certificate Examination[1] (WASSCE) is a status symbol for most youngsters. Male youngsters in possession of a BECE or WASSCE rise to the level of inmate teachers who teach other youngsters. *Brannies*, or youngsters in dorms one and two, who are in possession of these certificates are however expected to undergo their mandatory observation period before assuming a teaching role. The status of a teacher is cherished by youngsters as they get to teach a class and, by so doing, command deference and respect from other youngsters, as though they were teachers and officers.

Youngsters who pass certificated national examinations also stand the chance of being supported by philanthropists, church groups, and charity groups so as to further their education upon discharge from these institutions. Youngsters who possess a certificate but who are not selected to teach, exercise another level of authority as they seem not to be subjected to the command of inmate teachers. These youngsters sometimes sit on classroom rails overlooking the class and talking among themselves. On the whole, possession of certificates and attainment of some level of education is highly rated by youngsters and facilitates social mobility among them.

On account of the high premium attached to education by both institutions and youngsters, those who are unable to obtain certificates or complete a required period of training express frustration as James indicated in the previous chapter.

At the SCC, youngsters who attain some level of formal education prior to committal are enrolled in formal education, which is organized and structured. Youngsters are assessed upon entry to correctional centres, to determine the appropriate level of placement. They are then placed in various classes depending on their level of education and then they progress from one level to the other. By enrolling in formal education, youngsters follow the designated national curriculum and syllabus and also sit national certificated examinations such as the BECE and the WASSCE. Formal classes are taught by trained teachers, some of whom are officers and National Service Personnel[2].

According to narratives in Chapter 3, youngsters enjoyed schooling while they grew up and the majority discontinued schooling at an early stage against their will. Youngsters attach an important role to educational attainment given the status symbol associated with it at the centres. Yet, in practice, youngsters demonstrate little interest in participating in formal lessons. Given that many youngsters have been out of school for a considerable length of time before committal, following a daily rigid and formal programme of education becomes a major challenge they encounter upon committal.

I observed a lesson attended by 15 students taught by staff. The class did not seem interactive; the teacher copied notes on the board after which he taught about the nuclear and extended family. The students sat bored as the teacher lectured most of the time with little eye contact and some students comfortably placed their heads on their tables and appeared to be sleeping. I was therefore presented with a paradox, while youngsters embraced certificates, they were not always interested in the lessons.

Officers have themselves expressed concern about youngsters' lack of interest in formal educational lessons during interviews and focus group discussions. Some were of the view that youngsters with minimal education tended not to be interested in lessons. While sitting under a tree with some female officers and observing lessons in progress, some female officers commented about youngsters' lack of interest. They said: 'Youngsters who have to be forced to study are usually those who hardly have any educational background. Those with substantial educational background know the benefits of education and are more interested' (136).[3]

Other officers cited educational programmes in adult prisons and commented that adult prisoners demonstrated higher level of interest in educational lessons and that even adult cattle keepers, herders, or *Fulanis* who had no educational background prior to imprisonment were all eager to learn to write. Others were of the view that children who do not show seriousness in their studies should be punished so they would sit up.

Educational provisions are also plagued with structural constraints. At the initial stages of fieldwork, one class was held under a tree and later moved to an open structure. Teachers lamented about resource constraints such as the lack of textbooks and teachers. An officer shared his views: 'We lack textbooks and teachers, the centre has only four teachers; the centre has however formally applied to the Ghana Education Service to take over the management of formal education' (136).

While no lessons were held under trees during later visits, 2019 and 2023, formal educational lessons at the SCC were still plagued with all kinds of challenges such as low patronage of lessons, resource constraints, and inadequacy of textbooks coupled with youngsters who were not as interested in participating in formal lessons.

Regardless of whether or not children showed seriousness in their studies, there came a time when youngsters had to prepare to write their exams. During this period, all youngsters appeared to show keenness in preparing towards their exams and it was not easy to distinguish between who was studious and who was not. Teachers and the chaplains also provide all the necessary moral support to ensure that youngsters were well prepared for their exams.

In contrast to the SCC, there is no provision of formal certificated education at the girls' institution, the JCC. Girls who attain some level of formal education before committal are unable to further their formal education while in detention. Yaa, a female juvenile, was qualified for Senior High School (SHS) and was in possession of a BECE certificate at the time of committal. However, there was no opportunity for her to advance her formal education during the period she was in detention. Though she participated actively in various types of vocational training offered and had acquired some relevant skills, these courses were not certificated. According to Yaa, by the time she had served her sentence, and was prepared to continue her education, her BECE certificate was already five years old and could not be accepted by the schools she had approached for admission. This required that she went back three years to start junior high school all over again. She was keen to do so but the timing of the academic year did not coincide with the period she was discharged from the centre. Later she resorted to being an apprentice at a hairdressing salon. In my final conversation with her at the time of discharge, she sounded very disappointed and shed tears, for though she was still interested in continuing her formal education and looked forward to becoming a Chartered Accountant, there was little hope of achieving this goal.

From 2010 onwards, a one-to-one mentoring un-certificated educational programme at the JCC was introduced by a volunteer group of women professionals, 'Women's Voice', a non-governmental organization (NGO). Girls could not hide their excitement about this educational mentoring programme as they unhesitatingly spoke about the topics they treated. I found out more about this programme in an interview with the head of the NGO:

> This programme is being organized by Women's Voice, an NGO, whose members underwent training from the non-formal department of the Ghana Education Service [GES] and came twice a week to provide literacy lessons and mentoring to the girls at the correctional centre. Each girl was assigned to one teacher with each session lasting for one and a half hours. The girls were very interested in the programme and tended to develop friendship ties with the mentors. (137–8)

In fact, it was after the introduction of this programme that Yaa mentioned that she was considering pursuing accounting upon discharge: 'I would either go back to Junior High School [JHS] grade 2 or continue to the SHS level. I am interested in studying accounting to become a Chartered Accountant and determined to go back to school' (138).

A 19-year-old girl who had no educational background prior to committal also started considering the possibility of pursuing formal education. She was determined that upon discharge she would start school and later study Mathematics and Social Studies at the JHS level.

Once youngsters are interested in an activity, they are inclined to overlook obstacles such as the duration of schooling or the difficulty of studying.

Vocational and Technical Education

Vocational and Technical Education (VTE) at the boys' institution is certified by the National Vocational Training Institute (NVTI). VTE focuses on the acquisition of practical skills and provides hands-on training and experience for youngsters. VTE at the JCC for girls is however un-certificated by NVTI and the performance of girls is not assessed based on external examinations as is the case at the SCC for boys. VTE at the SCC comprises practical and hands-on instruction in car mechanics, blacksmithing, tailoring, shoe making, carpentry, car and general electrical, and ceramics making.

Vocational lessons are attended throughout the day from 9.30 am till 4.30 pm. As already indicated earlier, youngsters upon admission are expected to undergo a mandatory minimum period of observation of six months. In practice, however, this is not the case as, according to youngsters, the period of observation usually lasts for a year.

At the JCC, VTE constitutes the only form of educational provision and includes beads making, batik, tie and dye, hairdressing, dressmaking, catering, plumbing, and manicure and pedicure lessons. Lessons are conducted daily and commence after breakfast from 9 am to 4.30 pm. The JCC shares the same premises with a vocational institution that admits girls with formal qualifications such as a BECE certificate. Girls generally show very little interest in their VTE lessons and the majority admit that they would not pursue any of the VTE courses upon discharge. At the time of the first field visit, girls who partook of plumbing lessons also sought the opportunity to interact with young boys who were on remand, as lessons are conducted on the premises of the latter.

Non-formal education

Non-formal lessons at the SCC are tailored to the needs of boys of low educational attainment and are not certificated nor follow a formal structure. The focus is on basic literacy and numeracy skills; the provision gives no regard to differences in age. Youngsters refer to non-formal education as well as all other forms of educational provision as *sukuu*, meaning school. Non-formal education, which is also referred to as basic or rudimentary classes by officers, runs from 8 am to 9.30 am daily. These lessons precede formal education and VTE at the SCC, which is conducted after 9.30 am.

Rudimentary or non-formal lessons are taught by officers and youngsters who are inmate teachers. To qualify to teach, youngsters must have graduated with a BECE or a WASCE certificate. Topics taught usually are at the discretion of teachers. Rudimentary classes do not usually use textbooks; youngsters employ jotters and exercise books to copy notes from the board. Often young people read out recitals written on the blackboard and are assisted by the teacher to memorize these poems. Most inmate teachers are observed teaching lessons with great enthusiasm and interest; classes are lively and usually elicit mass responses (one could hear loud responses far off) as well as mass punishments.

Inmate teachers in the name of class control sometimes punish their students at will and also reward deserving students by calling for applause by the class; inmate teachers generally exercise a level of command and domination over others. By keeping a cane by the side, they keep their classes active, alert, and their students seldom doze off. Additionally, the cane is used when students are not attentive, do not behave well in class, are unable to respond to questions, or provide incorrect answers.

On the contrary, the cane is seldom used by teachers during formal lessons; it is employed more as a pointer and hitting the table to draw attention to what is taught. I noticed that youngsters are generally reluctant (not only in the classrooms) to give one another away publicly, mass punishments are therefore frequent and sometimes about a third of an entire class is made to kneel down as a form of punishment.

Youngsters during focus group discussions and one-to-one interviews could not conceal their interest in non-formal lessons. Interviews also revealed that most youngsters were interested in basic literacy and numeracy skills as they constituted entry points to vocational and technical careers. Generally, youngsters expressed the need for additional hours on non-formal education. Richard said: One thing I was not happy about is the duration of lessons; the school lessons were too short' (140). Others such as Yaw were pleased they could write their names: 'When I came here the second time, I made up mind to be serious with my work and also my schooling because I could not even write my name but the school has helped me very much and now I can write my name and write some few words' (140). However, schooling for Yaw meant more than just knowing how to write his name: 'I have benefited much from lessons. Even though I am 18 now, I would like to go to back to school as I realize that I need to know the names of the tools I work with. I am therefore determined that I would attend school and also learn a trade' (140).

Thus, compared to formal lessons where youngsters may have to be coaxed in order to attend, interest in non-formal lessons is undisputably high.

An appropriated form of non-formal education at the SCC

In contrast to the earlier observation of a formal lesson attended by 15 students and taught by staff, which lacked interaction and reflected little learner interest, I also witnessed a non-formal lesson led by one of the youngsters. Interest in such non-formal lessons was strikingly high, as illustrated by the case of William, an inmate teacher. William sidetracked from the formal methods typically used by staff, instead appropriating approaches rooted in his custodial and pre-custodial experiences. His methods, though unconventional and often described as crude, proved effective. They produced outcomes such as strong class control, focused attention, and improved reading skills, outputs that, while based on appropriated goals, still contributed to institutional objectives.

William actively engaged his peers, drawing on his experience in police custody prior to committal. He ensured that every learner participated, paying close attention to each individual's effort. His discipline was strict; he frowned upon those who could not read, used caning to enforce compliance, and quickly restored order when whispering or teasing disrupted the class. Wrong answers attracted lashes from peers who had answered correctly, and William reinforced discipline by demonstrating how punishment should be administered. He introduced practices such as rhythmic applause for good performance and required students to answer questions with their hands behind their backs. Despite the severity of his methods, the class progressed rapidly – from learning alphabets in English and Twi to reading and writing two and three-letter words, and later reciting short passages with ease.

William's lessons did not follow a formal syllabus or timetable. He worked independently, with minimal interference from staff, though an officer was usually present. His sensitivity to the movements, comments, and subtle behaviours of his peers was remarkable. Youngsters often display sharp attention to small details, detectable through rapid eye movements, yet in the presence of unfamiliar adults they adopt a neutral, disengaged stance. William's attentiveness to these cues was therefore not accidental but deeply connected to his shared experiences with the class. He commanded respect and maintained full control. When a student failed to respond promptly, he would ask, 'Is that not your name, or did you pick your name from the police station?' (142). This remark, while humorous, carried deeper meaning. Focus group discussions revealed that some youngsters had changed their names or ages at the point of arrest, making it possible they did not recognize or respond to their new identities.

William's case demonstrates that, although youngsters often show little interest in formal education, they creatively construct non-formal learning experiences by drawing on familiar methods and shared realities. His appropriated pedagogy highlights the importance of contextual approaches, methods that resonate with learners' lived worlds and sustain their engagement, while still contributing to institutional goals.

On the usage of the cane or corporal punishment, youngsters tend to have their own connotations. During focus group discussions they attributed diverse meanings to corporal punishment, which is seldom employed by officers during formal educational lessons, but administered in the yard or during parades. While staff are aware that corporal punishment contravenes the provision of the United Nations Convention on the Rights of the Child (CRC), they justify the usage of corporal punishment on the grounds of correction. Some staff also unhesitatingly state concerning youngsters that, without applying corporal punishment, 'youngsters will never change'; and most staff especially dorm warders tend to share this view thus focusing on the objective of control, order, discipline, and compliance, which, according to staff, augurs better for the smooth functioning of the institution (Carrabine, 2004).

Youngsters have their constructions about corporal punishment, shared during focus group discussions. Some say it toughens them and gives them more recognition among peers, as a result of which they command better respect and are able to stand up to harsher treatment. Such youngsters regard corporal punishment as a training that offers them progression from one level of toughness to the other. Few youngsters share the views of staff by regarding corporal punishment as a form of discipline to civilize them to conform to the rules of the institution. Others consider corporal punishment by officers as a demonstration of love. In other words, officers are ascribed a parental status by children and youngsters who consider corporal punishment not only as a form of discipline but as an expression of love stemming from a commonly used adage: 'A child who is disciplined is one that is loved by the parent.'[4]

Thus, whereas correctional institutions may not formally sanction the usage of corporal punishment as a form of correction along with some youngsters who embrace this objective, other youngsters may have their perspectives on this type of punishment.

In the next section I discuss religious provisions, which, like educational observances, serve a vital objective in correctional centres. Again, youngsters and sometimes staff have their own ways of appropriating institutional religious observances.

Religious activities

In Ghana, religious activities in the form of church services, Bible studies, and prayers permeate the entire formal fabric of correctional institutions. One who has oversight of religious activities at the boys' institution (SCC) is referred to as a chaplain. In an interview, the chaplain explains that most religious activities are Christian and that, though other religious organizations such as Muslim groups express interest, their organizations have been irregular. The chaplaincy annually reviews religious activities and on the basis of this review decides whether or not to renew permits to conduct religious service or activity at the centre. The chaplain detailed the nature of religious activities: 'Morning devotions are held twice a week on Mondays and Wednesdays. On Fridays, institutions hold a prolonged service commonly referred to as a Padre hour'[5] (143). During weekends (Saturdays and Sundays), church services are held twice a day and religious organizations also take turns to provide moral lessons and literary classes in late afternoons after workshop lessons.

According to the chaplain, although many churches express interest to conduct various religious activities, not all are allowed as some only seek to use correctional institutions to pursue their own interests. Some churches, by virtue of the services they organize at the correctional institutions, apply for funds from other organizations. Churches raise funds in the name of these institutions, yet such church organizations do not make donations to the centre.

The chaplain stressed that the institution regulates church organizations very strictly and investigates the genuineness of applications before endorsing them.

The conduct of church services, stemming from the interview with the chaplain, is voluntary and so the institution does not pay pastors, churches, or religious organizations involved in the institution's religious activities. Offertories taken during church services are strictly for the institution and are utilized for purchases such as hymn books, chairs, and other needs. The chaplain said: 'the institution boasts of one hundred chairs recently purchased using monies collected during offertories' (144).

Correction centres employ religious activities as a tool of correction and change. Staff and youngsters admit to the positive impact of church services, prayer, and Bible studies in the behaviour of youngsters. The chaplain explains this in the interview: 'In most prisons and correctional centres, religion is used as a tool to reform or bring about change in youngsters. It is not easy to reform but over time, we have noticed a lot of change' (144). The chaplain also spoke about external support from other churches besides the institution's own religious programmes:

> Many of the boys have engaged in bad behaviour for so long and it is our duty to encourage them to worship God and change from their bad ways. This is our main preoccupation. It is difficult for institutions to bring about change by themselves and that is why churches need to complement this function. In fact, we notice that inmates respond better if they hear sermons from other preachers. (144)

Youngsters such as Kofi commented about the usefulness of religious observances: 'Church activities are a good source of comfort and happiness, pastors encourage us a lot and I have noticed a lot of change. If I had not been brought here, I would have been killed or something bad would have happened to me' (144–5). Kofi also said: 'Church activities have helped me a lot; I was Methodist before my sentence and did not attend church regularly but now I do' (145).

During church services, pastors have often pledged to sponsor the education of youngsters upon discharge from correction centres. Other youngsters upon discharge have moved to reside with pastors. Thus, churches and pastors also somehow assume some parental role for youngsters. In discussions that follow, I explain how youngsters and staff appropriate religious observances for their own interests.

Appropriation of institutional forms of prayer and worship by staff at the SCC

I now discuss the appropriation of formal religious observances by staff to meet their own spiritual needs. In other words, the institution, in a bid to allay certain fears and superstitions, adapts or re-reshapes established forms of prayer and worship, in ways that may be different from or appear to run counter to the institutional established objectives and methods.

Whereas at the SCC, religious observances keep a formal appearance and are structured along traditional approaches of hymn singing, Bible reading, and prayer at definite times, sometimes, such observances take other forms. For instance, services sometimes feature clapping, dancing, unstructured movements, and episodic happenings of people falling in trance during the course of prayer or the service. In the process of such occurrences, pastors, staff, and youngsters seek to construct their various spiritual meanings. Such appropriated forms of religious observances or what I term 'Deliverance prayer sessions' have their own aftermaths, which sometimes are not in keeping with institutional expectations.

One Friday morning, the OIC said at a staff meeting that she had decided to cancel an intended visit of a group of pastors as the cost of hosting the pastors could not be borne by the institution. She however added: 'You are however free to make your own contributions and invite the said pastors.' After the service I met one of the officers for further clarification. She said:

> We had held a successful prayer session where there were various revelations by a group of pastors and we were considering holding a second prayer session. The institution bore the cost for the first prayer service. The centre's budget is however limited and so it cannot sponsor the second one and this is what the OIC raised. (146)

The officer explained that some pastors who were invited for a church programme in the past said, while they prayed, they saw coffins, an indication (according to the pastors) that some officers were likely to die in the near future. The pastors had predicted that about five officers would die and in fact three had actually died and so they all became very fearful as they did not know who was to be the next. Officers were actually thrown into some sort of confusion and so they decided to invite the pastors to pray so as to avert any occurrence of death or misfortune. The OIC did seem to be in agreement with the arrangement.

Deliverance prayer sessions also target youngsters as beneficiaries. I spoke with the chaplain briefly one morning when I saw some staff praying and carrying out an exorcism exercise, commonly termed deliverance. He said: 'Most of the boys come to the institution with charms and amulets and these things bother them spiritually and sometimes the boys request prayer themselves' (146).

This discussion was further advanced later, with the chaplain:

> Boys resort to spiritual powers and sometimes these powers manifest during the service and so the boys are brought to my office for prayer.

> Some come willingly for deliverance and for those who manifest at the church by suddenly falling to the ground at the church; we assist them, there and then. They manifest all sorts of spirits including witchcraft spirits. Once, one of the boys said to me that he could see through me when he closed his eyes. The OIC encouraged prayers for the boys and invited pastors from outside to assist, there were times she attended the prayers herself. (146)

Religious activities primarily seek to perform a key function of bringing about change and correction in youngsters, an objective that correctional centres seek to fulfil through regular conduct of religious services, counselling sessions, and other activities. However, in the process of pursuing this end, this objective is sidetracked. These appropriated forms of religious activities sometimes pose financial constraints on the institutional budget and also evoke thoughts of death as well as spiritual manifestations coupled with feelings of fear and anxiety. Whereas appropriating institutional goals in correctional centres tends to run counter to institutional norms, staff and management do not oppose such appropriated forms given that they yield some benefits to the institution.

Female youngsters at the JCC sidetrack from institutional religious services

In the following section, I explore how female juveniles at the JCC disengage from religious services, often choosing not to participate meaningfully in these institutional ceremonies. While such services are designed to foster moral reform and personal transformation, girls, like their male counterparts who show limited interest in formal education, frequently sidetrack from these efforts.

Although the girls are punctual and appear appreciative of the food and gifts provided by faith-based organizations, their actual engagement during church services remains minimal. They typically remain silent throughout, refraining from answering questions posed by pastors, much to the latter's frustration. These observations stem from Sunday morning services held prior to breakfast, where pastors often begin with a recap of the previous week's sermon. Yet, most girls remain unresponsive.

Preachers at the JCC often operate under the assumption that the juveniles are inherently deviant and in need of reform. However, as discussed in earlier chapters, children in conflict with the law conceptualize change differently. Many view their parents and the state, not themselves, as the entities requiring transformation. This inversion of responsibility frequently leads to resistance or disengagement from reform-oriented activities.

During one Sunday service, the pastor welcomed Esenam, a newly committed girl, and asked her to publicly recount the circumstances of her committal. Seated behind the girls, I observed their surprised expressions, suggesting that such a question was unexpected and perhaps inappropriate. Through ongoing interactions, I had come to understand that juveniles generally resent discussions centred on their offences. Attempts to shift focus away from systemic neglect and towards personal culpability often provoke anger.

Esenam responded with a giggle. When the pastor asked the group to summarize the previous week's sermon, they again remained silent. He threatened punishment, but the girls simply giggled. After the service, he confided in me: 'I've conducted church services for the girls for ten years, but I've seen little change' (149).

On another Sunday, following a similar silence, the pastor remarked: 'You girls are lucky to be here, you receive many things free of charge, so make good use of your time.' The girls giggled again, subtly signalling their disagreement. He repeated that they were fortunate to be fed three times a day, prompting another round of giggles. Yaa, the group captain, interjected: 'If only the food tasted better.' She added, 'The government benefits from us, we serve the government.' When asked what kind of service they provided, she replied, 'We scrub gutters and sweep madam's office.' Yaa continued: 'The government doesn't care for us. Let us go home! I don't pay for anything at home either, I get everything for free and I have more freedom' (149–50). The pastor then asked if they missed home and wanted to see their mothers. Yaa retorted, 'We would never go' (150). The other girls laughed and giggled throughout, while the pastor appeared visibly confused.

To the girls, the state benefits from their labour and therefore bears the responsibility of ensuring decent conditions during their committal. If it fails to do so, they believe it should release them.

A similar disconnect emerged during another Sunday service. After his sermon, the pastor invited questions, but the girls remained silent. He began calling on them individually. At one point, he said, 'I know what brought all of you here,' and directed a question to Afua. She remained silent. He urged her to speak, referencing her childbirth, her escape, and subsequent return. Suddenly, Afua burst out: 'I did not do anything' (150). Her anger was palpable, she sat with her hands firmly on her waist, her body tense. The pastor looked visibly surprised.

Although the girls' regular attendance might suggest that they find value in these services, their responses reveal otherwise. Their silence and occasional retorts signal not only resistance to the pastor's assumptions but also discomfort with the intrusion into their personal lives. As one girl confided to me after a service, the pastor had crossed into their private sphere. While he appeared to lead the service, the girls exercised their own subtle forms of control, deploying silence and non-participation as tools of resistance.

Unlike services at the SCC, where officers are present, those at the JCC are largely unattended by staff (save for the occasional caretaker). As a result, staff remain unaware of the girls' actual levels of interest and engagement.

In the next section, I turn from religious and educational provisions to examine how juveniles deliberately disengage and sidetrack from conversations with staff and visiting professionals, opting instead for their own appropriated forms of interaction.

Reform claims and sidetracked conversations

Youngsters sometimes consciously or unconsciously appropriate institutional rhetoric to present themselves as 'changed or reformed'. At other times, they divert or sidetrack from institutional interrogations to create space for their own narratives. This section begins by examining how youngsters appropriate the language and expressions of staff and professionals to align with institutional expectations or secure favour. The chaplain speaks about religion's role in effecting change:

> Many of the boys have engaged in unacceptable behavior for so long and it is our duty to encourage them to worship God so they can reform from their bad ways. This is our main preoccupation. It is difficult bringing about change and that is why we permit churches to complement our work. (153)

Youngsters such as Kofi also accord importance to change:

> On the whole I think I have really changed. I am glad I came here, if I had not, maybe something more terrible could have happened to me. When I watch what people suffer as a consequence of bad behavior, it scares me and I do not want to be part of that. Sometimes when I watch TV and see people being killed for committing crimes I get really scared. If I was spoken to when I was young, I would not have gotten myself into this. (153)

Although the kind of transformation Kofi describes can indeed be authentic, such transformation is often short-lived. At times, youngsters adopt the institutional language of change primarily to secure certain benefits or rewards rather than to reflect genuine change.

Just as juvenile and young offenders appropriate educational and religious programmes to construct meaning and belonging, they also divert or sidetrack from institutional interrogations to create space for their own narratives. Whether through silence, tale telling or emotional displays, youngsters demonstrate that they are not passive recipients of institutional interrogation or reforms.

In daily everyday life in correctional centres, one frequently observes situations where staff question young people about certain events, a practice I term interrogative encounters. By remaining silent, providing mechanical responses, resorting to tale telling or exhibiting open resistance, young offenders sometimes are able to deliberately divert or sidetrack from the focus of the conversation, so as to conceal information. A direct question such as: 'What is your name?' is likely to attract a series of responses such as 'My name is Kweku, I am 15 years old, I come from Obuasi, my offence is stealing.' By providing additional responses, youngsters situate themselves in positions of control, where they determine what direction a conversation should follow.

Other times, youngsters employ tale telling and dialogue with themselves (one poses a question and provides answers to the question himself or herself) and by so doing keeps the enquirer or interrogator partly out of the conversation, and rather place themselves on the centre stage of the encounter. An officer questioned a young offender as to the cause of a small fresh cut on his forehead and he responded dialoguing his way through a long narration (interspersed with further questions from the officer) that a mango fruit fell and hit him, though he had then come direct from the dormitory and not from the farm. Later, another youngster confided to me that the injury was likely the result of peer punishment inside the dormitory for stealing (see Chapter 6, section Supernatural practices and culprit identification).

While at the Hair Salon with the girls one afternoon, one of the female youngsters, namely Akua, entered, crying and looking gloomy. A female officer questioned why she was not participating in the lessons that afternoon and Akua responded that she was unwell. There was a long exchange of questions and responses with the young girl sometimes switching from tears to laughter with interjections from some of the other girls. Eventually the young girl seemed to have won the encounter with the officer and went back to the dormitory. Days later, having closed from a morning service and chatting with Akua and another girl on their way to the dining room, I asked Akua about her health condition: '[Chortled] I am fine. The last time I feigned it; there was almost nothing to do in the class and it was too boring' (152).

These interrogative encounters are characterized by poses such as begging, crying, and at the same time drawing on the support of other inmates as was depicted in Akua's encounter with the officer. In most cases, such bargaining exchanges are usually a means to fulfilling some material or non-material need, such as skipping lessons to afford some sleep, escaping punishment, or simply for the fun of it.

In conversations with professionals such as human rights officers, clinical psychologists, social workers, NGO staff, youngsters similarly make an attempt to conceal certain information. On one occasion I was with some girls in the hall where they usually sit while a clinical psychologist held one-to-one meetings with other youngsters in the office. The girls looked happy and were chatty, particularly Afua and Yaa. Afua, who had returned from meeting the psychologist, commented: 'This white lady is very troublesome, she continued to ask us what bothers us even when we continually say to her that we did not have any problems and that we were just fine [There were giggles from the others]' (153).

I noticed that, whereas staff, researchers and other professionals are very eager for information from youngsters, the latter are just as eager to withhold information unless they realize this is in their interest.

Final thoughts

Conceptually, the foregoing underscore the relational nature of reform. Whereas correctional centres frame questioning as a pathway to ascertain behavioural correction, youngsters reshape and appropriate such interactions for self-expression, or alignment with institutional discourses.

Centrally, this chapter emphasizes that youngsters are not passive recipients of educational and religious instruction, knowledge or reform; they actively sidetrack from and appropriate interventions that align with their realities. William's case demonstrates that effective education requires attentiveness to learners' micro-behaviours, lived contexts, and shared experiences. It also shows that institutional goals can be achieved more meaningfully when teaching methods are flexible, interactive, and rooted in the learners' worlds. When pedagogy ignores these realities, disengagement follows.

The case of William, alongside the broader framework of convict criminology, highlights the need to engage inmate teachers and peer instructors not only during custody but also after their release. These individuals embody a unique blend of lived experience, contextual pedagogy, and practical innovation. They can contribute innovatively to rehabilitation and correction efforts by promoting relatability, coaching, and mentoring as they tend to connect better with juveniles than staff and professionals. Former inmates could in turn be supported through scholarship programmes that link them to higher education, thereby echoing convict criminology's model (Ross and Richards, 2003, Jones et al., 2009, Earle, 2016, 2018, 2019, 2020, Richards et al., 2018, Davies and Earle, 2020) of contributing to a vibrant criminological research culture as is the case in the United States, United Kingdom, and other countries.

Conclusion

This chapter has examined the various ways in which youngsters subtly sidetrack from institutional programmes, particularly formal education and religious services designed to promote correction and reformation. These forms of sidetracking could serve as tacit expressions that either signal youngsters' agency or a disconnect between youngsters and agents of reform.

Most children in conflict with the law have experienced prolonged periods of school absence prior to committal, making adherence to daily formal education programmes a significant challenge. While educational attainment holds symbolic value and is often associated with social status, in practice, youngsters show limited engagement with structured lessons, preferring instead to pursue their own appropriated learning strategies, which they often find more relevant and effective. William's appropriated approach, though unconventional and often described as crude, produced remarkable results. When pedagogical approaches fail to consider the lived contexts of youngsters before and during incarceration, it may adversely impact the corrective rationale behind institutional education, despite its centrality to reform efforts.

Relatedly, although young inmates tend to attend services punctually and consistently, giving the appearance of active participation, their engagement often reflects personalized appropriations of these practices. They develop techniques for disengaging or 'switching off' during services, signalling a potential disconnect between inmates and those delivering religious instruction, including pastors and other agents of moral guidance.

Largely, youngsters' understandings of education, reform, and related constructs suggest that, rather than conforming to formally prescribed goals, children in conflict with the law often gravitate toward appropriated, locally constructed alternatives that reflect their lived experiences and aspirations.

9

Follow-Up Visits and Concluding Reflections

Introduction

This concluding chapter begins by highlighting the limited progress achieved over the past decade, drawing on follow-up visits. Many of the challenges identified during the initial assessment remain unresolved, even though Ghana's local, regional, and international legal frameworks for protecting incarcerated juveniles and young offenders are relatively strong. While some gains, particularly in healthcare provision, have been observed, the broader picture, as outlined in the following section, reveals that overall progress has been minimal.

The chapter then turns to closing reflections on recurring themes throughout the book, especially the persistent and troubling pattern of neglect by both parents and the state, as well as the everyday relational and social life in correctional centres, which is inherently complex.

I conclude with some recommendations, centrally, to genuinely respect children in conflict with the law, recognizing them as full human beings and rightful rights holders, capable of actively contributing to decisions and actions that affect their lives.

Follow-up visits: limited change over the past decade

Across the visits (Ayete-Nyampong, 2013a, 2019, 2023), one recurring theme has been the absence of consistent parental and family support. Girls at the JCC generally experienced greater parental involvement compared to boys at the SCC. Follow-up assessments revealed that SCC management made deliberate efforts to encourage visits from parents and guardians. Yet, as in 2009, interviews during subsequent visits indicated that most male juveniles had minimal family contact either before arrest or during committal. In fact, nearly half of the parents were unaware that their sons had been arrested and committed, making it difficult for police to reach them during trial proceedings. Even among those who did know, visits remained infrequent. Some boys went through their entire three-year committal without a single parental visit, and this disconnection often persisted after release. In one striking 2019 case, an officer escorted a boy home upon discharge, only to find his parents away at the farm. When approached, the father pointed a gun at his son, declaring that he was better off without him and refusing to take him back. Because the SCC is the country's only senior correctional facility, children are admitted from across all regions, requiring families to travel long distances to visit. Staff emphasized the urgent need for additional SCCs nationwide, particularly for female juveniles, who currently lack such facilities.

Adjustment and observation period

Juveniles continued to undergo an observation phase intended for counselling and adaptation to their new environment. As in 2009, this period was difficult and often traumatic, with youngsters confined for long hours and rarely engaged in educational or vocational training. Ethnographic evidence showed that most escape attempts occurred during this stage.

Pre-committal detention

Both boys and girls were still held in police cells before committal, though typically for shorter durations. Follow-up visits in 2019 and 2023 revealed that, in few instances, some boys remained on remand for over a year, though conditions had slightly improved.

Juveniles described an informal economy within police cells, similar to findings in 2009. They paid 'cell fees' to leaders, who sometimes used the funds to buy food when relatives failed to visit or to purchase cleaning supplies. Adult cells, which also sometimes held juvenile suspects, remained overcrowded, forcing detainees to sleep in rows, and the heat was often unbearable.

Educational opportunities

The SCC continued to provide both formal and non-formal education, alongside vocational and technical training certified by NVTI exams. As in 2009, most juveniles preferred non-formal programmes and were less interested in formal educational programmes. At the JCC, the Head oversaw a vocational school for non-offending girls, offering skills such as hairdressing, catering, and dressmaking. JCC girls were sometimes allowed to join these classes informally, fostering interaction with non-offenders. However, by 2023, participation was barred after instances of collusion to escape. For more than a decade, girls have been denied benefiting from nationally certified and standardized education, which constitutes gender-based discrimination against them.

Health

A notable improvement was in healthcare provision. By 2023, most SCC inmates were registered under the National Health Insurance Scheme (NHIS). During one visit, 157 inmates received renewals, replacements, or new NHIS cards. The SCC also had an infirmary staffed by a doctor and seven nurses. At the JCC, all but one girl were registered under NHIS.

Informal hierarchies and governance

During follow-up visits, leading questions revealed details about informal governance, hierarchies, and economies as was the case during the initial visit. At the SCC, inmate hierarchies included captains, assistant captains, senior men, and bathroom commanders. Initiation rituals persisted, such as *Abodwe Down*, including new ones such as *Boster no Good* and *Kangaroo.* No information on such informal practices was obtained at the JCC during follow-up visits.

Reintegration into society

Although reintegration of young offenders fell outside the formal remit of my research, it surfaced repeatedly during fieldwork as a matter of acute concern. The lack of relevant skills acquisition hampers children's educational progress and limits their entry into the labour market. The absence of familial support exacerbates these challenges, leaving many children without a home to return to. As a result, they become susceptible to precarious post-release trajectories including recidivism or entanglement with armed groups, extremist factions, or other high-risk networks. According to staff at the SCC, they did not have the mandate to follow up on youngsters following their discharge. Interviews at the JCC, revealed that resource constraints had also contributed to the Social Welfare Department not being able to conduct effective follow up.

Some NGOs such as the Child Research and Resource Centre (CRRECENT) provided some support to male youngsters following their discharge. There was the consideration by CRRECENT to establish a half-way home, where discharged male inmates with disadvantaged backgrounds could further be supported to advance their skills.

Overall, progress in the past decade has been modest, though the follow-up visits yielded useful insights. This demonstrates that practitioners, without the advantage of extended fieldwork, can still draw meaningful observations from such engagements.

Drawing on earlier chapters and preceding discussions, the ethnographic evidence presented here exposes a significant disconnect between institutional narratives and the lived realities of young people. Such misalignment has the potential to undermine interventions and reform initiatives. When reforms consistently fail to deliver on their intended goals, it becomes necessary to question whether these centres can truly be regarded as spaces of 'reform' and 'correction'. The reflections that follow, grounded in the discussions throughout this book, are intended to foster deeper engagement among scholars, practitioners, and policymakers, encouraging a critical re-examination of prevailing assumptions and practices within juvenile justice systems.

Beyond the rhetoric of reform: reflections

The notion of 'reform' has long been central to the discourse surrounding juvenile justice, yet the realities within correctional centres often reveal a disjuncture between rhetoric and lived experience. By drawing on ethnographic evidence and insights from earlier chapters, these reflections aim to provoke deeper engagement among scholars, practitioners, and policymakers, urging a reconsideration of entrenched assumptions and practices that continue to shape juvenile justice systems.

Implementing laws without context

Current laws and reforms often assume that children come from stable family structures (Ayete-Nyampong, 2024, 2025a). This assumption is misaligned with the realities of juveniles in this study, many of whom face neglect. Implementing legislation concerning children risks falling short when children's perspectives and lived experiences are excluded.

Recognizing children's voices – particularly those of boys – and their need for support

Discussions in this book do not intend to glorify harmful behavior, but it is important to recognize the different meanings children attach to their words and actions. For example, when boys describe 'illicit' economic activities as a way to cope or find social fulfilment, they may be expressing genuine needs that should not be dismissed. Similarly, statements from youngsters such as they were very bad and wicked; they would jail their parents and the police carried deeper meanings about their experiences and frustrations. If correctional measures ignore these meanings, they risk being disconnected from the realities children face. The anger voiced by boys, directed at fathers, police, and other authority figures, shows that their grievances are systemic, not just personal. With defilement remaining the most common offence at the SCC for over a decade, it appears that some boys are already turning harm, vengeance, and anger into weapons against neglect and betrayal. This makes it critical to support the boy child in his developmental journey. Early interventions that provide emotional guidance, mentorship, and safe spaces for self-expression can help redirect anger into constructive forms of agency, fostering healthier pathways into adulthood.

Oversimplifying childhood contexts

Prevailing literature in Ghana tends to reduce children's engagement in street life, labour, or migration to mere survival or criminality. Yet these contexts also hold social, spiritual, and relational meaning. Viewing them only through economic or criminal lenses obscures the multiple realities shaping children's lives.

The role of grandparents

Youngsters' narratives point to the caregiving role assumed by grandparents, most often grandmothers, who sometimes also tend to abuse them. This is a key issue and yet has been underexplored. Despite facing vulnerability, neglect, and social isolation (Van der Geest, 2002, 2008, 2016), and probably lacking resources, these grandparents may grow frustrated, occasionally directing anger towards the children in their care. With Ghana's extended family structures weakening, little has been done to address this paradox.

Disjunctures between narratives

Justice systems often label youth as delinquent, while many young people see themselves as victims of adult irresponsibility and neglect. This clash highlights the limitations of singular conceptions of youth in conflict with the law.

Interconnected life worlds

Custodial and post-custodial experiences are not separate from pre-confinement realities. Young offenders carry interconnected social experiences that shape their encounters within correctional institutions.

Peer learning and contextual pedagogies

Observations show that formal lessons often lack interaction and relevance, leaving students passive and uninterested. In contrast, appropriated peer-led lessons rooted in pre-committal and everyday custodial experiences such as those conducted by inmate teachers generate strong engagement, discipline, and rapid literacy gains (see Chapter 8). Education in correctional centres must move beyond lecture-based methods that disengage learners despite their pursuit of certificates.

Harnessing peer instructors for juvenile justice reform

The case of William, viewed alongside the broader framework of convict criminology (Ross and Richards, 2003, Jones et al., 2009, Earle, 2016, 2018, 2019, 2020, Richards et al., 2018, Davies and Earle, 2020), underscores the importance of engaging inmate teachers and peer instructors not only during custody but also after their release. These individuals embody a distinctive blend of lived experience, contextual pedagogy, and practical innovation. Their relatability allows them to connect with juveniles more effectively than many staff or professionals, offering mentorship, coaching, and guidance that resonates with young offenders. By supporting former inmates through scholarship programmes and linking them to higher education, their contributions can be formalized and expanded. This approach echoes the model of convict criminology where personal experience of imprisonment is combined with academic research to enrich criminological practice. As demonstrated in the United States, United Kingdom and elsewhere, such integration fosters a vibrant research culture and opens new pathways for innovative juvenile justice reforms.

Permeability and fluidity of physical, social, and virtual boundaries

Confinement, as Goffman observes, may appear rigid and isolated, yet its boundaries are in fact porous (Martin and Jefferson, 2019, Cunha, 2020, Weegels et al., 2020, Ellis, 2021) and fluid. Within correctional life, the social underlife, shaped by peer hierarchies, friendships, and rivalries, is continually negotiated and redefined, rendering social boundaries unstable, fluid, and porous. Access to television and the illicit use of cell phones connect young people to wider networks of entertainment, fashion, and criminal activity, as well as to virtual communities. At the same time, external interactions, such as visits from professionals, escapes, and other points of contact with free society, link inmates directly to the outside world. Correctional spaces, therefore, are not sealed environments but are embedded within broader physical, social, and virtual networks, which in turn penetrate and reshape the confines of incarceration.

Multiple realities of confinement

Detention life is complex and contradictory, marked by performances, negotiations, and strategies that defy simplistic categorization. Reforms that rely solely on singular realities risk overlooking these differentiated realities.

The logic of keeping appearances

Correctional institutions often operate under a performative logic, appearing to maintain control even when disciplinary power falters. Staff acknowledge their inability to enforce total compliance, yet the institution sustains the illusion of producing 'reformed' individuals. This performativity risks stifling innovation and reflection, raising questions about the true purpose of correctional spaces.

Concluding discussion

The relevance of the discussions in this book lies in their ability to complement conventional legalistic framings. By shedding light on the diverse ways children in conflict with the law and related actors respond to seemingly homogenous and constraining conditions, I portray these individuals not as passive subjects of confinement but as active participants in shaping their lived realities and actions concerning them. While my findings contribute to debates on structure and agency, particularly regarding confined youth as social actors, I move beyond the simplistic recognition of youngsters as 'bad' actors to demonstrate the practical ways they negotiate everyday boundaries and contribute to detention life. These coping strategies must not be overlooked in policy and programmatic interventions. Yet it is equally important to acknowledge that agentic youngsters remain firmly within the grip of confinement. Their powerlessness underscores the need to value, listen to, and provide appropriate support and protection.

From a rights-based perspective, respecting children as rights holders requires that their opinions be taken seriously, regardless of whether these views align with adult expectations, normative standards, or established principles. Although the narratives and lived experiences of children in conflict with the law may not directly reflect conventional understandings of human rights, my ethnographic evidence shows that they assert claims to human rights in differentiated ways. They articulate rights to be heard, to play, to survival and development, to education, to decision-making, and to participation.

Conceptual insights drawn from everyday correctional life – such as mortification procedures, underlife, public and hidden transcripts, sidetracking, and appropriation – constitute the mechanisms that sustain the confinement system and shape its outward appearance. Reform efforts that ignore these practical contexts risk remaining superficial. Overlooking such realities may also cause laws and policies to miss the significance of youngsters' agency, including inmate leadership, governance, peer teaching, and educational practices.

As earlier discussed, interventions that prioritize expanding prison infrastructure, such as building additional correctional facilities as staff of these centres recommend, may inadvertently attract more occupants and entrench cultures of criminality rather than mitigate them. Greater priority should be given to preventative strategies – strengthening parental and family bonds, while also fostering stronger collaborations with industry to ensure that discharged youngsters are effectively absorbed into the labour market during their transition.

Methodologically, this book contributes to the expanding scholarship on confinement ethnography in Africa. My initial fieldwork, conducted over a decade ago, remains the only long-term ethnographic engagement within juvenile and youth correctional centres in Ghana, underscoring its continued relevance. The ethnographic lens employed here highlights the importance of African prison researchers sharing their narratives, thereby enriching and complementing conventional accounts of carceral institutions across the continent.

The insights offered here hold value for disciplines such as anthropology, sociology, law, social work, criminology, and human rights. I advocate for policy interventions, future research, and scholarly debates to be grounded in these often, overlooked perspectives of confinement life.

This book is especially timely given Ghana's ratification of the Optional Protocol to the Convention Against Torture (OPCAT) and its ongoing efforts to establish a National Preventive Mechanism (NPM). As the country moves towards operationalizing the NPM, this book contributes to the emerging discourse by advocating for the integration of complementary methodologies, that foreground practical, insider, and contextually grounded perspectives. These approaches provide critical insights that can enrich and inform preventive frameworks beyond formal legal and institutional mechanisms.

Recommendations

My book emphasizes that dominant models of juvenile correction often overlook the lived experiences of detainees. With rising youth incarceration, I advocate for urgent, radical rethinking. Practitioners and policymakers must engage with confinement realities and adjust theory and practice accordingly. By re-centring the views and lived experiences of children rather than committing predominantly to poor material conditions and underperforming institutions in terms of human rights compliance, I offer an ethnographically rich contribution to the scholarship on incarcerated juvenile and young offenders and everyday correctional practice.

My book emphasizes the urgent need for human rights professionals to engage with children and vulnerable individuals as full human beings and rightful holders of rights. Building trust and gaining acceptance from those whose rights are at stake is essential for understanding their lived realities and ensuring that interventions are meaningful rather than imposed. Genuine respect requires not only advocacy but also reflection and reflexivity – professionals must continually examine their own biases and assumptions.

In response to the parenting deficiencies that have surfaced strongly in this book, I call for multi- and intergenerational strategies that strengthen intergenerational care, support, and connection within families and communities. Child Panels, which currently function primarily as referral mechanisms, could be repurposed to provide practical diversionary alternatives, particularly for children whose families are absent during legal proceedings. Early intervention is equally critical, especially through policies that support working parents – both formally and informally employed – by expanding access to high-quality childcare services.

Ethnographic evidence establishes that theft has remained the most prevalent offence among male youth, not only in the past decade but tracing back to the colonial era, (see Chapter 1) underscoring the urgent need to address youth development, employment, and survival challenges. Since 2009, defilement has also emerged as the second most prevalent offence among children in conflict with the law, revealing deep systemic issues around youth and sexuality. Importantly, this pattern cannot be understood solely as acts of perpetration as boys who commit sexual offences may have themselves endured histories of abuse, neglect, or exploitation. Also, boys may already be acting out their anger and vengeance against society, thus creating cycles in which harm suffered becomes harm inflicted. This troubling dynamic underscores the need to appreciate the views and lived experiences of male offenders, while acknowledging the dual reality of victimhood and perpetration. Urgent societal response is required as prolonged abuse threatens children's rights to life, liberty, and security, while exposing them to long-term emotional, physical, and health risks. Attention must also be directed to the initial phase of confinement in correctional centres. Many children arrive already traumatized by their upbringing and pre-custodial experiences, making this period a crucial opportunity to begin meaningful rehabilitation.

Persistent gender disparities in educational opportunities for girls in correctional centres must be addressed without delay, and rehabilitation and reintegration programmes for discharged youth require immediate review to ensure they are adequately prepared for life beyond confinement. Further research into informal governance structures, hierarchies, and economies within correctional centres such as SCC and JCC is also necessary. These systems, if properly harnessed, could be transformed into platforms for peer mediation, non-violent communication, and grassroots leadership training.

This book serves as a wake-up call to focus on children and youth in difficult and vulnerable circumstances. Empirical evidence suggests that many are ill-prepared for the labour market upon release, leaving them prone to retaliation, reoffending, long-term incarceration, or recruitment by radical and extremist groups. In the context of rising global instability, the need to prioritize prevention, rehabilitation, and intergenerational support has never been more pressing.

Correctional sites are increasingly assuming geopolitical significance in a world where boundaries between states, non-state actors, militias, mercenaries, extremist networks, and terrorist organizations are fluid and deeply entangled. In Ghana, the rising number of young people in detention, coupled with the suppressed anger, desire for retaliation, and resentment among juveniles in correctional facilities, alongside the recent escalation of physical and sexual violence among youth in broader society, particularly within Senior High Schools[1] (see Chapter 8), underscores the urgent need for collective action. Society must prioritize the healthy development of children, foster non-violent behaviour, and confront the wider challenges of youth incarceration and societal security.

Notes

Chapter 1

1 Names of youngsters and staff in this book are pseudonyms and not actual names.

2 An extract from a UN report on youth participation in the implementation of the SDGs (www.un.org/ohrlls/news/young-people%E2%80%99s-potential-key-africa%E2%80%99s-sustainable-development).

3 According to Ghana Statistical Service, Ghana has a young age structure, with approximately 57 per cent of the population under the age of 25 (www.statsghana.gov.gh/ghfactsheet.php). Also according to UNFPA, Ghana has 38.2 per cent youthful population, which translates to 12 million youth (https://ghana.unfpa.org/en/news/world-population-day-2024).

4 Interview with the Deputy Director of Prisons during the second follow-up fieldwork in 2023 points to a substantial proportion of youth incarcerated in Ghana's prisons.

5 By his efforts, Professor Norman Long positioned Wageningen's Development Sociology and Anthropology group within a large international network and which also attracted many PhD students from virtually all over the world to Wageningen. Although he had retired when I commenced my research, my interpretative framework benefited from the actor theoretical perspective. My research from 2008 to 2013 was under the supervision of Professor Leontine Visser and co-supervisor, Associate Professor Roy Gigengack.

6 The conference, which was held from 1 to 3 December 2010 brought together members of Global Prisons Research Network (GPRN) for the third time following the inauguration of the network in December 2009 and a panel presentation at the British Society of Criminology's Conference in July 2010. The workshop was hosted by the Netherlands Institute for the Study of Crime and Law Enforcement (NSCR), Amsterdam.

7 The revised Bill refers to *Child Justice* rather than *Juvenile Justice*. Since the Bill has not yet been passed, this book continues to use the term *Juvenile Justice* to reflect the current legal context.

8 The situation of youngsters committing petty thefts has persisted over past years through the period of my sociological research.

9 The major ordinances between 1944 and 1946 to deal with the problem of juvenile delinquency included (1) The Courts (Amendment) Ordinance (1944), (2) The Courts Ordinance 1945, (3) The Industrial Schools and Institutions Ordinance (1945), (4) The Probation of Offenders Ordinance (1944), and (5) The Courts (Amendment) Ordinance (1946).

10 These industrial homes were under the supervision of the Social Welfare Department. In the mid-1950s the Prisons Service assumed oversight of the Borstal home.

11 See www.crimeandjustice.org.uk/publications/cjm/article/keeping-tough-appearances-age-criminal-responsibility; and a related recent guidance (General Comment No. 24,

from 2019), the Committee strongly recommends that all countries raise the minimum age of criminal responsibility to at least 14 years.

12 Such as the preparation of Social Enquiry Reports; these are detailed reports prepared by a social worker based on investigations conducted with respect to the family, school, and general environment in which the juvenile offender resides and other factors that must have influenced the committal of crime. See Act 653 of 2003, section 24.

13 These two laws have been reviewed but the revised bills have since 2023 not been passed.

14 The Vienna Guidelines, 1997. See www.ohchr.org/en/instruments-mechanisms/instruments/guidelines-action-children-criminal-justice-system.

15 General Comment No 24 (2019). See www.ohchr.org/en/documents/general-comments-and-recommendations/general-comment-no-24-2019-childrens-rights-child.

16 It is hoped that the current review of the Juvenile Justice Act will affect the necessary changes to ensure that juveniles are kept separately from young people. Holding children in the same facility with young people was discussed at a consultation in 2019 on the review of the Juvenile Justice Act from 2 to 6 July 2019 at Volta Serene Hotel, Ho.

17 The CHRAJ however sought to ensure that juveniles were not kept in adult prisons or police cells. This was difficult to achieve as youngsters usually inflated their ages to spend shorter periods in adult prisons as discussed in this book. In CHRAJ's latest monitoring visit, juveniles were still found in adult prisons.

18 Consultative meetings such as the National Legislative Consultative workshop on the Children's Act, the Juvenile Justice Act, and the Human Trafficking Act, 3–5 July 2017 at the Volta Serene Hotel, Ho; National Legislative Consultative Meeting on the Review of the Children's Act on 31 October 2017 at the Golden Tulip Hotel; Justice for Children's Operational Plan Validation Workshop, La Palm Royal Beach Hotel, 5–6 April 2017; Justice for Children Mini Consultative Meeting, Chances Hotel, Ho. 13 February 2017; Justice for Children National Consultative Workshop, Chances Hotel, Ho 13 January 2017; The National Child Protection Committee meeting, Coconut Grove Hotel, 19 October 2016; The Launch of Justice for Children Policy. Accra International Conference Centre, 27 September 2016.

I was actively involved in the above consultations as well as part of a team of consultants who reviewed the Child Panel system in Ghana.

On the launch of the Justice for Children Policy and Child and Family Welfare Policies in 2016 I contributed anecdotal evidence from my ethnographic research to my employer's address, as part of the launch.

I was also part of consultations and discussions that culminated in the review of the Juvenile Justice Act and the Children's Act in Ghana, though these Bills, since the finalization of the review in 2023, have not yet been passed.

19 Also, see CHRAJ's Annual Reports from 1995 to 2021.

Chapter 2

1 Total number of staff (subordinate and superior) at the SCC is 212. This number is exclusive of prison support staff that numbers 30. The total number of subordinate staff is 202, comprising 95.3 per cent of total staff, whereas superior staff are only 10, constituting 4.71 per cent. Out of ten superior staff, only two are female. The JCC has a total of 31 staff, 4 male and 27 female. These officers serve other centres such as a remand centre for boys, a shelter for girls who have suffered various forms of abuse, and also a vocational training institute.

2 This is besides the numerous spontaneous conversational interviews and observations held daily.

3 I have employed pseudonyms for youngsters and staff throughout this book. The decision to allow the passage of time, more than a decade, before sharing the entirety of my

research also provides some protection for the identity of youngsters and staff as well as other research participants.

4 See CHRAJ's annual reports, https://chraj.gov.gh/.

5 In 2009, I conducted 95 interviews at the SCC and 90 interviews at the JCC; I also conducted 51 participant observations at the JCC and 65 participant observations at the SCC. I held 15 focus group discussions at each of the institutions. Narratives were provided mostly by male youngsters. Conversational interviews (these are interviews I held while participating in activities with the children) were virtually held daily for the two years. See Ayete-Nyampong (2013, 2015).

Chapter 3

1 Some children also endured the loss of one or both parents early in life; an area worth exploring in future research.

2 I had, before these interactions, observed Kwesi during school lessons, meal times, and while participating in various activities, and also during a focus group discussion.

3 All subsequent quotes draw on the same reference: Ayete-Nyampong, L. (2013). *Entangled Realities and Underlife of a Total Institution* (PhD Dissertation), Wageningen University, Wageningen.

4 Basic Education in Ghana comprises six years of primary education and three years of JHS Education, after which one proceeds to the SHS.

5 This conversion and subsequent ones were based on the exchange rate during the period of my initial fieldwork which was one dollar to GHS 4.00. At the time of finalizing this book in February 2026, the exchange rate was a dollar to GHS 11.04.

6 Grace's father was one of the very few parents I managed to speak with.

7 Kasapa is a telephone company in Ghana.

8 As previously noted, over the past decade, defilement has consistently ranked as the second most common offence leading to the arrest and committal of children.

9 A favourite local dish made of rice and beans.

10 Since the passage of the Juvenile Justice Act in 2003, the SCC has carried its present name. Yet, staff and young people alike still commonly refer to it as 'Borstal'. The term, originally linked to reformatory centres in the United Kingdom that sought to reform young offenders through discipline, education, and training, has over time taken on negative connotations due to its association with punishment and harsh regimes.

11 A senior officer of the social welfare department commented that committal is usually considered a last resort when all other alternatives to committal – most of which seek the involvement of the parent or relation to provide some support to the child in the community – are exhausted.

12 As earlier indicated, this conversion and subsequent ones were based on the exchange rate at the time that I was compiling my field reports, in 2012. At the time of finalizing this book in February 2026, the exchange rate was a dollar to GHS 11.04.

13 Youngsters sometimes refer to robbery acts as operations.

14 These are spiritualists and also adherents of the Islamic faith.

15 CHRAJ's reports on monitoring prisons and police cells.

16 CHRAJ's prisons monitoring reports have also documented some instances when police officers use their own money to feed suspects as there is usually no state provision for suspects.

17 See US State Report, Ghana. www.State.gov/documents/organization/160124.pdf www.internationalcure.org/Afrcontry/ghana.htm. Accessed 6 July 2012. Remand homes also house youngsters whose cases are on trial before court.

18 It is the direct responsibility for police officers to ensure that children and youngsters are conveyed to court regularly, but this is not always the case. Police usually attribute this inability to inadequacy of resources, for instance, non-availability of a vehicle to convey juvenile offenders to court.

19 See www.ghanaweb.com/GhanaHomePage/NewsArchive/5-times-Senior-High-Schools-have-recorded-violent-clashes-within-the-last-two-months-1972918; www.modernghana.com/news/1471684/gnat-condemns-assault-on-wass-teachers-after-viole.html; www.myjoyonline.com/severe-sanctions-await-culprits-in-shs-violence-clement-apaak/.

Chapter 5

1 See Chapter 3, note 3.

2 Unless otherwise stated, all the subsequent quotations draw on this reference.

3 See CHRAJ's annual reports from 1996 to 2021.

4 As a matter of policy, all staff at the JCC are female. At the SCC, most dorm wardens are female.

Chapter 6

1 Sometimes occupants of dorm six can suffer demotion when they do not comply with institutional rules, in which case such inmates may not necessarily be occupants of dormitory six prior to discharge.

2 These leaders were previously elected by inmates, but this is no longer the case. Staff are of the view that it is better to appoint captains. An instance was cited by an officer in an earlier chapter, when in the past a leader betrayed the trust of staff.

3 Sanitary facilities are cleaned regularly and yet this pervasive smell is unavoidable given that an average of 20 inmates share one lavatory and bathroom.

Chapter 7

1 According to official data during follow-up visits, an average of two escapes occurred at the SCC.

2 At the JCC, official records of female youngsters in committal over the past years (2005–09) were unavailable reportedly due to poor record-keeping and documentation. In an interview with the head and assistant (JCC, 21 June 2010), they said that no proper records were available at the time they assumed duty. I however managed to extract 22 old cases from 2005–09 from which the escape information of girls was obtained. According to these records, 12 out of 22 girls absconded while six girls completed their period of committal. No records exist for the escape history of four girls. Follow-up visits in 2019 and 2023 showed little improvement in the record keeping and documentation at the JCC. According to official data during follow-up visits, an average of one escape occurred at the JCC.

3 As was earlier indicated, a hacksaw blade commonly known by correctional centres as an *asor* blade is a small knife-like metal instrument that youngsters use to cut metal gauze and burglar proofing, in order to escape.

4 Follow-up visits indicate that this situation has virtually remained the same.

5 During the course of the fieldwork, an older youngster who was admitted with her baby related some concerns about plans to have her baby adopted. This was the period that monitors had visited from the CHRAJ and so the case was referred to the CHRAJ.

6 This is at the exchange rate during the initial visit, as stated in previous chapters. At the time of finalizing this book in February 2026, the exchange rate was a dollar to GHS 11.04.

7 www.ghanaweb.com/GhanaHomePage/NewsArchive/5-times-Senior-High-Schools-have-recorded-violent-clashes-within-the-last-two-months-1972918, Ghana Web, Tuesday, 25 February.

8 See www.modernghana.com/news/1471684/gnat-condemns-assault-on-wass-teachers-after-viole.html.

9 www.myjoyonline.com/severe-sanctions-await-culprits-in-shs-violence-clement-apaak/.

Chapter 8

1 In Ghana, the West African Examinations Council (WAEC) is responsible for several examinations. The main ones are the Basic Education Certificate Examination (BECE) for Junior High Schools and the Senior Secondary Certificate Examinations (SSCE) for Senior High Schools. The WASSCE was adopted to replace the SSCE in 2006.

2 All tertiary graduates are obliged to do a national service for a year before they can enter formal employments.

3 All pages cited in this chapter are attributed to this reference, unless otherwise indicated.

4 This is a biblical verse and so is 'spare the rod and spoil the child'. Such adages are not restricted to correctional centres only but often used in other spheres such as the home and school, where corporal punishment is administered.

5 Padre hour is a military term, according to the chaplain, for a church service.

Chapter 9

1 See www.ghanaweb.com/GhanaHomePage/NewsArchive/5-times-Senior-High-Schools-have-recorded-violent-clashes-within-the-last-two-months-1972918; www.modernghana.com/news/1471684/gnat-condemns-assault-on-wass-teachers-after-viole.html; www.myjoyonline.com/severe-sanctions-await-culprits-in-shs-violence-clement-apaak/.

References

Ababio, H. & Mawusinu, A. 2000. Trokosi, woryokwe, cultural and individual rights: a case study of women's empowerment and community rights in Ghana. Master Thesis. Saint Mary's University, Halifax, Nova Scotia.

Abbink, J. & Van Kessel, I. 2005. *Vanguards or Vandals: Youth, Politics and Conflict in Africa,* Leiden, Brill.

Abbott, L. & Scott, T. 2019. Reflections on researcher departure: closure of prison relationships in ethnographic research. *Nursing Ethics,* 26, 1424–41.

Abdullah, A., Cudjoe, E., Emery, C. R. & Frederico, M. 2020. Moving towards independent living in Ghana: narratives from young adults about their kinship care experience. *Journal of Adolescence,* 79, 148–56.

Abdullah, A., Huynh, I., Emery, C. R. & Jordan, L. P. 2022. Social norms and family child labor: a systematic literature review. *International Journal of Environmental Research and Public Health,* 19, 4082.

Abebe, T. 2019. Reconceptualising children's agency as continuum and interdependence. *Social Sciences,* 8, 81.

Abebe, T. & Ofosu-Kusi, Y. 2016. Beyond pluralizing African childhoods: introduction. *Childhood,* 23, 303–16.

Abekah-Carter, K., Boateng, A. & Dako-Gyeke, M. 2024. Pushed and pulled onto the streets: perspectives of street children in Accra, Ghana. *Children and Youth Services Review,* 159, 107514.

Abotchie, C. 1991. *Juvenile Correctional Institutions,* University of Ghana, Legon.

Abotchie, C. 1997. *Social Control in Traditional Southern Eweland of Ghana: Relevance for Modern Crime Prevention,* Ghana, Universities Press Accra.

Abrah, P. 2014. *The Transition from Juvenile Delinquency to Adulthood Criminality in Ghana; The Predisposing Factors,* Ghana, University of Ghana.

Aderinto, A. A. 2000. Social correlates and coping measures of street-children: a comparative study of street and non-street children in south-western Nigeria. *Child Abuse and Neglect,* 24, 1199–213.

Adewale, A. & Schepers, S. 2023. African pre-colonial social and political structures. *Reimaging Africa: Lifting the Veil of Ignorance,* Cham, Switzerland, Springer.

Adinkrah, M. 2011. Child witch hunts in contemporary Ghana. *Child Abuse and Neglect,* 35, 741–52.

Agozino, B. & Dastile, N. 2022. Criminology in Africa. *The Oxford Handbook of Sociology of Africa,* New York, Oxford University Press, 407–24.

Akoko, R. M. 2007. *Ask and you shall be given: Pentecostalism and economic crisis in Cameroon,* PhD, University of Leiden.

Alhassan, A.-R. K. & Ridwan, A. 2023. Identity expression – the case of 'Sakawa' boys in Ghana. *Human Arenas,* 6, 242–63.

Ame, R. 2013. Traditional religion, social structure, and children's rights in Ghana: the making of a trokosi child. *Vulnerable Children,* New York, Springer, 239–55.

Ame, R. 2018. The origins of the contemporary juvenile justice system in Ghana. *Journal of Family History,* 43, 394–408.

Ame, R. 2019. Towards a relevant and sustainable juvenile justice system in Ghana. *Journal of Global Ethics,* 15, 250–69.

Ame, R., Agbenyega, D. L. & Apt, N. A. 2011. *Confronting the Challenges,* Lanham, Rowman and Littlefield.

Ame, R., Ayete-Nyampong, L. & Gakpleazi, D. A. 2020a. Ghana's juvenile justice system: assessment of selected formal juvenile justice institutions and agencies. *Ghana Social Science Journal,* 17, 24–24.

Ame, R., Ayete-Nyampong, L. & Gakpleazi, D. A. 2020b. 'There's no functioning child panel in this region': an assessment of child panels in Ghana's juvenile justice system. *Contemporary Justice Review,* 23, 373–400.

Amenyendzie, A. 1998. The impact of reformation on young offenders. Academic Thesis, Accra, University of Ghana.

Anarfi, J. K. & Kwankye, S. O. 2005. The Cost and Benefits of Children's Independent Migration from Northern to Southern Ghana. Children and Youths in Emerging and Transforming Societies. *International Conference on Childhoods.* Oslo, Norway.

Anarfi, J. K. & Kwankye, S. O. 2009. *Independent Migration of Children in Ghana,* Accra, ISSER, University of Ghana.

Angrossino, M. 2007. *Doing Ethnographic and Observation Research,* Los Angeles, CA, Sage.

Annamma, S. A., Cabral, B., Harvey, B., Wilmot, J. M., Le, A. & Morgan, J. 2024. "When we come to your class… we feel not like we're in prison": resisting prison-school's dehumanizing and (de) socializing mechanisms through abolitionist praxis. *American Educational Research Journal,* 61, 3–47.

Aptekar, L. 1994. Street children in the developing world: a review of their condition. *Cross Cultural Research,* 28, 195–224.

Arce, A. & Long, N. (eds) 2007. *Forging a New Anthropology of Development: Common Ground and Contentious Issues,* Paris, Karthala.

Archambault, C. S., De Laat, J. & Zulu, E. M. 2012. Urban services and child migration to the slums of Nairobi. *World Development,* 40, 1854–69.

Ardayfio-Schandorf, E. & Amissah, M. 1996. Incidence of child fostering among school children in Ghana. *The Changing Family in Ghana*, 179–200.

Arowolo, D. 2010. The effects of western civilisation and culture on Africa. *Afro Asian Journal of Social Sciences,* 1, 1–13.

Arthur-Ewusie, E. 2024. The 'African concept of human rights': justifiable on grounds of cultural relativism? A particular focus on Ghana's Trokosi system: sexual slavery in Ghana. *Journal of Social Welfare and Human Rights.* doi: 10.15640/JSWHR.V10A1

Arthur, J. A. 1997. Rehabilitation of juvenile offenders in Ghana. *Journal of Offender Rehabilitation,* 24, 22–37.

Asamoah-Gyadu, J. K. 2015. Witchcraft accusations and Christianity in Africa. *International Bulletin of Missionary Research,* 39, 23–7.

Asare, S. 2009a. *The Impact of Rehabilitation on Recidivism in Ghana.* Academic Thesis. Accra, University of Ghana.

Asare, S. 2009b. Rehabilitation of juvenile offenders in Ghana: focus on the social context of delinquency. *Journal of Offender Rehabilitation,* 24, 22–37.

AUACRWC. 1990. Organization of African Unity (OAU), African Charter on the Rights and Welfare of the Child, CAB/LEG/24.9/49 (1990).

Awortwe, V., Litela Asare, J., Logoniga Gariba, S., Rakibu Mbamba, C. & Ansie, V. 2025. Witchcraft accusations and older adults: insights from family members on the struggles of well-being. *Journal of Religion, Spirituality & Aging,* 37, 167–79.

Ayete-Nyampong, L. 2010. Juvenile and young offenders in Ghana muddling their way through uncertainties of everyday life in detention. Paper presented at the Global Prisons Research Network (GPRN) Workshop *Dissecting the 'non-western' prison.* Amsterdam, the Netherlands Institute for the Study of Crime and Law Enforcement (NSCR).

Ayete-Nyampong, L. 2011. Situating CRC implementation processes in the local context of correctional institutions for children in conflict with the law in Ghana. *In:* Ame, R., Debrenna, A. & Apt, N. (eds) *Children's Rights in Ghana: Reality or Rhetoric?*, Lanham MD, Lexington Books.

Ayete-Nyampong, L. 2013a. *Entangled Realities and Underlife of a Total Institution,* PhD Thesis, Wageningen University, www.wageningenur.nl/.

Ayete-Nyampong, L. 2013b. Ethnography of confinement sites in Ghana for juvenile and young offenders. *Terrferme Conference on Confinement viewed from the prism of the social sciences: contrasting facilities, continuing approaches.* Pessac, France, Bordeaux University.

Ayete-Nyampong, L. 2015. Changing hats: transiting between practitioner and researcher roles. *In:* Drake Deborah, H., Rod, E. & Jennifer, S. (eds) *The Palgrave Handbook of Prison Ethnography*, Hampshire, Palgrave Macmillan.

Ayete-Nyampong, L. 2017a. Disjunctures: towards correction and education of young offenders in committal in Ghana. *Journal of Relational Child and Youth Care Practice*, 34, 35–47.

Ayete-Nyampong, L. 2017b. Practicalities and complexities surrounding escape occurrences in Ghana's correctional centers for children in conflict with the law. *International Journal of Research in Sociology and Anthropology*, 3, 1–7.

Ayete-Nyampong, L. 2019. Fieldnotes on a First Follow-up Visit to Correctional Centres for Juvenile and Young Offenders in Accra.

Ayete-Nyampong, L. 2023. Fieldnotes on a Second Follow-up Visit to Correctional Centres for Juvenile and Young Offenders in Accra.

Ayete-Nyampong, L. 2024. Vulnerable children and youth in conflict with the law in Ghana. *Conference on "Ghana's Youth Bulge: An Opportunity and a Challenge for Nation Building – Youth, and Security Concerns" organized by Child Research and Resource Centre (CRRECENT) on the 5th of September 2024*. Accra, Ghana.

Ayete-Nyampong, L. 2025a. Ghana's Juvenile Justice Act in practice for children in conflict with the law in the last decade. *E-journal of the International Child and Youth Care Network (CYC-Net), June 2025*, 51–82.

Ayete-Nyampong, L. 2025b. Trokosi and child abuse: the role of older adults as perpetrators. *African Journal of Ageing Studies (Manuscript in Print)*.

Ayete-Nyampong, L., Fleku, M. & Annankra, R. 2025. CHRAJ'S efforts in past years to promote and protect the rights of persons banished to witch camps in Ghana. *African Journal of Ageing Studies (Manuscript in Print)*.

Baffour, F. D., Francis, A. P., Chong, M. D., Harris, N. & Baffour, P. D. 2021. Perpetrators at first, victims at last: exploring the consequences of stigmatization on ex-convicts' mental well-being. *Criminal Justice Review*, 46, 304–25.

Bah, I. 2025. Sub-Saharan Africa's Progress towards the Sustainable Development Goals (SDGs). Starred paper, M.S. in Applied Economics, Saint Cloud State University.

Bandyopadhyay, M. 2007. Reform and everyday practice: some issues of prison governance. *Contributions to Indian Sociology*, 41, 387–416.

Bandyopadhyay, M. 2010. What chaos can offer method: ethnography in prisons. *"Dissecting the 'non-western' prison." Global Prisons Research Network (GPRN) Workshop, hosted by Netherlands Institute for the Study of Crime and Law Enforcement (NSCR)*. Amsterdam.

Bandyopadhyay, M. & Jefferson, A. M. 2010. Entangled interactions: prisoner-staff relations in India and Sierra Leone. *"Dissecting the 'non-western' prison." Global Prisons Research Network (GPRN) Workshop, hosted by Netherlands Institute for the Study of Crime and Law Enforcement (NSCR)*. Amsterdam.

Bauer, B. L. 2017. Cultural foundations for fear of witchcraft in Africa. *Journal of Adventist Mission Studies*, 13, 1–12.

Becker, H. S. (ed) 2001. *The Epistemology of Qualitative Research,* Prospect Heights IL, Waveland.

Begho, T. & Daubry, T. P. 2025. A review of the pathway to reducing youth unemployment in Sub Saharan Africa through agriculture and agribusiness. *Discover Global Society,* 3, 81.

Bentum, H. & Manful, E. 2022. Reunification in informal foster care child placement: examining the different pathways in Ghana. *Journal of Social Service Research,* 48, 672–81.

Boakye, A. O. 2012. *Juvenile delinquency in Ghana: a qualitative study of the lived experiences of young offenders in Accra.* Master Thesis, Norges teknisk-naturvitenskapelige universitet, Fakultet for samfunnsvitenskap og teknologiledelse, Psykologisk institutt.

Boakye Boaten, A. 2008. Street children: experiences from the streets of Accra. *Research Journal of International Studies,* 8, 76–84.

Boakye Boaten, A. 2009. Changes in the concept of childhood: implications on children in Ghana. *Afroeuropa: Journal of Afroeuropean Studies,* 3.

Boakye Boaten, A. 2010. Changes in the concept of childhood: implications on children in Ghana. *The Journal of International Social Research,* 3/10.

Boakye, K. E. & Akoensi, T. D. 2021. Doing time: young people and the rhetoric of juvenile justice in Ghana. *The Palgrave International Handbook of Youth Imprisonment*, Cham, Switzerland, Palgrave Macmillan.

Boaten, B. A. 2001. The Trokosi System in Ghana: discrimination against women. *African Women and Children: Critical Response*, 91–103.

Bonsu, O. 2021. *The Impact of Tuition-Free Policies on Schooling and Child Labour Incidence in Ghana,* Canada, University of Lethbridge.

Bosiakoh, T. & Andoh, P. 2010. Differential association theory and juvenile delinquency in Ghana's capital city – Accra: the case of Ghana Borstal Institute. *International Journal of Sociology and Anthropology,* Vol. 2, 198–205.

Bourdieu, P. 1990. *The Logic of Practice.* Translated by Richard Nice, Stanford, Stanford University Press.

Bourdieu, P. 2000. *Pascalian Meditations,* Cambridge, Polity Press.

Bourdillon, M. F. C. 1994. Street children in Harare. *Journal of the International African Institute,* 64, 516–32.

Boyatzis, C. 2011. Agency, voice, and maturity in children's religious and spiritual development. *The Study of Children in Religions*, 19–32.

Brown, A. 2015. Awkward: the importance of reflexivity in using ethnographic methods. *Game Research Methods.*

Buscatto, M. 2018. Doing ethnography: ways and reasons. *The SAGE Handbook of Qualitative Data Collection*, 327–43.

Callon, M. 2007. Actor network theory. *In:* Asdal, K., Brenna, B. & Moser, I. (eds) *The Politics of Interventions.* Oslo, Norway, Oslo Academic Press.

Carrabine, E. 2004. *Power, Discourse and Resistance: A Genealogy of the Strangeways Prison Riot,* Aldershot, England, Ashgate.

Chikoko, W. 2025. Utilising the Ubuntu philosophy among street children in sub-Saharan Africa: an overview. *The Palgrave Handbook of Ubuntu, Inequality and Sustainable Development*, 339–54.

Chopra, V. 2020. Focused ethnography: a new tool to study diagnostic errors? *Diagnosis*, 7, 211–14.

CHRAJ 2001. Report on Inspection of Prisons and Police Cells in 2001. Accra, Ghana, CHRAJ.

CHRAJ 2021a. CHRAJ's Monitoring Visits to Prisons. Accra, CHRAJ.

CHRAJ 2021b. A Qualitative Study of Child Labour in Ghana's Fishing Communities along the Volta Lake. Accra, Ghana, CHRAJ.

CHRAJ 2022. Baseline Study Report on Access to Justice and Gender Based Violence Against Elderly Women Alleged as Witches in Ghana. Accra, CHRAJ and Crossroads International.

Christiansen, C. 2006. Youth, Religiosity and the AIDS Pandemic. Faith Friends and Family Virtues in Uganda. *Youth and the Global South*. Dakar.

Christiansen, C., Utas, M. & Vigh, H. E. (eds) 2006. *Introduction. Navigating Youth, Generating Adulthood: Social Becoming in an African Context*, Uppsala, Nordiska Afrikainstitutet.

Copland, F. & Creese, A. 2015. *Linguistic Ethnography: Collecting, Analysing and Presenting Data*, London, Sage.

Côté-Boileau, É., Gaboury, I., Breton, M. & Denis, J.-L. 2020. Organizational ethnographic case studies: toward a new generative in-depth qualitative methodology for health care research? *International Journal of Qualitative Methods*, 19, 1609406920926904.

Cotton, C. 2021. An enduring institution? Child fostering in Sub-Saharan Africa. *Population and Development Review*, 47, 1179–206.

Cramer, C., Hammond, L. & Pottier, J. 2011. *Researching Violence in Africa: Ethical and Methodological Challenges*, Leiden, Brill.

Crewe, B. 2009. *The Prisoner Society*, Oxford, Oxford University.

CRRECENT. 2024. Panel Discussions on Ghana's Juvenile Justice System on the 5th of September 2024, Accra.

Cunha, M. I. 2020. Inside out: embodying prison boundaries. *The Cambridge Journal of Anthropology*, 38, 123–39.

Curtis, S. 2013. 'Compassionate containment'? Balancing technical safety and therapy in the design of psychiatric wards. Contemporary carceral geography and the 'total' institution. (1st Key note speaker) Confinement viewed through the prism of the social sciences: contrasting facilities, confronting approaches. Pessac, France, University of Bordeaux, 16 to 19 October 2013.

Dako-Gyeke, M., Adam, A. & Mills, A. A. 2022. The quagmire of juvenile delinquency: perspectives of inmates and officers in a correctional facility in Accra, Ghana. *Deviant Behavior*, 43, 241–57.

Darke, S. 2012. Estação Carandiru. *Alternative Representations of Imprisonment. Prisons Service Journal*, 26–8.

Davies, W. & Earle, R. 2020. Glimpses across 50 years of prison life from members of British Convict Criminology. *Prison Service Journal*, 13–19.

Davis, D. A. & Craven, C. 2020. Feminist ethnography. *Companion to Feminist Studies*, 281–99.

De Boek, F. 2005. *Children, Gift and Witchcraft in the Democratic Republic of Congo,* Dakar, Codesria.

De Castro, L. R. 2020. Why global? Children and childhood from a decolonial perspective. *Childhood,* 27, 48–62.

De Graft-Johnson, K. 1965. Social control in a changing society (Ghana). *Ghana Journal of Sociology,* 1, 47–55.

Drake, D. H., Earle, R. & Sloan, J. 2015. General introduction: what ethnography tells us about prisons and what prisons tell us about ethnography. *The Palgrave Handbook of Prison Ethnography*. New York, Palgrave Macmillan.

DSW 2005a. A Report on the State of Juvenile Justice Administration in Ghana. Accra, Ghana, Department of Social Welfare.

DSW 2005b. A report on the State of Juvenile Justice Administration in Ghana. Accra, Ghana, Department of Social Welfare and UNICEF.

Durham, D. 2000. Youth and the social imagination in Africa: introduction to parts 1 and 2. *Anthropological Quarterly,* 73, 11320.

Dvoryanskov, I. V. & Sika, A. M. 2022. Criminal subculture influence on criminal behavior of those sentenced to forced labor. *Пенитенциарная наука,* 16, 372–9.

Earle, R. 2012. 'Who's the daddy? Ideas about fathers in a young men's prison'. *Theoretical Criminology,* 16, 140–55.

Earle, R. 2016. European origins, perspectives and experiences of convict criminology. *Convict Criminology*. Policy Press.

Earle, R. 2018. Convict criminology in England: developments and dilemmas. *The British Journal of Criminology,* 58, 1499–516.

Earle, R. 2019. Narrative convictions, conviction narratives: the prospects of convict criminology. *The Emerald Handbook of Narrative Criminology*. Emerald Publishing Limited.

Earle, R. 2020. Doing time for convict criminology. *Convict Criminology for the Future*, London, Routledge.

Ellis, R. 2021. Prisons as porous institutions. *Theory and Society,* 50, 175–99.

Emerson, R., Fretz, R. & Shaw, L. 1995. *Writing Ethnographic Fieldnotes*, Chicago, The University of Chicago Press.

Emerson, R., Fretz, R. & Shaw, L. (eds) 2001. *Participant Observation and Field Notes,* London, Sage.

Englund, H. 2006. *Prisoners of Freedom: Human Rights and the African Poor* California, University of California.

Ewing, S., Mcgowan, J. M., Speed, C. & Bernie, V. C. 2011. *Architecture and Field/work*, Abingdon, Routledge.

Foucault, M. 1977. *Discipline and Punish: The Birth of the Prison,* Trans. Alan Sheridan, New York, Vintage.

Foucault, M. 1978. *History of Sexuality: An introduction, Volume 1,* New York, Vintage.

Fourchard, L. 2006. Lagos and the invention of juvenile delinquency in Nigeria, 1920–60. *The Journal of African History,* 47, 115–37.

Garces, C. 2012. Prison climates in the south: insider views from Africa and Latin America. *Resisting the Eclipse: An International Symposium on Prison Ethnography.* London, Milton Keynes.

Gatsinzi, A. & Hilson, G. 2022. 'Age is just a number': articulating the cultural dimension of child labour in Africa's small-scale mining sector. *Resources Policy,* 78, 102779.

Gillepsie, K. 2013. A post-apartheid prison? Confinement viewed through the prism of the social sciences: contrasting facilities, confronting approaches. Pessac, France, University of Bordeaux, 16 to 19 October 2013.

Glasser, B. G. & Strauss, A. L. 1967. *The Discovery of Grounded Theory,* Chicago, IL, Aldine.

Goffman, E. 1968. *Asylums: Essays on the Social Situation of Mental Patients and other Inmates,* Harmondsworth, Penguin.

Golo, H. K. 2018. The court and police protection of the rights and welfare of juvenile offenders during arrest, detention and trial in Ghana. *Global Journal of Arts, Humanities and Social Sciences,* 6, 48–67.

Government of Ghana, 1960. Criminal Offences Act, 1960 (Act 29). Accra, Ghana Publishing Corporation.

Government of Ghana, 1992. Constitution of the Fourth Republic of Ghana. Accra, Ghana Publishing Corporation.

Government of Ghana, 1993. Courts Act 1993 (Act 459). Accra, Ghana Publishing Corporation.

Government of Ghana, 1998a. The 1998 Children's Act of Ghana (Act 560). Accra, Ghana Publishing Corporation.

Government of Ghana, 1998b. The 1998 Criminal Code Amendment Act (554). Accra, Ghana Publishing Corporation.

Government of Ghana, 1998c. The 1998 Criminal Code Amendment Act (554) of Ghana. Accra, Ghana Publishing Corporation.

Government of Ghana, 2003. The 2003 Juvenile Justice Act of Ghana (Act 653). Accra, Ghana Publishing Corporation.

Government of Ghana, 2015a. Child and Family Welfare Policy. Ministry of Gender Accra, Ghana Publishing Corporation.

Government of Ghana, 2015b. Justice for Children Policy. Ministry of Gender Accra, Ghana Publishing Corporation.

Halsey, M. J. 2006. Negotiating conditional release: juvenile narratives of repeat incarceration. *Punishment and Society,* 8, 147–81.

Hammersley, M. 1994. Introducing ethnography. *Researching language and literacy in social context*, 1–17.

Hammersley, M. 2015. Research 'inside' viewed from 'outside': reflections on prison ethnography. *The Palgrave Handbook of Prison Ethnography*. Springer.

Hammersley, M. 2018a. What is ethnography? Can it survive? Should it? *Ethnography and Education,* 13, 1–17.

Hammersley, M. 2018b. *What's Wrong with Ethnography? Methodological Explorations*, London, Routledge.

Hammersley, M. & Atkinson, P. 1995. *Ethnography: Principles in Practice,* London, Routledge.

Hammersley, M. & Atkinson, P. 2007. *Ethnography. Principles in Practice: Third Edition,* London, Routledge.

Hassen, I. & Mañus, M. R. 2018. Socio-economic conditions of street children: the case of Shashemene Town, Oromia National Regional State, Ethiopia. *International Journal of Sociology and Anthropology,* 10, 72–88.

Hebinck, P., Den Ouden, J. & Verschoor, G. 2001. Past, present and future: Long's actor-oriented approach at the interface. *Resonances and Dissonances in Development: Actors, Networks and Cultural Repertoires*, 1–16.

Heikkilä, E. 2020. The Ethnographer as a Storyteller. *Memoriamedia.*

Hensley, C., Wright, J., Tewksbury, R. & Castle, T. 2003. The evolving nature of prison argot and sexual hierarchies. *The Prison Journal,* 83, 289–300.

Higgins, E. M., Smith, J. & Swartz, K. 2022. "We keep the nightmares in their cages": correctional culture, identity, and the warped badge of honor. *Criminology,* 60, 429–54.

Hoffmann, S. & Baerg, C. 2011. *A Study to Assess the Status of Juvenile Justice in Ghana,* Accra, Ghana, Commonwealth Human Rights Initiative.

Holzscheiter, A. 2020. Affectedness, empowerment and norm contestation – children and young people as social agents in international politics. *Affectedness and Participation in* International Institutions. London, Routledge.

Honwana, A. & De Boeck, F. 2005. *Makers and Breakers. Children and Youth in Postcolonial Africa*, Dakar, CODESRIA.

Hynd, S. 2018. Pickpockets, pilot boys, and prostitutes: the construction of juvenile delinquency in the Gold Coast [Colonial Ghana], c. 1929–57. *Journal of West African History,* 4, 47–74.

Iheme, W. 2020. Religious Intolerance, Witchcraft, Superstition, and Underdevelopment in Africa. *Skeptic*, 25, 13–21.

Isiugo-Abanihe, U. C. 1985. Child fosterage in West Africa. *Population and Development Review*, 53–73.

Jefferson, A. 2007. Prison officer training and practice in Nigeria: contention, contradiction and re-imagining reform strategies. *Punishment and Society,* 9, 253–69.

Jefferson, A. & Gaborit, L. 2015. *Human rights in prisons: comparing institutional encounters in Kosovo, Sierra Leone and the Philippines*, Basingstoke, Palgrave Macmillan.
Jefferson, A. M. 2015. Performing ethnography: infiltrating prison spaces. *In*: Drake, D. H., Earle, R. & Sloan, J. (eds) *The Palgrave Handbook of Prison Ethnography*, New York, Palgrave Macmillan.
Jefferson, A. M. & Martin, T. M. 2014. Editorial comment: everyday prison governance in Africa. *Prison Service Journal*, 212, 2Á3.
Jefferson, A. M. & Schmidt, B. E. 2019. Concealment and revelation as bureaucratic and ethnographic practice: lessons from Tunisian prisons. *Critique of Anthropology*, 39, 155–71.
Jefferson, A. M., Caracciolo, G., Korner, J. & Nordberg, N. 2021. Amplified vulnerabilities and reconfigured relations: COVID-19, torture prevention and human rights in the Global South. *State Crime Journal*, 10, 147.
Jefferson, A. M., Martin, T., Bandyopadhyay, M., Darke, S., Ayete-Nyampong, L., Lindegaard, M. R. & Ryberg, A. E. 2009. Inaugural Meeting of the Global Prisons Research Network (GPRN) 3–4 December 2009. Rehabilitation and Research Centre for Torture Victims, Borgergade 13, Copenhagen.
Jewkes, Y. & Johnstone, H. 2006. *Prison Readings. A critical introduction to prisons and imprisonment,* US and Canada, Willan Publishing.
Jindra, M. 2020. Social Instability, Churches, and Child Witchcraft. *OKH Journal: Anthropological Ethnography and Analysis Through the Eyes of Christian Faith,* 4.
Jones, R. S., Ross, J. I., Richards, S. C. & Murphy, D. S. 2009. The first dime: a decade of convict criminology. *The Prison Journal,* 89, 151–71.
Julien, G. 2024. Rehabilitating street children: the great paradox. *International Journal of Sociology and Anthropology,* 16, 1–8.
Kakuru, D. M. 2022. Towards a localized understanding of violence against children and adolescents in Africa. *International Journal of Child, Youth and Family Studies,* 13, 1–9.
Kassa, S. C. & Abebe, T. 2016. Qenja: child fostering and relocation practices in the Amhara region, Ethiopia. *Children's Geographies,* 14, 46–62.
Kielland, A. & Maurizia, T. 2006. *Children at Work. Child Labour Practices in Africa,* London, Lynne Rienner.
Knoetze, J. J. 2015. Spiritual transformation: reaching and equipping sub-Saharan African children. *In die Skriflig,* 49, 1–8.
Koomson, B., Manful, E., Dapaah, J. M. & Yeboah, E. H. 2022. I agreed to go because … examining the Agency of Children within a phenomenon conceptualised as trafficking in Ghana. *Children & Society,* 36, 101–17.
Koomson, B., Manful, E., Yeboah, E. H. & Dapaah, J. M. 2021. Work socialisation gone wrong? Exploring the antecedent of child trafficking in two Ghanaian fishing communities. *Children's Geographies*, 1–12.

Kwarteng, K. A. 2012. *Duties & Responsibilities of Children in Ghana: Perspectives of Children and Adults in Kumasi*. Master Thesis. Accra, University of Ghana.

Kyei, P. S. 2024. Child fostering and school attendance in West Africa over time. *Vulnerable Children and Youth Studies,* 19, 505–17.

Liebling, A. 2004. *Prisons and their Moral Performance: A Study of Values, Quality and Prison Life,* Oxford, Oxford University Press.

Lindegaard, R. 2009. *Coconuts, Gangsters and Rainbow Fighters. How Male Youngsters Navigate Situations of Violence in Cape Town, South Africa.* PhD dissertation, University of Amsterdam.

Long, N. 1992. *From Paradigm Lost to Paradigm Regained. The Case of an Actor Oriented Sociology of Development,* London, Routledge.

Long, N. 2001. *Development Sociology: Actor Perspectives,* London, Routledge.

Maclean, K. 2022. *Crimes in archival form: human rights, fact production, and Myanmar,* University of California Press.

Martin, T. 2009. Taking the snake out of the basket. *In:* Jefferson, A. M. & Jensen, S. (eds) *Repopulating State Violence and Human Rights: State Officials in the* South. London, Routledge-Cavendish.

Martin, T. 2010. Reasonable caning and human rights. *"Dissecting the 'non-western' prison" Global Prisons Research Network (GPRN) Workshop, hosted by Netherlands Institute for the Study of Crime and Law Enforcement (NSCR), Amsterdam.* Amsterdam.

Martin, T. 2015. Witnessing and accessing Ugandan prisons: fieldwork within a post-colonial bureaucracy. *Palgrave Handbook of Prison Ethnography. Hampshire,* Palgrave, 424–41.

Martin, T. & Chantraine, G. 2018. *Prison Breaks: Toward a Sociology of Escape,* Springer.

Martin, T. & Jefferson, A. M. 2019. Prison ethnography in Africa: reflections on a maturing field. *Politique Africaine,* 155, 131–52.

Mathiesen, T. 2006. The defences of the weak: a sociological study of a Norwegian correctional institution. *In:* Johnston, Y. J. A. H. (ed) *Prisons Readings: A Critical Introduction to Prisons and Imprisonment.* US and Canada, Willan Publishing.

Mauthner, N. S. & Doucet, A. 2003. Reflexive accounts and accounts of reflexivity in qualitative data analysis. *Sociology,* 37, 413–30.

McGranahan, C. 2018. Ethnography beyond method: the importance of an ethnographic sensibility. *Sites: A Journal of Social Anthropology and Cultural Studies,* 15.

Mechlinski, T. M. 2007. *Negotiation and Supplication, the Social, Cultural and Political Interactions of West African Mobility Control,* Santa Barbara, University of California.

Medlicott, D. 1999. Surviving in the time machine: suicidal prisoners and the pains of prison time. *Time & Society,* 8, 211–30.

Mensa-Bonsu, H. 1990. The young offender and the criminal justice system. *U. Ghana LJ,* 18, 49.

Mensa-Bonsu, H. 1995. Human rights and the juvenile justice system: the Ghanaian experience. Annual conference-African Society of International and Comparative Law, 321–47.

Mensah-Akorah, E. 2005. *The Role of Juvenile Correctional Centres in Character Formation of Juvenile Offenders,* Legon, University of Ghana.

Merry, S. E. 2006. *Human Rights and Gender Violence: Translating International Law into Local Justice,* Chicago, University of Chicago.

Merry, S. E. 2011. Measuring the world: indicators, human rights, and global governance. *Current Anthropology,* 52, S83–S95.

Merry, S. E. 2016. *The Seductions of Quantification: Measuring Human Rights, Gender Violence, and Sex Trafficking,* University of Chicago Press.

Merry, S. E. & Levitt, P. 2019. Remaking women's human rights in the vernacular: the resonance dilemma. *Rethinking Gender Equality in Global Governance: The Delusion of Norm Diffusion,* 145–67.

Meyer, B. 1996. Powerful Pictures: Popular Christian Aesthetics in Southern Ghana. *Africa: Journal of the International African Institute* 66, 343–68.

Mhaka-Mutepfa, M. & Maundeni, T. 2019. The role of faith (spirituality/religion) in resilience in sub-Saharan African children. *The International Journal of Community and Social Development,* 1, 211–33.

Midtlyng, G. 2022. Safety rules in a Norwegian high-security prison: the impact of social interaction between prisoners and officers. *Safety Science,* 149, 105690.

Mizen, P. & Ofosu-Kusi, Y. 2013. Agency as vulnerability: accounting for children's movement to the streets of Accra. *The Sociological Review,* 61, 363–82.

Morelle, M., Le Marcis, F. & Hornberger, J. 2021. *Confinement, Punishment and Prisons in Africa,* London, Routledge.

Mukasa, B. 2021. *Parenting Styles and Juvenile Delinquency: A Case of Selected Families in Rwoho Town Council Ntungamo District-Uganda.* University of Kisubi.

Mumo, P. M. 2016. The role of Sunday schools in Christian socialisation of children in Africa: a case study of Africa inland church in Kenya. *Ilorin Journal of Religious Studies,* 6, 47–58.

Nugent, R. 2005. Youth in a global world. *World,* 1, 1–845.

Nukunya, G. K. 2003. *Tradition and Change in Ghana. Second and enlarged edition,* Accra, Ghana Universities' Press.

Nyarko, J. A. 2023. Assessment of the Social Changes of Colonialism: Ghana 1874–957. *Available at SSRN 4498517.*

O'Reilley, K. 2005. *Ethnographic methods,* London, Routledge.

Odetola, T. 1980. Social policy, modernization and crime among the African youth: a comparative analysis. *Journal of African Studies,* 7, 213.

Ogunkan, D., Adeboyejo, A., Adejumobi, D. & Giwa, T. 2024. Unveiling the shadows: investigating the substance use among street children. *International Journal of Human Capital in Urban Management,* 9.

Okafor, E. E. 2010. Child labour dynamics and implications for sustainable development in Nigeria. *Journal of Sustainable Development in Africa,* 12, 8–21.

Olivier De Sardan, J.-P. 2005. *Anthropology and Development: Understanding Contemporary Social Change,* London, Zed Books.

Olivier De Sardan, J.-P. 2008. Researching the Practical Norms of Real Governance in Africa. *The Africa Power and Politics Programme.* London, Overseas Development Institute.

Onyinah, O. 1997. Contemporary "witchdemonology". In Africa. Edinburgh, Edinburgh University Press, 67, 223–41.

Onyinah, O. 2020. "The Person I Hate Most in Life is My Mother". *OKH Journal: Anthropological Ethnography and Analysis through the Eyes of Christian Faith,* Tulsa, Oklahoma, Oral Roberts University, 4, 24–39.

Oppong, C. & Bleek, W. 1982. Economic models and having children: some evidence from Kwahu. *International African Institute,* 52, 15–33.

Orme, J. A. & Seipel, M. M. O. 2007. Survival strategies of street children in Ghana. A qualitative study. *International Social Work,* 50, 489–99.

Papadopoulos, D., Stephenson, N. & Tsianos, V. 2008. *Escape Routes: Control and Subversion in the Twenty-First Century*, Pluto Books.

Petrus, T., Uwah, C., Davids, D. & Jonas, B. 2022. Softening the 'Iron Hand': re-thinking punitive approaches to addressing gang subcultures in South Africa. *Artha Journal of Social Sciences,* 21.

Piacentini, L. 2004. *Surviving Russian Prisons: Punishment, Economy and Politics in Transition,* Cullompton, Willan.

Pilon, M. 2003. Foster Care and Schooling in West Africa. The State of Knowledge. Background Paper, the UNESCO 2003 EFA Monitoring Report.

Plummer, K. 1983. *Documents of Life: An Introduction to the Problems and Literature of a Humanistic Method,* London, Unwin Hyman.

Porter, G., Abane, A., Blaufuss, K. & Owusu Acheampong, F. 2011. *Children's Rights, Mobility, and Transport in Ghana: Access to Education and Health Services,* Lanham, Maryland, Lexington Books.

Reid, G. W. 1978. Missionaries and West African nationalism. *Phylon (1960–),* 39, 225–33.

Rhodes, L. 2009. Ethnography in sites of total confinement. *Anthropology News,* 50, 6.

Rhodes, L. A. 2010. 'This can't be real': continuity at HMP Grendon. *In:* R. Shuker, R. & Sullivan, E. (eds) *Grendon and the Emergence of Forensic Therapeutic Communities: Developments in Research and Practice*, MA, Wiley-Blackwell, 187–202.

Riby-Williams, J. 1954. The treatment of juvenile delinquency in the Gold Coast of West Africa. *International Review of Criminal Policy,* 6, 1–14.

Richards, P. 2005. To fight or to farm- Agrarian dimensions of the Mano River conflicts. Liberia and Sierra Leone *African Affairs,* 104, 571–90.

Richards, S. C., Ross, J. I., Newbold, G., Lenza, M. & Grigsby, R. S. 2018. Convict criminology. *Routledge Handbook of Critical Criminology*, London, Routledge.

Ross, J. I. & Richards, S. C. 2003. *Convict Criminology*, Belmont, CA, Wadsworth/Thomson Learning.

Routley, L. 2023. Doing God's time: time, religion and reform in Ghanaian prisons. *Political Geography,* 106, 102955.

Rowland, A., Sugie, N. F. & Turney, K. 2025. Reaching incarcerated people in jail: the case of Prison Pandemic. *Sociological Methodology*, 00811750251331970.

Rubin, H. J. & Rubin, I. S. 1995. *Qualitative Interviewing. The Art of Hearing Data: Choosing Interviewees and Hearing What They Say,* Thousand Oaks, Sage.

Sabates-Wheeler, R. & Sumberg, J. 2022. Breaking out of the policy enclave approach to child labour in sub-Saharan African agriculture. *Global Social Policy,* 22, 46–66.

Sarbah, J. 1904. The Gold Coast When Edward IV. Was King. *Journal of the Royal African Society*, 10, 194–7.

Sauls, H. 2009. Delinquency or Resilience? How Interpretations of Violence Translate into the Daily Management of Children in a Place of Safety in Cape Town. *Medical Anthropology at Intersections: Celebrating 50 years of interdisciplinarity*, Yale University Press.

Schatz, E. 2013. *Political Ethnography: What Immersion Contributes to the Study of Power*, University of Chicago Press.

Schliehe, A. K. 2016. Re-discovering Goffman: contemporary carceral geography, the "total" institution and notes on heterotopia. *Geografiska Annaler: Series B, Human Geography*, 98, 19–35.

Schimmel, N. 2006. Freedom and autonomy of street children. *International Journal of Children's Rights,* 14, 211–33.

Scott, J. 1985. *Weapons of the Weak: Everyday Forms of Peasant Resistance,* Yale University Press.

Scott, J. 1990. *Domination and the Arts of Resistance: Hidden Transcripts*, Yale University Press.

Sibeoni, J., Verneuil, L., Manolios, E. & Révah-Levy, A. 2020. A specific method for qualitative medical research: the IPSE (inductive process to analyze the structure of lived experience) approach. *BMC Medical Research Methodology,* 20, 1–21.

Stein, J. 1955. Time, space and social discipline: factory life in Cornwall, Ontario, 1867–1893. *Journal of Historical Geography,* 21, 278–99.

Sunstein, S. B. & Strater, C. E. 2007. Writing self, writing cultures: understanding field writing. *In: Fieldworking,* Boston, Martins.

Sykes, G. M. 1958. *The Society of Captives. A Study of a Maximum Security Prison,* Princeton, New Jersey.

Tooth, G. C. 1949. *A Survey of Juvenile Delinquency in the Gold Coast,* Great Britain, Colonial Social Science Research Council, Research Department.
Tracy, S. J. 2012. The toxic and mythical combination of a deductive writing logic for inductive qualitative research. *Qualitative Communication Research,* 1, 109–41.
Twum Danso, A. 2009. Reciprocity, respect and responsibility: the 3rs underlying parent-child relationships in Ghana and the implications for children's rights. *International Journal of Children's Rights,* 17, 415–32.
UN 1985. United Nations Standard Minimum Rules for the Administration of Juvenile Justice ("The Beijing Rules"): resolution/adopted by the General Assembly. GA 40/33.
UN 1990a. United Nations Guidelines for the Prevention of Juvenile Delinquency ("The Riyadh Guidelines"): resolution/adopted by the General Assembly. Guidelines; GA 45/112.
UN 1990b. United Nations Rules for the Protection of Juveniles Deprived of their Liberty (Havana Rules): resolution/adopted by the General Assembly, A/RES/45/113.
UN 1990c. The United Nations Standard Minimum Rules for Non-custodial Measures (The Tokyo Rules), adopted by General Assembly resolution 45/110 on 14 December 1990.
UNCRC 1989. Convention on the Rights of the Child. U.N. General Assembly. Document A/RES/44/25, 12 December 1989.
UNICCPR 1966. International Covenant on Civil and Political Rights, 19 December 1966, 999 U.N.T.S. 171, 6 I.L.M. 368.
UNICEF 2005. Access to Justice by Children. Judicial Service of Ghana, UNICEF & CUSO.
UNICESCR 1966. International Covenant on Economic, Social and Cultural Rights, 16 December 1966, 993 U.N.T.S. 3.
UNOPCAT 2002. The Optional Protocol to the Convention Against Torture and Other Cruel, Inhuman or Degrading Treatment or Punishment (OPCAT), adopted in 2002 (A/RES/57/199).
Van Der Geest, S. 2002. Respect and reciprocity: care of elderly people in rural Ghana. *Journal of Cross-cultural Gerontology,* 17, 3–31.
Van Der Geest, S. 2008. Resilience and the whims of reciprocity in old age: an example from Ghana. *Medische Antropologie,* 20, 297–311.
Van Der Geest, S. 2016. Will families in Ghana continue to care for older people? Logic and contradiction in policy. *In*: Hoffman, J. & Pype, K. *Ageing in Sub-Saharan Africa: Spaces and Practices of Care.* Policy Press.
Wacquant, L. 2002. *The Curious Eclipse of Prison Ethnography in the Age of Mass Incarceration,* London, Sage.
Weegels, J., Jefferson, A. M. & Martin, T. M. 2020. Introduction: confinement beyond site: connecting urban and prison ethnographies. *The Cambridge Journal of Anthropology,* 38, 1–14.

Weiss, R. P. & South, N. 1998. *Comparing Prison Systems: Toward a Comparative and International Penology*, Amsterdam, Gordon and Breach Publishers.

Yeboah, T. & Boafo, J. 2024. The social significance of children's work in cashew supply chain activities in Ghana. *Children's Geographies,* 22, 149–64.

Yoder, H. N., De Jong, J. T., Tol, W. A., Duncan, J. A., Bayoh, A. & Reis, R. 2021. Child witchcraft confessions as an idiom of distress in Sierra Leone; results of a rapid qualitative inquiry and recommendations for mental health interventions. *Child and Adolescent Psychiatry and Mental Health,* 15, 1–15.

Yushawu, A. & Jaishankar, K. 2025. Sakawa in Ghana: the influence of weak ties on economic cybercrime offender networks. *Deviant Behavior*, 1–21.

Yusuf, S. A., Daud, M. N. & Arshat, Z. 2021. Perception on the role of parenting style on juvenile delinquency among adolescents in the Government remand homes, Lagos State Nigeria. *International Journal of Academic Research in Business and Social Sciences,* 11, 1425–41.

Ziman, R., Espin, S., Grant, R. E. & Kitto, S. 2018. Looking beyond the checklist: an ethnography of interprofessional operating room safety cultures. *Journal of Interprofessional Care,* 32, 575–83.

Index